# ■ TALKING DIRTY

# TALKING DIRTY

glittering moments
with the mad, the bad
and the brilliant

**SUSAN CHENERY**

SCEPTRE

SCEPTRE

Published in Australia and New Zealand in 1997
by Hodder Headline Australia Pty Limited,
(A member of the Hodder Headline Group)
10–16 South Street, Rydalmere NSW 2116

Published in association with
Belladonna Books
39 Palmer Street, Balmain NSW 2041

Reprinted 1997

**National Library of Australia Cataloguing-in-Publication data**

Chenery, Susan.
Talking dirty.

ISBN 0 7336 0556 7.

1. Celebrities—Interviews. 2. Authors—Interviews.
I. Title.

080

Text design and typesetting by Bookhouse Digital, Sydney
Printed in Australia by Griffin Press Pty Ltd, Adelaide

*Dedicated to the memory of my brother Hugh Warren.*
*With love and sorrow.*

# Contents

# Contents

# Contents

# ■ Acknowledgements

With mucho thanks to John Alexander, editor in chief of the *Sydney Morning Herald*. Much of the travelling and work for this book was done under the auspices of the *Sydney Morning Herald* and I am greatly indebted to my boss for allowing me the latitude and the freedom to do it. And for not getting really, *really* mad when it took longer than I thought. Without his support there is no way I could have done this.

Thanks also to all the *Herald* section editors who put up with me for the duration: Richard Glover, Jenny Tabakoff, Peter Cochrane, Ian Hicks and Susan Wyndham. I trust you have all recovered sufficiently. Now, about my next assignment . . .

I must also thank Shona Martyn, Fenella Souter and the erstwhile team at my alma mater, *HQ* magazine, where I learned how to do this stuff and who stood by me through some very bad phases during those dire freelancing years.

And with love and gratitude beyond words to Susan and Clare Haynes, who not only let me stay for months after I came for two days but for many years' sustaining friendship besides. Without you I would not be.

A great deal of thanks to those well met along the way and the kindness received: Deborah Leser, Tim Hatfield, Jane Kent, Gaynor Fennessy, Simon Kent, Garech Browne and Roderic O'Connor.

Thanks too to Jason Romney for galloping to the rescue with technology, to my colleague and friend Anne Susskind, with whom I continue to argue, in a caring way, every day, and to Maryanne O'Sullivan for being there.

To my publisher Alison Pressley, I thank her for her courage in dragging this book out of me. The last chapter is in the mail, Alison, I promise . . .

The characters in this book are real, and any resemblance to fictitious persons is all in your mind and purely coincidental. I could not have made these people up. They are true originals. I thank them for giving me their time. And a few other things as well. For their courage, their intelligence, for refusing to conform, for placing their imprimateur on the world. For living their lives as they have. More power to them all.

# Prologue

This is it, I inwardly screamed, squashed between a Christian with a bad haircut and a toothless Japanese man. This is *It*, I wanted to run up and down the aisle and shout wildly as the plane hit 591 miles an hour and blasted across New Zealand at 33,000 feet. Instead I drank. With conviction. Free at last. This indeed was It. Here we go, here we go, here we go. Away out across the Pacific. I was the passenger everyone dreads sitting next to on a long flight. The one who wants to chat. The one who drinks. The one who sings out loud with the earphones on. The one who doesn't sleep. Who takes up too much room. Oh yes, it was me, me, me who smoked a cigarette in the toilet.

■ ■ ■

I was languishing fitfully on the sofa when I got the idea, hatched the plan. Things were bad at the time. For reasons of my own I needed to get out of town for a while. But first I needed money and I needed it fast. One day on the sofa it hit me. A book advance. Yes.

So that was how it started. Buy the ticket, take the ride.

I had no way of knowing when I started what a hell of a trip it would be. I didn't really know where I was going. Just that I was going. On the road. Baby, baby, baby. Where I ended up going depended on who agreed to be interviewed. I sat in hotel rooms firing off faxes, pestering agents and managers, trying it on. Ready and willing for action. The people who magnanimously agreed to give me their time shaped this book.

One by one they came through. The famous, the mad, the brilliant, the bad, the merely interesting. Nearly all of them have chosen, or been forced, to live outside conformity. There is no easy transition in that. To sing, and to dance, and to write, to think; to be free. To live out there as Hunter S. Thompson says "where the *real* winds blow". And that is where I found them.

Do we collude in mythologising the famous? How does one person transcend the rest of us? The journalist gets up close and reports back. Do we create myths around people? Yes. But to get famous and stay famous takes, I think, exceptional brains, beauty or talent. And the desire to do so. The powerful need to create. To make an art out of living. To offer up their work and themselves for our consumption. Some of them simply fascinate without doing very much at all. These people are aberrations, they *are* different, they are luminous. But, hey, you decide.

"Charisma," says Steven Berkoff, "is testosterone. Men and women both have it." But it is something else too. It is a living.

Between these covers lies an odyssey. It was a journey that was wild and fast and sexy and slow.

And I am feeling a whole lot better now.

Thank you and goodnight.

When I phoned Hunter S. Thompson in Aspen, in that disturbed valley in Colorado, he was howling into his answering machine. Howling into the alpine night and under the impression that it was Christmas. Christmas in Texas. Christmas, furthermore, in May. Maybe there was white stuff in the sky. Maybe there were men on camels bathed in celestial light and bearing gifts up there on his ranch. Maybe the carpenter was having delusions of grandeur again. But on his answering machine he was howling along with a blues band. "Merry Christmas, hot dog. Santa Claus is here. Yes. Christmas Eve, man, it will cost you $4.98 to hear the second verse. Oh yeah. Christmas in Texas. Hot dog man."

Things were weird of course in Woody Creek. As per usual.

When I arrived in Aspen, I phoned from the Limelight Lodge. This time, Hunter's machine said he had finished the treatment, he was sick, and the caller should send $100,000 right away.

# Fucked and Far from Home

There is violence and then there is murderous interruptus. Hunter S. Thompson is white line fever somewhere in between. And as for me, I should have known better. I should have known that when history repeats itself it goes from bad to completely fucked. No other way to describe it. Well, OK, me. Not after the drugs began to take hold. And that was after I got drunk. Maybe it was altitude. Maybe it was nerves. But the last time I left Owl Farm it was from the foetal position on the doorstep, silently screaming for mercy, my head convulsing on my luggage, taxi driver feeling for a pulse.

Well I was younger then, but to this day the smell of new paint makes me nervous. They had been painting at Owl Farm that week, real nice brushwork too; but the fresh fumes had curdled in the cortex and turned a bad hangover into something else again. Whatever way you look at it, it was bad then. And it was worse now. A lax moment in journalism, even by my low standards. A Rocky Mountain low.

But then again, as the great Gonzo himself wrote in *Generation of Swine*, 'I have spent half my life trying to get away from journalism, but I am mired in it—a low trade and a habit worse than heroin, a strange seedy world full of misfits and drunkards and failures. A group photo of the top ten journalists in America on any given day would be a monument to human ugliness. It is not a trade that attracts a lot of slick people; none of the Calvin Klein crowd or international jet set types.'

The problem, though, with being a practitioner of Gonzo journalism is that you have to be inhuman to pull it off with elegance, élan, a life expectancy beyond 42 hours and not being quarantined for rabies. You have to live in deep caves in undiscovered valleys or on high, vertiginous mountains where deep winter snow dulls the screaming and shooting and buries the bodies until spring.

There is only one man for the job. Hunter Stockton Thompson. And he is one scary dude.

**HUNTER S. THOMPSON**

Hunter is what happens when rehab fails. When case-hardened specialists examine the patient then go shrieking into the night. When weird and dangerous creatures carrying guns and staggering and screaming across mountains are not lassoed, filled with tranquillisers and sent away to scientific laboratories in cages. He is unreconstructed drugus fiendus. Full-blown psychosis. The last lurching guest at the party that was the '60s.

Let the good times roll, as he says often and demonically as the rest of us flop and twitch and plunge around him. 'I'm by myself. The last dope fiend. It's hard to find the right people to party with,' he admitted to the *Los Angeles Times* back in 1987.

The first time I met Hunter Thompson he gave me a strange smile and hit the accelerator of his red Chrysler convertible: the great red shark. Long and sleek and shining, it has co-starred in nearly all of his books. It was dusk, the top was down and there appeared to be snowflakes swirling in the sudden rush of wind as the car took off; except it was late summer and couldn't possibly be snowing, not even in Aspen. Nup, the white stuff had to be something else. Something more sinister than snow.

I might as well have not got off the plane. Already I was flying fast at 30,000 feet and straight up the side of a mountain. Hunter did not, I felt, pay any attention to the road. As Aspen and civilisation as I knew it flashed away and was gone, gone, gone, he poured himself a tumbler of straight Scotch on the dashboard, jabbed at the buttons on the stereo, steering with his knees and pretty much ignoring the corners on the winding road. I was, I realised around about then, i.e. too late, alone on a mountain with a maniac.

Things were weird before I even met the great Gonzo journalist. At Denver airport I had literally tripped over the legs of a dead body. A man had sat down in a green plastic airport seat and quietly expired from a heart attack. It was in the departure lounge of all places. He had departed, all right, but not like he had planned. This had made me miss my connecting flight and up at Aspen airport Hunter had passed the time by creating a minor disturbance—something to do with an Indian hunting knife that had been on display in a glass case in the souvenir shop. I later, but not much, realised that the ground staff's effusive greeting was not down-home hospitality but massive relief at my taking Hunter off their shaking hands.

Events of the next few days are not entirely clear but sometime later that night I sent a fax to our mutual friend Susan Haynes in London. It said: 'Things are getting crazy around here. There are sharks in the garage and white stuff on the ceiling.' Hunter's fax to the same friend was, perhaps, more succinct: 'Susan is flapping around like an idiot savant penguin.'

At least if I was flapping I was, presumably, up and walking. This would definitely be progress. Up until then I had been lying on the floor, staring unblinking at the ceiling, where the archangel Gabriel appeared to be coming forth to carry me home, or so it seemed to me, and the Doctor of Gonzo journalism was spoon-feeding me a strange home-made medicine in a gallant attempt to reacquaint me with planet Earth. Not to mention being stuck with a corpse on the rug. Was that before or after he picked up one of the loaded guns lying around the kitchen and shot up his own house? Don't ask me. I was having problems of my own. But it may have been around about then that a tiny bit of paranoia started to set in. The mind plays tricks, I know, but I have evidence. In the photo fir trees stand tall against a blue sky and are reflected in a window riddled with bullet holes. As the sun came up across the steep rocky mountains casting pink light across ridges and turning snow into sparkling fairy floss, Hunter handed me a high-powered rifle. We were standing in the backyard in towelling bathrobes. Fresh out of the hot tub where he had lain on his back on the bottom with his eyes open for an unnerving amount of time. When he surfaced spraying water, like some kind of steaming bald beast from the broiling deep, he proceeded to his nightly task of dictating memos into a tape recorder; incomprehensible memos that no secretary has ever been able to transcribe.

Hunter arranged a row of cans on a log out on the grass. The rifle shots echoed across the sleeping valley and up into the hills, sending startled elk skittering up the mountain. By some extraordinary fluke (and the fact that I once did the weapons training course on a story about a police academy) I managed to hit two cans in a row. Hunter put his arm around me and called me "buddy". I had, it seemed, passed some kind of hideous test. Hey, maybe I even had the potential for violence.

It was later that week that I had found myself running through the woods in the dark, wild-eyed, jabbering and muttering about "the devil", gunshots ringing ominously from the house. And by then things had gone seriously wrong. Call it cocaine psychosis, call it crazy, call it anything you like, but when I saw evil cloud that man's face, I too skittered up that mountain. I didn't even hang around long enough to check for cloven hooves. I was out that door and into the piney woods. Pronto. There is always a point, it seems, when the visiting journalist gives up on the interview and starts fearing for their life. Hunter, after all, has his image to consider. "I was keeping it down to secondary yelling," he told me later, much later, when I returned, feeling better and covered in pine needles. "You should hear primary yelling." I don't think so. The Scream, trust me on this, is awesome. It echoes ominously through the rocky canyons for miles.

So. You'd think I would have learned. All in all. But no, ho, ho, not me.

Aspen was preternaturally quiet that morning in May, as the plane came in through the canyons on a blast of cold wind. From the foot of the mountain the snow was blinding in the late morning sun. And from the window of the Jerome Hotel it streaked across fir trees and away up the mountain. Hunter sat at the bar drinking whisky, wearing a slouch hat rakishly angled, and baggy army fatigues. With him was an attractive blonde whom he introduced as Angie. Though this was not, it would turn out, her name. They had not slept, they said, for quite a while. That would be about 30 years in Hunter's case. But he seemed kinder somehow, mellowed. Less menacing.

A lone guitarist in the corner picked desultorily at his guitar. Stale cigarette smoke hung in the still, thick morning air.

A huge, large-limbed and fleshy man with a cigarette drooping from a holder in his mouth, Hunter, against all the sizeable odds stacked by himself, seemed not only to have halted the ageing process but thrown it into reverse. He had gained weight and he actually looked younger than he did five years before. This defies medical science. He is, after all, a man whose doctor says should have been dead 20 years ago. This is a man whose daily consumption of liquor, tobacco and drugs would kill a mere human being and several passing rhinoceros. At the very least, require the use of a padded cell in an understanding institution for a while. Just until those walls stopped talking and the eyes stopped swivelling.

And now, and now, astonishingly, he is 60. The 60-year-old from hell and still stone-crazy. Ageless, unrepentant and brutally strong. The constitution of a mule. I remember he told me back then that withdrawal from any of his many addictions would probably kill him. His body would shrivel up in shock. His heart would burst from boredom. His is not the kind of constitution that runs on empty. So he might as well keep going. Faster and faster. The wild party that never ends. At six o'clock one morning, as we were idly horizontal on the floor watching a weird televangelist in a toupée explaining his strange interpretation of the Crucifixion using a flip chart, I asked Hunter if he was on a suicide mission. If he secretly wanted to die quite soon, since that could surely be the only immediate outcome of his nocturnal activities.

"Oh yes," he said thickly. "I welcome death."

But the 'terminal psychosis' he described in *Fear and Loathing in Las Vegas* has failed, incomprehensibly, to reach terminal velocity. Unlike Kerouac or Faulkner or Fitzgerald, he has not managed to sagaciously check out while he was still ahead. He did not die the early, violent or dramatic and timely death so popular in the great alcoholic American literary tradition. The death that ensures that your early peaking genius is enshrined and unsullied by the indignity of age. Though God knows he has tried. It is something of an uncomfortable surprise to him, I think, that he is still here. We will get to see the full catastrophe. The Gonzo journalist growing elderly. The hellion on a zimmer frame, dribbling and past his prime. Unless he does turn out to be, as evidence would suggest and many people suspect, indestructible.

As he explained in *Generation of Swine*, he really is just 'a lazy drunken hillbilly with a heart full of hate who has found a way to live out there where the *real* winds blow—to sleep late, have fun, get wild, drink whiskey and drive fast on empty streets with nothing in mind except falling in love and not getting arrested . . .'

Soon after he wrote that he did get arrested, alas . . . the porn purveyor who said he hit her and molested her and threw a drink regretted it later—but not as much as Hunter, whose house got raided in a full-scale investigation . . . explosives and drugs removed . . . charges laid . . . but who stood before the courts defiant and said, "everyone's house is a little safer now: the Fourth Amendment has been protected. If we had lost this case they'd have been at your house next" when all charges were dropped. But man oh man, what a drama.

Hunter and I hunched over the Jerome bar and engaged in some idle conversation, catching up. It had been a while, after all, since he last tried to shoot me. We drank some Scotch. We drank some more Scotch. The blonde was strangely silent. Sort of stunned. She had a haunted look about her. A look I had seen before in accident victims . . .

Hunter reached across and patted my knee. Friendly and sort of green. Like a large lizard in a hat. His legs jerking as if to some distant rhythm only they could hear. Heavy metal maybe. The deep, fast baritone voice that scatters sentences into small pieces. "So, Susan," he growled, "what do you want tonight? Explosions? Serious talk?" And then it came back to me. The exploding jeep. The searing chemical flash in the night. The sickening tearing of stricken metal. The smoking crater in the ground. The photograph. 'This could happen to you' Hunter had scrawled savagely across that photograph of flaming metal before sending it to Somebody-Junior-the-Third in New York, a publisher who was failing to deliver a $2 million advance, in cash, that night, in a brown paper bag for a novel that was, at the time, still largely in the planning stages. "All my books have been best sellers," he explained innocently, conveniently forgetting the awesome rootin', tootin' and shootin' involved in writing those books, the trail of weeping broken-down editors in his wake.

'You don't really know until you've been through it,' said one battle-fatigued editor in the book *Hunter*. 'I'd heard the stories— but I didn't know. Nobody knows except veterans.' Oh, my *God*, I realised on the bar stool at the Jerome, Hunter was planning on putting on a show. "A good bomb is high art, you know," he smiled encouragingly.

"Er, I don't think that will be necessary, Hunter," I said, acting insouciant. "Let's just, you know, talk."

It is not a huge consolation up there in the dark, dark night with a compulsively violent, drug-crazed maniac who is busy blowing the place up, to remember that he wrote in *Fear and Loathing in Las Vegas*: 'I did, after all, have weapons. And I liked to shoot them—especially at night, when the great blue flame would leap out, along with all that noise . . . and, yes the bullets too. We couldn't ignore that. Big balls of lead/alloy flying around the valley at speeds up to 3700 feet per second . . . But I always fired into the nearest hill or, failing that, into blackness. I meant no harm; I just liked the explosions. And I was careful never to kill more than I could eat.'

Hunter carefully examined his newspaper. That the ground at Woody Creek was not split by dynamite and the valley lit up by high-octane explosives that night was due, in the end, to the fact that there was a big basketball game on television. Orlando v. Florida.

They were no doubt already putting their money on the bar up at the Woody Creek Tavern. A short hell-drive in the shark down the mountain from his house, the Tavern is Hunter's 'office'. A shabby backwoods bar frequented by hillbillies, cowboys and gamblers nearly as crazy as Hunter, where everyone owes everyone else money from betting on the ball games and anything else worth betting on, but the exact amounts seem to be lost in the mists of time and alcohol. Hunter once let off a smoke bomb in there just to have something to write about in his weekly column for the *San Francisco Examiner*. And, well, because he likes bombs. Now there is a signed statement on the wall: Hunter Thompson promises not to let off any smoke bombs.

Loud country singing and the occasional primordial howl float from the kitchen and the décor is dodgy at best. In the corner is a massive stuffed bison head, a bison that looks distinctly surprised to be there, mounted like that and everything. When it falls off the wall, as it often does, it could easily maim or kill an unsuspecting patron. None of the locals, needless to say, sits in the chair under the bison head.

Hunter and I freshened our drinks at the Jerome. Straight Scotch on an empty stomach. Burning all the way down. The guitar player's heart was just breaking into itty bitty pieces over there in the corner. Hunter frowned into that folded up newspaper through half moon glasses, thoughtfully circling numbers on the sporting pages. "Right," he said, standing up and staggering back, casting a long shadow; rangy and gangling and completely uncoordinated, "come up to the house at five o'clock. We'll have a party."

Well, that man has always unsettled me. And by then I was having a party of my own. So when Gary the guitar player said, "Mind if I join you?" because his wife had run off with a drug dealer, I just kept right on drinking.

I am not proud of this. And it was, as it turned out, a serious mistake. But that guitar player was a wreck, man. He needed a friend nearly as much as he needed a drink. And I could use a friend myself sometimes. When I finally stood up in the white afternoon to stroll through the cold mountain village I was staggering and weaving and singing a sad song. I remember the flowers though, all around Aspen, bright flowers in window boxes and tubs. And stopping to stand awed at the huge misty thunderhead clouds playfully rolling around and carrying on up there in the sky.

I asked the taxi driver what alcohol I should get for Hunter. He laughed a nervous, knowing laugh. "Chivas," he shuddered. We cruised in companionable silence along the mountain roads. It looked so peaceful out there, like a pastoral painting, the horses and barns and gorges dropping to clear surging rivers. Fields of dandelions and white fluffy cottonwoods. Corrugated mountain rockfaces, dusted with snow and reflected in still, clear water. Incredibly beautiful.

Until you reach the high wire fortress gates of Owl Farm, that is. Welcome to white line fever. And up here nothing has changed. Up here a full daylight moon hangs so big and close you could reach out and touch it. The peacocks still strut among the dumped cars (and human wreckage) that litter the grounds.

Over 30 years ago, after living with the Hell's Angels for 18 months and writing a best-selling book in their defence—serious journalism about the way they had been negatively mythologised which only hinted at what he was to become—he retreated here to the mountains and began mythologising himself instead. Nowadays, apart from occasional and often disastrous forays out into the real world, he lives reclusively. "A crazy loon out here in the woods," he once told me. He shuns society and hates going out to parties. His friends are the locals and he frequently feuds with his neighbours. Shooting their pets, for example, doesn't necessarily help neighbourly relations a whole lot. Ignored mail spills from his letterbox, phones go unanswered, and visitors and acolytes who have come to pay homage often find that he has locked himself in to avoid them. Those who do gain entrance will wonder later what hit them.

It was here in the privacy of his own strange home that he became Dr Hunter S. Thompson the great Gonzo journalist. Perhaps the only one in captivity. It was here that the drugs began to take hold. Here in this log cabin he became the monster of his own creation. To visit *chez* Thompson is to meet a man who is even more exaggerated and violent than his myth. 'When the going gets weird the weird turn pro,' became his motto. A man who has lived at top terrifying speed. 'And it has always been with the total, permanent finality of a thing fed into an atom smasher,' he noted in the author's note to *Songs of the Doomed*. The writer did not invent the character. The character was already there and going about his grisly daily business. The writer simply wrote about his life. Hell, he was only writing the truth and isn't that what journalists are supposed to do? "My way of joking is to tell the truth," Muhammad Ali once told him. "That's the funniest joke in the world." Indeed, agreed Hunter with alacrity in one of his finest pieces, a devastating profile of the champ in decline. 'And that is also as fine a definition of "Gonzo journalism" as anything I've ever heard, for good or ill.' And as Jim Harrison rightly pointed out in E. Jean Carroll's biography *Hunter*, 'personal journalism depends on the writer having an actual personality'. Hunter's alarming personality is there leering over your shoulder in all his work. 'Hunter,' his mother told E. Jean Carroll, 'was difficult from the moment of his birth.' Hunter seems to have been off the rails from birth. But his condition worsened when his father died and his mother hit the booze.

In *The Great Shark Hunt* he explained just exactly what Gonzo journalism is. 'It is a style of "reporting" based on William Faulkner's idea that the best fiction is far more true than any kind of journalism—and that the best journalists have always known this . . . My idea with *Fear and Loathing in Las Vegas* was to buy a fat notebook and record the whole thing, *as it happened*, then send in the notebook for publication—without editing. That way, I felt, the eye and mind of the journalist would be functioning as a camera . . . But this is a hard thing to do, and in the end I found myself imposing an essentially fictional framework on what began as a straight/crazy piece of journalism. True Gonzo reporting needs the talents of a master journalist, the eye of an artist/photographer and the heavy balls of an actor. Because the writer *must* be a participant in the scene, while he's writing it—or at least taping it, or even sketching it. Or all three.'

"You changed everything, Hunter," I said, participating in his drugs. Pharmaceuticals, of course, stream through the veins of Gonzo journalism.

"Gonzo journalism came from total despair," he tells me, "total failure. I would be on assignment somewhere missing the deadline, the editor would be panicking so I would have to send my notes. So I would just pull my notes out of the pad and send them. Eventually I became very good at keeping notes."

'Thompson's talent—and it really is his only talent—lies in his ability to describe his own manic plunge into drink, drugs, and madness through a use of controlled exaggeration that is truly marvelous' wrote Vivian Gornick in *The Village Voice* in 1979. The only problem with this argument is that he is not exaggerating, he is playing it down.

He does not even begin writing until he is stoned out of his gourd each night And drunk. I once saw him ingest an ounce of marijuana, a gram of cocaine, a bottle of whisky, some gin and a tab of LSD, alternating the cocktail until he was ready to write, around midnight. This is business as usual for Hunter S. Thompson. The elegant sentences and savage satire do not come easily. "Sometimes they do," he says when I tell him this, "but the punctuation and rhythm don't always. I see writing as riffs, as pure music." Most of his work comes out of a lot of yelling, shooting, drugs, and torment, usually of other people. It is a team sport, usually involving a secretary (a fairly high turnover on this front), girlfriend (also a high turnover, but generally young), trusted friends, dealers, a roaring open fire, the stereo at full volume, and the constant flickering of the television across the stations looking for ideas and ball games. By the time he hits the hot tub, a nightly ritual, he is, in his own words, "raving and jabbering".

He told P. J. O'Rourke in *Rolling Stone* that 'It took me about two years of work to be able to bring a drug experience back and put it on paper. And to do it right means you must retain that stuff at the same time you experience it. You know, acid will move your head around and your eyes, and whatever else you perceive things with. But bringing it back was one of the hardest things I ever had to do in writing.'

Whether he is one of the great contemporary stylists living out his art or a sad gibbering old wreck whose time has passed is a question of taste, I guess. Much of his early work was brilliant: seminal, peerless journalism. Informed, hilarious, wide-ranging. The Ali piece, the Kentucky Derby, the piece that launched his career and changed journalism as we know it (though it seems rather juvenile now, getting shitfaced at a horse race and writing about it), a piece on travelling with Teddy Kennedy to visit Governor Jimmy Carter in Georgia, the piece on the Roxanne Pulitzer divorce trial in Palm Beach in which the illustrious Pulitzer name was considerably blackened by tales of cocaine sluttishness and wanton sex with everyone from the help to other women.

"There was a tortured and smouldering love affair between me and Roxanne," he admits with an uncharacteristically coy smile. "It was one of the best kept secrets. I went back to Palm Beach and it plunged me back into the vortex of lust and madness that Roxanne represented. It always will to me. Yeah. Roxanne is one of my loves, which we denied for a while during the trial. She got nothing from the settlement. She was not quite beautiful enough for Palm Beach. I have never told anyone that. Goddamn it, Susan, if you want to interview me you have to realise that I was always really out there."

Through all of it he lopes on fast forward: staggering, loaded, shouting, carrying cans of beer and bottles of Wild Turkey, drunk in the morning, scaring the shit out of his subjects, not giving a goddamn. He went to Zaire, New Orleans, the Nixon resignation, Vietnam on expenses and never got around to writing anything when he got back. When he arrived for his first combat mission in Vietnam at six o'clock in the morning he was wearing Bermuda shorts, sneakers with no socks, a Hawaiian shirt, baseball cap, shades, cigarette in cigarette holder. Two room-boys carried his

chest of ice with beer. Nick Proffitt in *Hunter*: 'Looked in the car—
no Hunter. We looked down the highway and there was Hunter, I
mean, a mile down the damn road. Walking along. Talking into his
tape recorder. Heading right toward where the troops were, the last
South Vietnamese presence on the highway. Well, first of all, we
debated whether to let the son of a bitch get himself killed. Then
we jumped in the Jeep and I sort of had to beat the driver about
the head and shoulders to get him to go down the road. We pulled
up alongside Hunter and grabbed him and threw him in the car.
I'd say we were no more than five hundred meters from the first
North Vietnamese outpost.'

It was the opium dens that got Hunter in Vietnam.

If his work seems thinner now and descends, occasionally, into
gibberish, if he appears to have lost it, he is just doing what he has
always done—drugs and writing.

"He works hard," his friend Dan told me later as we eased
back down the mountain; wired, the morning light creeping across
the sky. "He is up there working every night, he is not always
partying and blowing things up. He works."

Therein, I think, lies the key to Hunter's continued presence on
the planet. He might put on a show for visitors to engineer his bad
boy image, he certainly vacuums a lot of substances, but he never
stops working up there on his mountain, and to work and do drugs
in tandem and live you have to know what you are doing.

In the author's note for *Fear and Loathing: On the Campaign
Trail* he wrote: 'In airport bars, all-nite coffee shops and dreary
hotel rooms all over the country—there is hardly a paragraph in this
jangled saga that wasn't produced in a last-minute, teeth grinding
frenzy. There was never enough time. Every deadline was a crisis.'

The great Gonzo was cooking as I arrived that night at five, a
sight to behold, as smoke billowed through the kitchen. "You may
notice I have a new refrigerator, Susan." He looms through the
smoke. "Er, no," I reply. "Call yourself a journalist?" he shouts
across the room. To even get to the stove had involved moving
stacks of documents, these being the archives, a lot of "goddamns"

and some playful secondary yelling. Hunter kept backing into the corner, like a caged animal, recoiling from my tape recorder as if it might be radioactive. "OK," he said at one point, lurking in the darker recesses of his kitchen, "fire away." Then he walked out the door. On my tape recorder, doors are slamming in the background, a gun is cocked, there is a lot of sniffing, ice clinks in glasses, and long silences are underscored by bouncing balls and hysterical screaming on the giant television. And we must rely on my tape recorder and scrawled notes from here on in because my memory of events by then could not be considered reliable. And he mumbles and mutters and slurs and changes direction so much that it is almost impossible to understand him anyway. There are glittering moments of lucidity though, every now and then.

Hunter's friends stood around the kitchen enveloped by smoke, drinking beer and avidly following the ball game, taking it personally and bitterly if their team lost a goal, whooping it up and dancing around the kitchen if they scored.

"So, Hunter, what did you think of the E. Jean Carroll biography of you?" I slur. In the book he is accused of wife-beating by his former wife, Sandy. "It is bullshit, all of it, except for about three or four things," he responds with feeling. "See those purple pansies to your left, right next to the .44 rifle—it is loaded, by the way—I bought those on the way home today."

Hearing this veiled threat, Dan valiantly wades in to my rescue and, heading off a homicide at the pass, offers to read Hunter's latest *Rolling Stone* piece aloud. And what should it be but *Polo is My Life*. This is clearly one of Hunter's favourite pastimes. Hearing his own work read aloud. He corrects the rhythm, chortles at his own jokes, makes Dan go back and re-read if he misses a word, opens a kitchen drawer and rummages around; all the while shaking his head and marvelling at his own audacity.

The kitchen is a command centre from which Hunter works like some spastic bad guy from a Bond film, often wearing only his bathrobe and chomping on a cigarette holder. He stays in touch with the evil empire with the help of a sometimes recalcitrant fax, a confusing telephone system and a satellite dish which allows him to beam into almost any television network anywhere. He views the follies of the rest of humanity on that television screen, never turned off and which during the incessant ball games can cause a person to duck for cover because it seems the ball is coming straight at you.

The décor is difficult to accurately describe. Arrested adolescence meets psychopathic hillbilly meets eccentric writer. The Stars and Stripes flag hangs across the kitchen window and a large lamp acts as a noticeboard. The rest is chaos. There are piles of papers, books and videos everywhere, an old upright piano literally buckles under their weight. Fairy lights glisten through the house. A full-size skeleton stands sentinel in the corner, a luckless visitor perhaps, overseeing a collection of stuffed animals poised in interrupted flight. Photographs cover every wall, fresh flowers sit in vases alongside Indian masks on tables. Loaded guns lie around, leaning in corners.

The walls and ceiling are covered with cards and notes and well, objects: a rubber face of Richard Nixon, presidential campaign buttons, drawings, mementoes of all those stories so violently executed, the stories that made all those journalism students yearn to ride wild and free; a kind of a shrine to the Doctor of Gonzo journalism. "It is so easy, Gonzo journalism," he mumbles. But it is a bad, bad mistake to use him as a role model. It leads to harder things.

By the time his book on the 1992 Clinton election campaign, *Better Than Sex*, was published, standards had clearly slipped. He didn't by this stage find it necessary to go out on the actual campaign, he communicated with pertinent people by fax and watched it on television, although he and Jann Wenner did meet with Clinton for lunch during the campaign, in a bid for *Rolling Stone* to deliver its audience. Hunter and the candidate, by Hunter's account, appeared to scare the hell out of each other. And he did make it to Little Rock for election night, shambling menacingly around the Capital Hotel, drunk, as always, on the job. Yep, maybe he is right. He shouldn't leave his house. For the good of the nation. There are enough lumbering psychopaths and sons of bitches out there as it is. "In politics," he mumbles now, "we can count Mr Bill as the number one pig. Sly, evil. Some are more equal than others. Clinton appears, er, er, sour, degenerate, er, er, all men are swine. If you don't listen to what I am saying, Susan, I am going to kill you."

Silence.

A throat clears nervously in the background.

More silence.

Cheering on the television.

"He is from a morally bankrupt position anyway," Hunter resumes. I am obviously listening to his satisfaction now. "People are swine from the start, people are whores."

I rally for a suicidal moment. "So are you getting sick of politics?"

"Yeah, I am getting sick of disease too." His friends laugh cruelly in the background. I am obviously out here on my own now. "But on any given day," he continues, "I will participate because I must. Yeah. I am addicted to politics in the sense that I have a vested interest in controlling . . . and if I don't someone else will. And if it happens you get a little flare up."

Foolhardy to the end, I gamely go on. "Why do you hate Clinton so much, Hunter?"

"He is a lunatic, he is like a romper stomper. A real badass. He really is one of the worst. He is white trash."

Even with a loaded gun waved around I just don't quit. "Worse than Nixon?" I coolly enquire as if this is a normal interview. Jesus how drunk *was* I? Who gives a fuck whether Clinton is worse than Nixon.

And Hunter seems to have calmed down. "Yeah, worse than Nixon. I have to admit. I have thought about it for a long time and I have to admit that I like Nixon better than Clinton. I had more fun with Nixon than I had with Clinton. That's funny. That tells you something. I had more fun with Nixon." Evil chuckle. Sound of footsteps, then Hunter says, "There are faxes coming in on the machine." Long and terrifying scream. Yep, The Scream still makes the hair on your arms stand up. "Warren Zevon," he shrieks. "I have to call him back." His voice drops, conspiratorial: "I am now getting deeply into songwriting, Susan."

I remind him that he once predicted Nixon would only last four years and that his political predictions have usually been deadly accurate. "Well," he says, pleased by the excruciating flattery, "I didn't realise it would be so easy to bring him down." There is an art to the flattery, I am dimly beginning to realise. And getting it right is a matter of survival. Straight out sycophancy only makes him want to kill you. It embarrasses him in front of his friends. You have to sit at the shrine, you have to worship, but you have to be subtle if you want to live.

Jimmy Carter, whom he championed, is "a mean person, humourless through and through" these days.

In her book, E. Jean Carroll quotes Hunter's friend David Felton saying: 'Two major changes occurred with Hunter. One of them was when he started to use cocaine . . . The second thing that got in his way was the celebrity.' Indeed he is a phenomenon. He represents the walk on the wild side that most people will never take. He seeks attention in his writing but he shrinks from its effects. "I don't want to meet my fans," he shakes his head. "Some of them are dangerous. I get the crazies."

For some reason I now ask him about similarities between John Kennedy and Clinton. Oddly, since this has never occurred to me before. "He was a Nazi and so is Clinton," Hunter responds. "Er, Clinton is an, er, robot. He is in favour of corporal punishment. I think Kennedy wasn't so big on punishment except to purge his enemies. The mob was all over those people. They were notional allies at the time. They were from Cuba. That was the connection to Cuba. All of a sudden Castro came in"—blurring on the tape—"he had to get out of Cuba because of Castro." My tape is turned off. And then turned back on again. "Clinton is in cahoots with the NRA. Those bastards. They are jackbooted thugs bursting into your house. The FBI murdered two people. I have never considered murder." This, I have to tell you, is something of a relief, since I am seriously starting to get on the Doctor's nerves.

More people arrive. "Walk in you alcoholic bastards," Hunter calls to them. Fortunately I shut up for a while here and then we are talking about writers. "Tom Wolfe would have been better, you know, would have realised his potential if he didn't have a drinking problem. I love Tom, he is a wonderful guy, but the drinking, it has been a problem for him." Coming from Hunter S. Thompson, this is an extraordinary statement.

I ask him if he knew what he was doing back in the '60s when he was pioneering Gonzo journalism. "I am professional," he says with great dignity. "I am who I am. Here we go"—and his great bald head leans forward into the trough.

*The Curse of Lono*, which many people consider to be the last book the Doctor wrote at the peak of his powers, has always been the book for which he has most affection. "I have a reasonable amount of affection for *Lono*. It was supposed to be a big book, an art book, I was only going to do the captions but it took a year and a half to find a publisher."

There is a disjointed conversation about a bomb Hunter let off last week. "Bombs are fun. Two thousand pounds of nitrate, it is a real buzz." His voice is loving now. "That first profane flash. I punctured a perfect shot. I just held that white gas. You get sucked into the vortex of the bomb and get blown back, whoosh. People hang out and look at each other and say 'oh that stupid fucker'. Goddamn it. All bombs are not spectacular. It isn't fun when a bomb hisses. If I don't hit that thing, if it doesn't go off, my life is a barrel of scum for a long time."

I tell Hunter he seems mellow, it must be love. Dan later tells me that this was a particularly stupid remark, since Hunter has only known Angie or whatever her name is for about two weeks. Hunter laughs. "Now isn't that a silly question. I am always in love. I am like a honey badger." My tape goes on and off. There are all kinds of antics swirling around us in the kitchen, jabbering and laughing.

Then quite suddenly there follows a long and lucid discussion about *Fear and Loathing*, how it happened and how all of it was true. He had been deeply involved in a story about the killing of a Chicago journalist, Ruben Salazar, in 1971 and was talking to his contact, lawyer and political activist Oscar Acosta, when things got heavy. Bodyguards were threatening to kill him. "I took Oscar to Vegas in order to be his bodyguard, to get him away from politics. Then he left me there with a pound of weed and a magnum revolver loaded with six shots and some bullets in his briefcase. It was because of the Chicago Seven. He had to get back to represent the people who burned down the big hotel in LA. I couldn't pay the bill, I was afraid. Suddenly I found myself in the kitchen of this hotel and I had to get out. I had to jump the hotel bill and take off in a red car. Vegas was a spin-off from that. Look can we go off the record"—his voice gets deep and scary—"don't talk, Susan".

To sit with Hunter until daylight, as I have done, is to experience some dark places. There is the good Hunter and the bad Hunter. The good Hunter still has the vestiges of the Southern Gentleman from Louisiana and can be a fascinating conversationalist with an encyclopaedic knowledge. His work is sprinkled with classical and biblical references. The bad Hunter is bullying and violent, snarls and twitches.

But call me crazy, for some reason I have never really felt frightened around Hunter Thompson. No matter what his state of mind he knows how to handle firearms, and to the best of my knowledge no one has ever come to any serious harm at Owl Farm—well, no one has died there, that we know of, and you do recover from trauma in the fullness of time.

At least I didn't go screaming into the night this time.

Dan and I are in a taxi going down the steep mountain. Going down to what Hunter calls Fat City. "I was broke recently," Dan is telling me, "and Hunter just pressed $500 into my hand. He was broke too, but he just did that for me."

And all the rivers run to the sea.

My nose was streaming as I stared dismally out at green grass strewn with buttercups at Aspen airport. The hangover and remorse were severe and unrelenting. Normal people appeared to be doing normal things all around me, getting on planes, flying away, stuff like that, but not me, oh no, I was seriously, grindingly, violently sick as I lay, filled with self-pity and hatred, on the hard bench seat. Darkly fantasising about a world without small shrill children running around and screaming like that. Now it was me who was green and acting like a large malign lizard.

I solved the hangover problem, I thought, by drinking heavily and passing out on the plane as the canyons and valleys and steep rocky mountains swooped and melted whitely below and finally receded into the mystic. But something troubling woke me from a deep, dead sleep. I looked down. Glurp. My nose had bled copiously and conspicuously down my shirt, a deep crimson flower, as if I had been shot. And for an alarming moment I thought I had missed something that might turn out to be important. My own death. But those nose-bleeds would continue for another three weeks, on and off. Every time I sniffed I would be transported back to the fear and loathing at Woody Creek. Reminding, reminding, reminding. Reminding me of what I could not remember. Never a good sign, that. Illustrator Ralph Steadman was not exaggerating when he said, "Every time I've been with Hunter I've been a wreck at the end of it. I always had the feeling that when I went on a job with him I might not come back."

I began to suspect that I had gotten out alive. Concussed perhaps, a twitching nervous condition, brain damaged even, but alive. The less generous of my acquaintances might even ask how anyone would know the difference.

# Shootin' the Shit at Charlie B's

They are hollerin' and hootin' and howlin' down Main Street. Roaring and ripsnorting and baying at the big ol' silvery moon. *oow, oow, oooow*. It's the Saturday night special, Missoula, Montana. Boogie-woogie.

Here they come now. Pick-up trucks blasting bluegrass slithering to a stop outside the Top Hat and Charlie B's. Cowboys tall in the saddle, huge in the sweat-stained hat and all spruced up for Saturday night. Drinking beer and shooting pool and looking real sharp for the ladies. Here they come now, swaggering past the Elk Club in scuffed boots, down past the Depo and the Oxford, all along the sidewalk; yowling and yelping and lurching from bar to bar; tomcatting tonight.

After a stopover in sanctimonious Salt Lake City, with its glistening snow-dusted hills, its cheap suits, unsullied complexions and its party-pooping persistent temperance, a town that is liquored and loud, a town with a drinking problem, a wild and crazy town smack in Big Sky country is, hey, my kind of town.

"Montana has a higher rate of alcohol consumption per capita than any other state in the US. Even Alaska," Otis tells me proudly at the bar of the dark and nefarious Top Hat as he casually downs tequila shots and a reggae band in cowboy hats inexplicably changes gear and lunges into an extended drum solo. "In Montana you go to church, the PTA or the bar. It is the only place they give you a drink to go. You can drink it in your automobile. I like that," he adds unblinking as the drum solo drones in the phosphorous neon of beer signs that glow green and pink in the feverish night.

Shootin' the shit over at Charlie B's a country singer is getting all choked up. "There's a lotta of words in this song," he says earnestly "I mean every one of 'em though. You look up at the sky and, dammit, you just kinda howl don't ya?" Yes siree. Ain't that turning out to be the truth. This is, after all, the wild, wild northwest.

**JAMES LEE BURKE**

Pretty much the only person not howling and drinking to excess in Missoula, Montana this hectic Saturday night is the person I have come here to see. James Lee Burke. Crime writer. And there is plenty of reason for that.

James Lee Burke and his wife Pearl are eating ice-cream on the riverbank. A river fringed with dandelions and buttercups and bright green grass that shimmers like silk in the moonlight. Crumpled James Lee Burke is savouring the sound of the rushing river, the fragrant air fresh on the face, the sweet syrup cold on the lips.

"As we say in AA," he cackles, "most of us have two speeds: Wide Open and Fuck It. Alcohol in the alcoholic goes almost immediately into the blood. It doesn't stop at the yellow light."

Well, it's Fuck It down there in the town tonight. No two ways about that. Fuck It all the way home.

Ageing elm and maple trees reach out across the wide empty streets of Missoula on a subdued Sunday morning. James Lee Burke cruises through the town in his new car; past wooden two-storey houses and neat green lawns, and swings up into the foothills of the sheer jagged mountains that surround the valley. Hills strewn with yellow, with firs and vestiges of melting snow as fierce winter recedes to sunsplashed summer. And my flea-pit hotel at the foot of a mountain, with a man's shavings still in the sink, fades away into panoramic Big Sky Montana. 'Montana was so beautiful,' the young James Lee Burke was once moved to write in *The Lost Get-Back Boogie*, 'that it made something drop inside me.'

James Lee Burke, a crime writer who transcends the genre, stopped saying Fuck It a long time ago. Crawled out of the black hole of booze. Slammed on the brakes and skidded to a stop at the yellow light. Sobriety, serenity and success have unfolded slowly from hard times.

"I tried many, many times to stop drinking on my own. I would go maybe a few days. Maybe 30 days; that was the longest I ever went without drinking. But I always went back to it. Finally I bottomed out. I reached a point where I never wanted to drink again.

I became what they call a white-knuckle recovering alcoholic. A person who tries to do it on sheer willpower. But I had reached a very desperate point in my life and I went five and a half years like that. Not wanting to drink, wanting to be sane. But finally I just went crazy. I didn't find relief in white-knuckle sobriety. I found a kind of madness. I became delusional. I was worse than I ever was when I was drinking. I didn't have any tools. I didn't have anyone I could talk to about the problems that beset me. It is like wrapping your head in tinfoil and putting it in a microwave. I could publish nothing, could not think of the world except as a place where you slid shards of glass across your palms. Probably with time I would have gotten drunk again. Then I went to my first meeting of the 12-Step Fellowship. When I heard all the other people talk about their problems I knew I had found a home. I walked out of the firestorm. Without it I wouldn't be here."

James Lee Burke speaks in the slow drawl of bayou, swamp and boogie; down home Louisiana. He comes here to Montana in the summer but his heart and his mind lie in the steamy, complicated South. "When good people die they go to New Orleans," he smiles from the shadow of a white Stetson as emerald pastures roll off the mountain into the huge blue sky. "I love the South. I love the civility. In Louisiana they are French Catholic and they have this sense of the *bon vivant*. Social life, food, huge family parties. They are ferociously Catholic but in the middle of their culture there is this pagan ambience. They know how to live in the world."

Burke grew up in that world of wooden porches, juke joints, superstition, dinners of crawfish and crab in the late evening sun under the cypress trees on Bayou Teche, fishing the Gulf with his father, digging those rhythm and blues. But southern Louisiana was a world, too, of old families, old resentments and old wars. The faded gentility of the Old South. A world of ancient grudges where all men are not created equal and never forget it.

That is the over-ripe, exotic, jiving and unjust world of James Lee Burke and his fictional Cajun cop Dave Robicheaux. It is always hot in Burke's books. Robicheaux is one tough son of a bitch: righteous, Catholic, a family man, a recovering alcoholic, a Vietnam veteran, haunted by his past, fighting oppression and his own demons all at once. A good, imperfect man who if angered can lose it in a big way. Go on a bender, beat the crap out of a recalcitrant hood, maybe even trash a joint. 'I saw the balloon of red-black color well up behind my eyes, heard a sound like wet newspaper ripping in my head, saw the startled and fearful look in his face . . .' (*Burning Angel*).

Sudden shots of violence that leave him as shaken as his slime-bag adversary is smashed up. Bad nights of bad dreams and flaying insomnia. But this is not the mindless violence of, say, a James Ellroy or an Elmore Leonard. "Dave," says Burke, "his anger and his violence are always expressed on behalf of another, it is always in defence of another. He absorbs most personal abuse. People in recovery maintain that the single greatest cause of a slip is anger. Anger born out of fear."

We drive along gravel to the end of a road at the head of a canyon. "We live in the poor white trash section," chuckles Burke as we pull up outside a wooden house set in a nest of firs. James Lee Burke is still a handsome man at 58, striding out in cowboy boots, Stetson and leather jacket; stopping to greet two hysterical dogs writhing in pleasure in the driveway.

"Gee whiz," he says to them. "Gee whiz, guys." A face creased by life and made beatific by a palpable peace within. A chivalrous, sweet-natured Southern gentleman; the kind of peace that comes from pain negotiated and parlayed into love. When Burke writes stuff like this from *Burning Angel* there is a sense of dues paid in full:

'He was a mercurial headcase, a functioning drunk, a physiological caricature, a libidinous nightmare whose sexual habits you tried never to think about, but, most important, Johnny, like all drunks, was driven by a self-centered fear that made his kind see blood in tap water and dead men walking out of the surf.'

Or this, from *Cadillac Jukebox*:

'If you seriously commit yourself to alcohol, I mean full-bore, the way you take up a new religion . . . you drink down. That means you cannot drink in well-lighted places with ordinary people because the psychological insanity in your face makes you a pariah among them.'

James Lee Burke is clearly no stranger to the alcoholic self-loathing that seems to feature in and fuel the lives of most crime writers. "When I was drinking I was bitter and jaundiced and virtually nihilistic. There was very little in the way of light in my work."

Since he stepped into the light his books have become more and more poetic, atmospheric and lyrical, bringing the mist-shrouded swamps and vine-wreathed levees to full living colour with the kind of deeply felt nature writing that elevates him from the realm of mere crime writing. And even when his characters are meaner than junkyard dogs, when their actions are sickening, the work is informed by humanity, morality and a strong sense of social justice.

The violence is, perhaps, ever more shocking set as it is under lavender and crimson sunsets, pecan and cypress trees, live oaks, wisteria and warm tropical rainstorms. But the gracious ante-bellum mansions and many-columned plantation houses do not come without the shacks of the poor scattered around the line of sight. In *The Lost Get-Back Boogie* he wrote of remembering 'the string of shacks by the rail yard where the whores sat on the wood porches on Saturday afternoons and dipped their beer out of a bucket.'

A common Burke plotline involves the corrupted scion of an old family and his exploitation of the black people on his plantation under the guise of benefactor. "The Cajuns are a very loving people, very gentle. They are easily taken advantage of by aggressive outsiders. I remember all the people of colour I knew; their kindness, I could trust them." Grudges are generations old, the shrieking past is always present; slavery, civil war. Throw into the mix white trash with a vengeance, seething Central America next door, the complexity of generations of racial relations, the Klan, the CIA and crime, and you got yourself characters like pimp Sweet

Pea Chaisson, ex-mercenary and grifter Sonny Boy Marsallus, the Giancano mafia family, corrupt Governor Buford LaRose, black hookers with attitude, Batiste the old black man who works in Robicheaux's bait and tackle shop, and private eye Clete Purcell, a human wrecking ball and "one of my favourite characters. Clete is one of those guys who always backs you. We used to have an expression in the '50s: 'I'm backing your action, Jackson'." Burke hoots with strange laughter.

Old friends and adversaries appear in book after book. Dave understands the bad guys because he grew up with them. We know how they got like they are, bad guys come from bad families, got beaten by their fathers, castrated by poverty; and all of it is bathed in the grace of a compassionate man. Burke unfailingly takes the side of the poor and oppressed, the damaged and wronged. "The stories are meant to be an idyllic journey. It is my own feeling that there has been a struggle between good and evil for control of the earth since the beginning of humankind. It is ongoing, it is daily. As Dave says, there are those who cross the line and deliberately murder all life that is in their soul. They are always in our midst. I have known a handful, they become visible only when we give them sanction. Interestingly, when I met them they weren't in jails, they worked in positions of managerial administration. I am convinced they were sociopaths."

Sun streams through skylights in the kitchen of this perfectly silent house. Out there somewhere are mountain, sky and pasture, bison roaming the range, grizzly bears, those scary dudes of the Montana Militia, but in here there is only the goodness and kindness that radiates from James Lee Burke, a godly man; goddamn it. This is fundamentally a state of grace . . . "I was raised in the church and the God I believed in earlier in my life was a vengeful God who punished and put people in hell. Today I am a practising Catholic and I can say honestly that I love the church. But I had to relearn my concept about God. I learned in the 12-Step Fellowship that God is of our own understanding. I believe there are two kinds of grace. The grace of God and the grace of our fellow men and women. Art has to be informed by that kind of grace, if it is not it won't be able to evolve." Burke has a deep, growling, cackling laugh that circles the room, bounces off the ceiling and then reverberates in the still afternoon. And he laughs and laughs. "He just works all the time," laments his small, Chinese-born wife Pearl, alighting momentarily outside the small study where her husband conducts his life of crime. "The story is always there," he agrees. "I never know where the book is going but I see it all the time. It is in my dreams. I write all the time. I would go crazy if I didn't."

On the wall are family photographs of their four children. He might have invented them himself as characters for his books. Or have they read too much James Lee Burke? It is genetic? Huge and long laugh. "Our kids have just always been wonderful children," he says, the accent sliding into the Bayou. "I just feel very blessed to have our children. Alafair is a county prosecutor, two of them are in law enforcement, and Jimmy the boy is a prosecutor in the US Attorney's office. He is a lawyer in the tradition of my grandfather who was a really famous lawyer in Louisiana, Walter Burke. He was known for his altruism and his courage. I have some letters downstairs from Roosevelt to my grandfather. And I tell you, when Jimmy prosecutes people they go up the road."

They were frequently on the road during the hard, drinking times. The family lived in a garage once, stayed in Okie motels, spent a year in a trailer park. The dream turned nightmare on wheels, a classic American story of survival and redemption. "We lived everywhere from Florida to California, and everywhere in between. Oh, we were poor, we were really poor. I would like to say it was romantic but it wasn't. After I got my degree I went to work on the pipeline in the oilfields. We had our first child when I was 23. You had to ride with the line, I would write at night in motel rooms in longhand. I taught in four or five colleges and universities. I have been a truck driver, a land surveyor. I was a newspaper reporter and I was a social worker on skid row in LA. I learned a lot. I don't believe anyone is beyond help. You would find very famous people, actors, very well known people on skid row. There was one guy the cops wouldn't put in their squad cars because he would just throw up. This pitiful creature from skid row was the bane of all Los Angeles county. Another guy would use his welfare ticket to check into a hotel and then he would throw all the furniture out of the window and run down and pick it all up and carry it up to the pawn shop to sell it for wine. These guys would literally stop the system. The jailer would put his hands over his face when he saw them coming."

These guys would also return to make a guest appearance in *Dixie City Jam*. All the time, he was writing and dreaming. All of it, all of that living, all those weird, working, maladjusted people would be poured into his books and given voice. "I published my first short story in 1956 and never wanted to be anything but a writer since . . . It helps if you are deeply neurotic because you have got this infinite well of neurotic material you can just stick your hand into." Another fearsome cackle.

"Many of the characters are biographical," he allows, eating butterless bread in his kitchen. "And many of the events are founded in real experience. It is ongoing. Writing about the South is a great advantage because it is an antithetical society that has had many histories that happened simultaneously. The treatment of people of colour in the South is an enormous wrong. We can only get rid of the past by owning up to it. I don't think we have dealt with it yet. I was with Amnesty International for nine years. Some terrible things went on in San Salvador and Guatemala during the Reagan era that the press wouldn't touch with a dungfork. The country could not deal with the fact that the administration was doing things that were truly horrible. I have written about it in *Burning Angel*. We lived in a little village in Mexico for a while. Out in this godforsaken place where life has no value at all. We dealt a couple of times with guys with big US Army machine guns. You look in their eyes and know they are going to kill. Mess with them and they will kill."

For a guy who graduated from high school "so dumb I could hardly write my name" he skyrocketed to success early with *Half of Paradise,* which he wrote at 24 and found a publisher for it a couple of years later. "I got a six-column review in the *New York Times.* Best review I ever had. I thought that was normal. If it comes later you can handle it better. I was arrogant, I was young. Alcoholism is characterised by grandiosity and arrogance, you think anything good that befalls you is because you are a great guy; there are better ways to learn it. Every artist who makes a lifetime career will discover that success has a lot to do with endurance. We learn at a certain point that we never wrote better because of an opiate. We just thought we did."

As he gets up to dust away some cobwebs a turquoise and silver ring in the shape of a cross catches the sun and throws a spray of light.

Two novels that followed that first one remain unpublished but his fourth, *To the Bright and Shining Sun,* and his fifth, *Down My Sword and Shield,* were published by the time he was 34. Then he went into a downhill slide for 13 years, into the deep and ugly black hole. His next book, *The Lost Get-Back Boogie,* was rejected by 52 publishers and reworked and reworked before it was finally published in 1986.

He only really got going again in 1985 with a collection of short stories called *The Convict.* Then damaged Dave Robicheaux, a character not a million miles away from his author, an alter ego perhaps, came into the plot and Burke has been on a roll ever since, winning a John Simon Guggenheim Fellowship and a Pulitzer nomination. "That was pretty neat." The profound humility he believes is essential to evolve as an artist.

He wrote his first Robicheaux book, *The Neon Rain,* because he wanted to get back in print and writing a literary novel within a genre was a crafty way of doing it. After years of rejection the book was an enormous success. "I was just dumbfounded." Set in sexy, bad New Orleans, it dealt with his ongoing concern with US corruption in Central America and with Latin American drug dealers.

Like so many crime writers he has moved, in the second phase of his career, from one-dimensional efforts to a body of work that grows more and more literary. "It is all rock and roll," he shrugs, chewing on a pumpkin seed. "You are in fashion and then you are out. My feeling is that every artist has an obsession to record history as he sees it. It is a vanity, a feeling that somehow you have captured the truth. A desperate sense that you have to somehow convey it to others."

James Lee Burke pulls on his battered boots and slams on his Stetson. Love, Keith Richards told me, wears a white Stetson. We cruise down through fir-covered hills.

Down by the river a homeless person wrapped in a blanket is reading a dictionary while his black mongrel dog stands shivering sentinel.

And sitting in the soda fountain of picture postcard Missoula eating a hamburger while Frank sings 'Mack the Knife' on the juke box and the mountains gleam with melting snow that runs to rushing rivers, it is hard to come to terms with the underbelly of violence that permeates the American small town. That is the horror of it, the sudden shock, the juxtaposition of fear and hatred, immaculate civic pride lawns, crimson blood on the sidewalk. Ugliness underlying beauty.

In literature and film culture a Freddy Krueger is all the more terrifying because he prowls ranch style, station wagon, God fearing, innocent family value suburbs. But out here in the wild west where men are men and women are crying into their beers, there was never an innocence to lose. Hell no. But still, but still. "I believe what has happened," says Burke, "is that what used to be confined to the underdog has one way or another spread laterally into the mainstream of American life. We are not equipped to deal with this. One political redress is to deny the existence of the problem, to cut education, to cut rehab programs, to cut money from law enforcement. This is madness. My own feeling is, and this is one guy's perspective, and that is that narcotics have been the third world's atom bomb. It is a deliberate and vicious agenda that not only makes billions of dollars for these criminals but has eviscerated American cities. The most important political event in the post-war era is the registration of the black vote. That was rescinded by the devisiveness, the chaos precipitated by massive cocaine addiction in the inner cities. I think we liberals are partially responsible for it. Their enabling of the industry and the black kid who maybe has a longevity of one year once he is on the crack. This guy is running around with a 9-millimetre Baretta."

And as night falls across the jagged mountains they are howling and hollering in the streets again. Standing in the street and going *oow, oow, ooow*. School is out for summer and the students from the University of Montana are leaping and roaring all over the joint. "I'm going to do boobs," screams a delirious medical student, arms spread wide to the wind. "Boobs, boobs, booooobs."

There are dogs everywhere in this dog town but their owners appear to do their howling for them. Walking on down past the Elk Club I hear a thin, strangulated sound. I look around for some kind of deranged critter on the loose. A hamster in distress, perhaps. An elk that has lost its way. But no. It was only me. Holy heck, I was howlin' too. Going native. And heading for the hills.

Los Angeles. So many different things to so many different people. So much concentrated and ostentatiously displayed wealth, so much poverty and despair, so much calibrated in between. It is not so much that the centre does not hold in Los Angeles as that there is no centre at all. It is hard to see immediately the Los Angeles so mythologised by its writers and film makers in the amorphous tangled mass of freeways, bungalows and unconnected clumps of fast food and fast everything shops that stretch away before you in the hard white light. The Los Angeles that so fascinates and appals writers like Joan Didion, James Ellroy and Dominick Dunne. Los Angeles, more than any other city, as Thomas Pyncheon has pointed out, belongs to the mass media. LA noir, movie stars, rhythm and blues, Disneyland, colonic irrigation, earthquakes; all waiting out there somewhere. The strange sight of oil wells near the airport, though, seems symbolic. This city was built on speculation, on the blind hope of hitting paydirt.

My shuddering cab joined the blur of traffic that never ends on the freeway to take me to my hotel in West Hollywood. The West Hollywood Ramada turned out to be a B-movie all on its own. A budget hotel frequented by gays, it served as a stage for ongoing comical dramas: huffs in the hallways, hissing by the pool, yearning in the dining room. Its reputation was such that my muscular new friend Sergeant Mario MuÉoz of the Los Angeles Police Department refused to park his car outside when he came over for a drink, lest it be recognised by colleagues at a 'faggot hotel'. For some reason I found it hilarious when he, off-duty, took his gun out of the waistband of his jeans and put it down on the table before he sat down. I never tired of watching him do this. It was so ridiculously tough. It was like being in a television cop programme. I almost expected him to blast his way out when he left. Where are you Michael Douglas when we need you? I still don't know if he was glad to see me, but that was definitely a gun in his pocket.

Hey, I was on the road. The plot was unfolding. And I could invent my own character. Everyone in California is busy inventing themselves. The place runs on pretending; on shedding the past and grabbing the opportunity, on reinventing to ever new and more fabulous specifications. You need never get old in LA. Go west. You can be making cocktails one day and millions the next. And they don't ask too many questions out here. You just make it up.

I became so ensconced at the Ramada that the dining room became my living room and I became part of the furniture. So much so that the staff, William the chef included, would come outside and wave me off to my interviews. And on one humiliating occasion double over in laughter as I, going native, staggered shakily across the four-lane highway to join the gym. They tried to hide it the next day as I limped into breakfast and eased myself painfully into the chair, but I heard the shrieks in the kitchen.

Oh yes. I listened to my fledgling friends tell their tales of heartbreak across the pool tables in the gay bars across the road and watched as the recently spurned found love anew the same night. I shared the elation of Larry the barman as the band for which he was a drummer entered the charts with their debut album and tried not to wince too openly at their crashing nightclub performance. I tried even harder to look sufficiently blonde and cool when he took me for a spin in his new two-tone Cadillac, polished and shined to the max, which he had bought with the profits.

"Help me out here," barked Dominick Dunne into his phone over at the Chateau Marmont when I called to confirm our interview. "Who are you?" I later found out that he is partially deaf. But I had found something else out too. It's hard being a nobody in Hollywood. I should have been grateful he took my call at all.

# Blood on the Socks

It was raining on Sunset Strip on that washed out Monday in Los Angeles. Wet and slippery. Fallen jacaranda splotched along the pavement of the slippery strip, sticking to your shoes, splashing them purple. Down past Tower Records, down past the House of Blues, past the Marlborough Man, down past the Hugh Grant memorial blowjob and the Thunder Roadhouse and on past the sinister black Viper Room. No great finely wrought monuments on the way here. Just monochromatic freeways and the tired suburbs that cling to them, indistinguishable.

The monuments are there all right, further up in Beverly Hills, monuments with clipped trees and wide cool landscaped lawns. Faux-tudor, elaborate castle, delicate pink confection, antebellum white with columns, elegant estate and mansion. Rolls Royce parked in the driveway, bronze sculpture on the lawn, staff discreet. Monuments to showgirls and slick hustlers and chiseled men; the Stars, ladies and gents, put your hands together please. Monuments to money and charisma, exquisitely displayed. Grandiose mansions to make believe. The houses range from large to larger to downright ridiculous and sprawling down the hillside.

This was once the world of Dominick Dunne. The mansion, the movies, the lot. "Our house was always full of people and parties," he says now, sadly. "The house was always lit like you were on stage. It was very theatrical." Back when he was a Hollywood producer the Reagans dropped by, Truman Capote vigorously cut the rug, Natalie Wood smoked from an elegant cigarette holder in the kitchen, Paul Newman swam gorgeously in the pool, Elizabeth Taylor and Richard Burton smooched in the living room, Lauren Bacall and Bogie tinkled ice in the Scotch. In their prime. Another time. So much youth and beauty. Gone now. Sick, old, disgraced, fat, dead. Time is so cruel. "This life that we lived was so extraordinarily glamorous." Dominick Dunne frowns. "I always knew it wouldn't last."

**DOMINICK DUNNE**

Down along Sunset, past the Rainbow Bar and Grill where Marilyn Monroe went on her first date with Joe Di Maggio and John Belushi bought his last round, on past that big, ugly barn the Whiskey Au Go Go, where The Doors first rode the storm and every square inch has been puked on since. Hendrix played there and so did Janis Joplin, dead now; sordidly, sensationally dead. Down on Sunset Boulevard bougainvillea splashes down the windows of the infamous Chateau Marmont, obscenely pink hibiscus flowers line the garden where Belushi checked out in a bodybag. From the window palm trees rise from the white haze then slump sideways in the rain.

In Dominick Dunne's room papers are piled on all the chairs, towering and teetering on tables, scattered across a desk, sliding to the floor; a writer's room. "It fascinates me to even be able to write. I think one of the reasons writing has worked for me is that I am not writing about a world I have never been part of. I know that world first hand, inside out. It is a world of privilege in which everything looks so pretty, but it isn't pretty at all."

Dominick Dunne has a way of bringing his tiny hands to his bespectacled face, his tiny mouth open in a wordless oohhh. As if he is about to hear something delicious and awful. Which he nearly always is. People tell him things. They just do. 'Gus listened, as he always listened when people told him things at dinner parties, which they always did,' he wrote of his alter ego Gus Bailey in *People Like Us*. As a tragic figure, solitary, apart, Dunne, the writer, walks through all his books, thinly disguised, slightly mysterious, listening quietly to the powerful and glamorous, watching, vicarious, guarding his secrets. A small, grey repository for confession.

'I have always enjoyed writing about people,' says Harrison Burns in *A Season In Purgatory*. 'People have always talked to me, even people who were reluctant to be interviewed. Claire has said to me on more than one occasion that I became involved in their lives as a way of not dealing with my own.' The past; the painful, painful past. The secret grief, the quiet rage. This man is a haunted house. 'I may appear to be a calm man,' explains Gus in *People Like Us*, 'but there is within me a rage that knows no limits.'

Orchids bloom in Dominick Dunne's light, airy hotel room. The watery afternoon light fills the room, turning leaves that press against the window translucent green. Suddenly the phone rings. Dominick Dunne barks into it. Crochety. "Oohhh." He is listening intently now though. A breathless, confiding female voice oozing silkily from the phone. "Oohhh." *Gossip*. Yes. They are doing it again. Telling him things. Then the neat little man, the repository for salacious and terrible secrets, crosses his legs carefully and settles into his chair, frowning. "I have never understood why people talk to me, but they do. I have an extraordinary knack for being given information. It is an odd thing." Even though they know that it is his role as a writer to betray them, they talk. And he in his turn takes them closer to the flame. To the scorching flame of celebrity. To the hottest show in town.

Dominick Dunne was a failure once. Here in this town. Down and out in Beverly Hills. Weaving around drunk and stoned, his wife gone in disgust, the phone shatteringly silent. Failed films, substance abuse, the full self-destructo. "After 28 years as a TV executive and studio executive I had a failed marriage I couldn't let go of and a career that had let go of me. I was out of work for several years. I was desperate and broke. I couldn't pay the rent. I was desperate in every way. Hollywood is a very cruel place for a failure to be. I had become known as a failure. They will forgive us our lies, forgeries, cheating, even your murders on occasion. But they will never forgive you for failing." Humiliation after humiliation. At the end there was only one option. He had to get out of town. Fast.

But it can be a mistake to write certain people off. To kick them when they are down, depressed, suffering, lost. Because if they are intelligent, if they have, after all, a life force, however diminished by circumstance, they might just come back. When Dominick Dunne came back it was in another incarnation. And when he came back, he came back with a vengeance.

His new career would be shaped by the sadness of loss, fuelled by the steepness of his social fall and rise, coloured by all the experiences of his life and driven, finally, by the desire to put things right. When you emerge from your own private hell you are forever changed.

With nowhere to turn, Dominick Dunne drove distractedly into the Oregon mountains and checked into a guest house, suicidal, everything that mattered gone. Thinking his life was over, he instead went deep into himself and began to heal. "I lived on cans of hash because I didn't have much money. I quit drinking and I quit smoking grass. In the loneliness I found that all the bull of Hollywood was bull that I had filled myself with." And he began to write. The perfect occupation for the troubled, broke and alone. No overheads, no studios, no stars, no budgets, no tantrums, no one giving a shit about how you look. Especially not yourself. Just you and your bruised imagination. A time of truth. At 51 he crashed, burned, left one lamentable life behind and began another. But, even so, for Dominick Dunne the pure crusading motivation was still to come. The impelling sorrow that would elevate him from good to great in his late-life career.

Dominick Dunne used to live in one of those abundant houses, staff discreet. If you live in a Beverly Hills mansion you doubtless got credentials, prestige and a shitload of money. "All the houses are in the three to five million range," says Dunne. And if you die in Beverly Hills make it spectacular if you can possibly manage it. Dying is good for the fame business. Everyone loves a celebrity death. 'Never underestimate the power of celebrity in Los Angeles,' Dunne once wrote in *Vanity Fair*. Dying of natural causes, or old age, however, is positively infra dig. A young dead star is infinitely more interesting than an old dead star. A young dead star is almost certainly doing something illegal and therefore fascinating at time of death.

Some losers, however, have to die in a terrible way to achieve celebrity. On the corner of North Elm Tree Drive, next to Dionne Warwick's routinely grand house, in Nick Dunne's upholstered and rarefied old neighbourhood, one of the most prestigious addresses in Beverly Hills, is a square brick Mediterranean mansion whose sightless windows gaze directly onto the street. Five million smackers' worth of real estate, it has, it needs hardly be said, swimming pool and tennis court, courtyard and guesthouse. What more, one wonders, could you want? Well, liquid cash as it turned out. The Menendez house acquired its starring role in the tree-lined street after those rich-boys Erik and Lyle Menendez pumped bullets into their parents until pieces of them were splattered all across the, ahem, family room in what could only be described as overkill. Dominick Dunne, by now a famous writer, pursued the case relentlessly in the pages of *Vanity Fair*, in a series of devastating articles, confessing up front to feeling 'not an ounce of sympathy for these two young killers', thereby entering into unarmed combat with Erik's formidable attorney Leslie Abramson, who was playing the sexual abuse card to the hilt. "She tells people I am evil." It really pissed her off when he wrote things like this in *Vanity Fair*: 'Even though I acknowledge that they lived a miserable life with a pitiful mother and detestable father, I happen to believe in the alternative solution of moving out. But that way, of course, you risk not getting the money, and these kids liked money.'

Like all Dunne's journalistic obsessions, this one had everything. Wealth, murder, sex, greed, privilege, glamour, a mansion of course and a cliffhanger court case. "It is amazing, isn't it?" he blinks behind his rimless glasses. "These people live so well. What is it that spawns this viciousness? People with such privilege. Those Menendez boys had everything. Granted their father was a shit and a martinet and all those things, but I don't believe for an instant that he sexually abused them. Not for an instant. They were spoilt and arrogant and they just couldn't wait for the money. I know that the defendant has to be given the best trial but I just think this whole thing of creating false stories of things that didn't happen is just shocking. The amount of lying that goes on."

In a particularly impassioned and hardhitting piece for *Vanity Fair* after two hung juries in the Menendez trial he confessed, reluctantly he said, that he had been psychologically and physically abused by his father. Beaten and mocked. His deafness is the result. He wanted his readers to know that he fully understood the gravity of child abuse in spite of his hardline stance in this case. 'I am unable to even visit his grave. But I never wanted to kill him. The thought never once entered my mind. There were alternatives. I went away to boarding school. I went away to war. I went away to college. I went away to my life.'

Dominick Dunne does not like murderers.

On a shelf in his hotel suite is a black-and-white photograph, faded and yellowing, of a young woman. Her thick dark hair swirls around her shoulders, her face is pale and fine, her dark eyes wide, lips slightly parted; she looks out of the frame with untramelled innocent curiosity. Her killer strangled his daughter for five and half minutes then left her to die. Her father will never get over her death. "I loved her," he says simply. "I think about her every day." Everything he does, everything he writes is atonement for the wrongful death of Dominique Dunne, actress. She had just completed her first feature film, *Poltergeist*. Filled with promise and choked to death at 22. Her killer got two and a half years. Her father got life. It is his sorrow. To the core. And his anger. Helpless, impotent, towering. May she rest in peace because her father never will.

"It absolutely changed my life. It is impossible to say in words what it did to my life. It made me a totally different kind of person. It was time to get serious. Hers was the first trial I had ever gone to and I began to understand this thing: that the rights of the killer on trial exceed the rights of the victim. The victims are forgotten. My ex-wife is a helpless invalid with multiple sclerosis. The defence even tried to stop her appearing in court in her wheelchair because she would arouse sympathy. When the killer got out of jail I hired a private investigator to follow him. I don't know what I was looking for or what I was going to do. I wanted to kill him. I was like a crazy person. I was obsessed with revenge. Finally I realised I couldn't go on like that. I had to put that rage into a positive thing." Now, like a man possessed, he writes for his life and for hers.

Her photograph stands there as a reminder, perhaps, a touchstone for what became his life's work. That fading face giving him the strength to persist. "I feel she protects me and has helped me. I ask for her help sometimes." The glass has cracked, jagged across her beautiful, porcelain face, seeming to poignantly symbolise the circumstances of her death and its aftermath. Her life was taken so callously by her former boyfriend, a chef with a history of violence towards women, who sweet-talked the jury and pretended to read the Bible through the trial. "He is not in love with me, Dad," Dominique had told her father, "he is obsessed with me."

No wonder her father went after O. J. Simpson. A history of obsession and violence towards his slaughtered wife. "He is a shit. Every woman is a fuck and that is it." Nick Dunne's voice hard and angry as he flicks across the evening news. 'Yes, of course he did it,' he wrote impatiently in *Vanity Fair*.

The dead eyes of O. J.

I managed to get into that bleak badly lit courtroom one day, level nine. One of the days when they were doing DNA, the blood on the socks evidence in the O. J. trial. Stains of Nicole's blood had been found on each of the socks on O. J.'s bedroom floor. The defence was saying the blood was planted. They were saying there was a 1/68 billionth chance that the blood could have come from someone else. Results that were pointing an accusatory finger of guilt at The Juice. The scientist doing the DNA match was shaking with nerves. In profile O. J.'s face looked as if it had been carved out of bronze. Even incarcerated, denied natural light, the skin tinged yellow under courtroom fluorescence and gaunt, this was a rare physical specimen: symmetrical sinew and muscle and perfectly portioned. His lips literally moved as he wrote on his yellow legal pad. And then those brown eyes lifted and looked sleepily sideways across the room; the skin seemed to be coming away beneath them. It was eerie. They were dead, those eyes. The man upon whom all of America was focused, the man vilified, the personification of something frightening and askew in the national psyche, simply wasn't there. He had left the building. Abdicated quite some time ago. Leaving lawyers, witnesses, jurors and all kinds of people climbing over the carcass to get rich and briefly famous. America.

"I look on this," said Dunne that day, "as an American pageant. A great drama that has been played out in front of the whole country and it is free and everybody has got a front row seat. Of course he is guilty. Of course he is. I mean who else could have done it? Did he ever say 'how dare you put these handcuffs on me'? That all came later when the lawyers told him what to say. This trial has changed all of us. I am an observer but I have become a part of it. It changed the lawyers and it changed the judge. He is an extremely bright and capable man but the fame changed him. Then the criticism that he lost control. He got tougher and tougher and meaner and meaner. The danger of it has been the mockery and humiliation of law enforcement. In order to save this killer every member of the LAPD, from the cop who taped around the crime scene through every policeman who was there that night, has been presented to this country as corrupt, as liars, as movers of evidence. This is a terrible thing. They put these criminal experts on the stand and then humiliate them in front of the country. Who is going to want to protect us now? This is very dangerous. This is evil. We need the police.

"And yet through all this I have become friendly with his two sisters. They are fabulous, wonderful women. One day one of them cried during the photographs that were shown of Nicole. On the way out afterwards I saw she was trembling and I leaned over to her and gave her a hug and said, 'This is awful.' I think people feel revulsion for it. It is disgusting what money can buy and what justice has become. It is a joke."

The O. J. case, too, had everything. Money, power, celebrity. A mansion, of course. And finally it had something else. Something against which Dominick Dunne constantly rails in his relentless crusade. The ineluctable fact that the rich in America can get away with murder. Literally. And often do. Everybody has their price. This makes Dominick Dunne really, *really* mad. All his best-selling books are morality tales around this theme. And he is everywhere in them. He may be tiny and tubby and grey and speak in a slightly quavering voice, he may appear harmless and amiable with the charm and manners of the East Coast WASP, but he is a fearless and forceful man. Unapologetic. After a dark night of the soul of the kind that he has experienced there is, perhaps, nothing left to fear. He is the rich and powerful defendants' dogged worst nightmare. The conscience that they lack. He follows their trials with morbid forensic fascination. Sits through months and months of quotidian legal argument, sifting through the evidence to make his own case, writing neatly in his little notebook. "People that get killers off get infuriated because I follow these cases so closely. When you have a million bucks to spend on your defence attorney you will win. If you can afford a high priced defence attorney with a huge staff and huge resources you will win. If you have money you can get justice. There is a genuflection to money and fame."

The rich, as Dominick Dunne knows only too well, are definitely different from you and me. The law is there to keep the rest of us in line. The rich simply assume that they are above it. 'It's the old story,' he wrote in his tirade against the Menendez brothers. 'Things are different for the rich in a criminal situation. Had the exact same killings been committed, the same shotguns used, the same number of shots fired, the same everything, by young defendants from a less swell part of town, South-Central Los Angeles, say, the trial would probably have lasted eight or nine days, and there would probably have been a different ending.'

One wall and the mirror in Dominick Dunne's room are covered with memos and notes from *Vanity Fair*. Even on this sultry summer day, relaxing in his room, he is wearing a tie, pulled tight at the neck over his monogrammed shirt. There is something utterly correct about Dominick Dunne. Something right. In the correct cut of his navy jacket. In his old-fashioned morality and integrity. In his work, where he never puts a word wrong. When he chronicles the casual, brutal carelessness of high society, he is writing about curved marble staircases, of country clubs and summers of sailing and tennis, of magnificent rooms with fine paintings, shot silk and high ceilings through which he has walked all his life. He moves through fashionable society. He knows those perfectly proportioned rooms. He knows the smooth athletic arrogance of its youth. He knows how efficiently they can close ranks and cover up unfortunate slips of conduct, regrettable peccadillos, profligate, messy lives. How they take care of things. Handle their own problems in their own way: privately. "It is a story," he says resignedly, "that I have always known."

Beyond the endless, glittering parties of mere movie money, it is a world of power and beauty for whom publicity and scandal are too vulgar to even contemplate.

'My father used to describe them as the kind of people who can keep things out of newspapers,' explains the Los Angelean old-money heiress, Camilla, in *An Inconvenient Woman*. 'There are about two or three hundred of us who dine together in various combinations, and we rarely widen the circle, and you rarely read about us in the newspapers . . . we never mix with the movie crowd, and only sometimes with the people from Pasadena, except for civic evenings or certain charities.' This was the glowing world of Pamela Harriman, Babe Paley and Betsy Bloomingdale, who ran grand houses and staggeringly rich and powerful husbands with equal élan, changing them efficiently when necessary, and of whom the aristocratic Pauline Mendelson in *An Inconvenient Woman* seems to be a composite. Van Gogh's *White Roses*, for example, hangs over the fireplace in the library of Pauline and Jules Mendelson. '"That's my treasure,"' Pauline tells the writer Phillip Quenell. '"It was my wedding present from Jules twenty-two years ago."' When Pamela Harriman died *White Roses* was part of her estate— valued at $101 million.

It is into this world with its elaborate etiquette and rituals that the beautiful flame-haired waitress Flo March came and by doing so brought it all, including herself, undone. When Alfred

Bloomingdale died on the job, so to speak, his socialite wife Betsy, understandably perhaps, abruptly cut his mistress out of his will. But Vicki Morgan did not go quietly. She was a desperate and therefore inconvenient woman. The ensuing scandal, my *dear*, was mortifying, the sniggering, the humiliation, the *newspapers*; just too, too awful. So common. Especially for such close personal and pretentious friends and advisors of the Reagans, who were then comically resident in the White House. Like Flo March, Vicki Morgan was later bludgeoned to death, and her male porn star friend found guilty. In *An Inconvenient Woman*, Dunne makes it clear that he believes the porn star is innocent. Flo got in the way of a rich woman, connected at the highest levels. Broke and frightened, she threatened to expose all in a book. You don't do that and get away with it. No siree. You do not forget your place with people like these. Not when the billionaire lover had questionable colleagues with secrets to keep. Too much, far too much, to lose. The waitress had to go. Simple.

Dominick Dunne seems to know absolutely everybody. And everything about them. When he turned on his own kind, betrayed his own background and breeding, he did it with a kind of knowing contempt. Says Flo March, whose mother had dragged her from welfare hotel to welfare hotel, not long before her murder: 'Like I felt sorry for Pauline Mendelson, this rich lady who'd had every whim of her whole life attended to.'

Dominick Dunne speaks in the same clear and measured way in which he writes. Attention to detail. "I come from a rich Irish Catholic family, I come from Connecticut, my father was a surgeon. We were not rich like the Kennedys. We were lower case Kennedys. But I went to the same kind of schools as they did. I have always known them. Jackie and my wife went to this young ladies' school. Jackie was a year ahead of my wife and Lee was a year below. She knew Jackie. I met Jackie but I didn't really know her. I wrote a tribute about her when she died. I went to Bobby and Ethel's wedding. And when I was young and married and lived in Hollywood and Santa Monica, our great friends were Peter and

Patricia Lawford, who had been Patricia Kennedy. We were two houses away from the beach in Santa Monica and Jack Kennedy would come in his helicopter and come for lunch when he was President. I mean it was a very glitzy glam time."

The Kennedys don't speak to him any more. Not since he covered the William Kennedy Smith rape trial. And then, as if that wasn't enough, *A Season in Purgatory*. For they are, after all, the model for everything he came to despise. He sees straight through the blinding charisma, always has. "I always thought they were great, the Kennedys. But after Chappaquiddick something happened to them. I just found that one of the most revolting episodes in our history. And then one thing after another happened. The Kennedys don't like me, no." Grimace.

In *Vanity Fair* he wrote of the Smith rape trial: 'The verdict, not guilty, was a disappointment to some, a cause for delirium to others, but a surprise to no one.' Certainly not to Dominick Dunne. A Kennedy in *jail*? Unthinkable. "It was so strange in Palm Beach after the trial. The Kennedy sisters were like dowager archduchesses of a royal house, believing in the divine right of kings, or Kennedys. They knew how to play it. The court was like a church. I was on one side of the aisle and they were on the other. I know them all and we never spoke. But I think the William Kennedy Smith trial was shaming for them all. Whether he got acquitted or not. It was a shameful episode of public tawdriness. I think it is a wonderful thing the way they all stick together when one of them is in trouble. They all arrive, the whole parade of the family was utterly fascinating. But somebody told me that they would stick by him through thick and thin but after it was all over, when they were alone, they would have kicked the shit out of him."

The rape trial scandal may have been over for a Palm Beach not entirely unused to sex scandals and a titillated public but it would go on to star, thinly disguised, in Dominick Dunne's next book, *A Season in Purgatory*, a damning composite of the Kennedys and a novelistic indictment of their assumption of impunity. Well, you can't let the playful high spirits of golden youth get in the way of a commanding future, now can you? Not for a little thing like murder. The narrator is a writer, of course, doomed to live as an outsider, but who as a poor but bright schoolboy is shown largesse by a dazzlingly rich, glamorous and mesmerising large Irish Catholic family. Largesse for a price, that is. The price of silence. Harrison Burns is a bought and paid-for family retainer. The deal? His school fees are paid if he never speaks of the sex murder he has witnessed, committed by his beautiful, witty, charming friend, scion of the family. "I really love *A Season in Purgatory*. That is the closest thing to me," Dunne confesses smiling, an oddly rare event.

As a boy Dominick Dunne, one of six, was small, stammering and 'sissy'. He did not cut a swathe through the debutantes and country clubs. He did not leave them gasping with his grace on the courts, field and water, and he does not, to this day, have the arrogance or bearing of the Eastern Seaboard Patrician. The assurance perhaps, the toughness certainly, the social mobility clearly, but not the sense of rightful, unquestioned ascendancy. He fights for the disempowered, for the victim, for a start. He has no room for compassion when privilege and power are abused. He can seem almost camp at times, waving a wrist limply to emphasise a point, speaking at a certain gossipy pitch. But the courage in this elfin man with his strict side parting, mocked by his father until he went away to World War II, was evidenced a long time ago when he came home from that war decorated for bravery, though his father died before rapprochement could be made. His two sisters died of cancer and his younger brother Stephen committed suicide. Such endless, endless loss. As the Irish do, he feuds with his brother, the writer John Gregory Dunne, who is married to Joan Didion.

"This story, *A Season In Purgatory*, was one I had always known. It is what I call a country club story." Dunne rests his freckled hand on his leg and obligingly gathers momentum. "People in the country clubs all knew about this. It was Ethel Kennedy's family, the Skakel family. There was a rumour that William Kennedy Smith was in Greenwich, Connecticut, on the night of this murder. He and the Skakel boy are cousins. I went back to check on the rumour. But it turned out not to be true. It's an incredibly rich community. Big houses. Private security. I called the mother of the deceased 15-year-old girl. This woman, Mrs Moxley, was a fascinating woman. It is outrageous. The guy who everyone knows did it has never even been questioned by the police. The girl was killed with a golf club and the head of the club had the initials of this family on it. The family told the police, 'If you have any questions, put them in writing and submit them to our lawyer.' Would that happen to you or me? This is power. You can't get bigger than that. I don't know what kind of life he has, but he has gotten away with this. So I wrote a story about it. In my book he comes to trial. But in life he never has. I copied all the trial part from the William Kennedy Smith trial in Palm Beach."

Some characters walk through all of Dunne's books: the patrician fixer lawyer Sims Lord, Dunne himself. The books interconnect: Flo March does a screen test for a role in *The Two Mrs Grenvilles*.

When Dunne left his cabin in Oregon he went back to Los Angeles and sold everything he owned. "I reduced my life to one suitcase and a typewriter." He moved to New York, joined AA and finished his first novel. It went absolutely nowhere. "I got one stinking review in the *New York Times*." But he was a writer now. And he had survived. While his former Hollywood friends were busy spontaneously combusting, Dominick Dunne was beginning anew. Coming to terms with his brother's suicide, he was in his apartment in New York when the phone rang at 5 o'clock one morning. It was the phone call that changed his life, the call that every parent dreads. His daughter was in a coma, dying. He flew to her hospital bedside. "She was on life support for a couple of days and before they took her off it, each member of the family spent some time alone with her. When I left her for the last time, I just said to her, 'Give me your talent'. And you know, I think she did."

He met Tina Brown, the editor of *Vanity Fair*, at a dinner party in New York just as he was about to go to Los Angeles for the trial of his daughter's murderer. "She commissioned a piece about it, she told me to keep a diary. It was the first article I ever wrote and it was her first issue. She is my dear friend. I came in with her from the first issue on. I work exclusively for *Vanity Fair* and have done for 12 years. It was the best place, it still is, I love it there. The people involved in those early years were all such huge personalities. Tina had this sort of unique thing of never wanting to hog the spotlight. She wanted to take the people she picked and turn us into our own kind of star. It is a very generous thing. She has a unique take on the USA. The things that we accept and take for granted because they are a part of us were new and exciting to her. She made me look at my country in a whole new way. I just find her endlessly interesting like that. She taught me everything really. She kept saying to me to 'put yourself into the story'. I would say 'c'mon' and be modest. She taught me how to do that. She also told me that with my von Bulow articles, that is when the magazine really took off. This sounds pushy and I am not that kind of person. She called me at my house in Connecticut and told me she was going to the *New Yorker*. I cried. That is how deeply affected I was. She told me then, we talked for about an hour, she said to me, 'With the von Bulow article you set the writing style for *Vanity Fair*'. I shouldn't say that, but it was thrilling. There was something about that article. I sort of found myself. I found my own style, my role as commentator, which I have subsequently built on." Murder, money, sex, glamour, betrayal. High stakes. The rich *in extremis*. "All the big stuff. That is what I love. It fascinates me."

His next book, *The Two Mrs Grenvilles*, which would later be made into a mini-series starring Ann Margaret, was a hit. Another country club story. Another story he has always known. "That was an actual case. When I was a young man, before I was married, I had a sort of a romance with a girl called Ruthie, now dead, whose father married into the Woodward family. She used to tell me about that family, how the son of the family had married this cheap showgirl and the whole family hated her. But the girl was beautiful. I loved hearing stories like this. I would hear about this showgirl who was after the guy's money and so forth. One night, years ago, in 1954, I was with Ruthie in the Stork Club. She said 'Oh, there she is.' And I looked across the room and there was this fabulous woman. She got up to dance, she was with her husband. She was in a blue satin strapless evening dress. She pulled up the dress and walked to the dance floor with her husband trailing after her. She got out on the dance floor and she started to dance and then she started singing in her husband's ear. I thought it was the most glamorous thing I ever saw. And about a year later she shot and killed him. I think they were both drunk and he had another girl, you know, sloppy lives. By that time I had broken up with Ruthie and I was going to get married. And I became obsessed with that case. I saved all the newspapers. Years passed, and my first novel came out, which was not successful. Michael Korda, my editor, who had liked the novel that flopped, sat me down. He said, 'There is nothing that the public enjoys reading about more than the rich and the powerful in a criminal situation.' I went *boing*. He clarified my life for me. I told him the story of all those years ago. And he said 'Well, there is your book.'

"At first, the thing was to write it as non-fiction. But, you see, what fascinated me so much was that the young woman's mother-in-law, who despised her, stood by her after she had killed the only son, and protected her in order to keep scandal from the family. I looked through all those old newspapers and read that the young wife, after the shooting, was taken to hospital. The shooting took place on Long Island. She was taken in an ambulance to a fancy rich people's hospital. The police were not allowed to talk to her for 20 days. Just think about that. Shot and killed the husband 20 days before they could question her. During that time the mother-in-law went to the hospital to see her for the first time since the shooting. That is all you knew. The mother-in-law in the hospital room. I kept thinking, 'What did they say? What did they *say* to each other?' I had to know what they said. I almost started the book by writing that scene. Think about what it was like: a mother-in-law facing her son's killer."

He once wrote of the widow in *Vanity Fair*: 'There are people in fashionable society who, throughout their lives, carry with them the burden of their scandals, as ineradicable from their personalities as a tattoo on their forearm. Ann Woodward, the beautiful widow of the handsome and very rich William Woodward, never again after her husband's death walked into a drawing room, or anywhere else, without someone whispering, "She's the woman who shot and killed her husband." Perhaps it was an accident, as she claimed. Perhaps not. It didn't matter. It was what people said about her, and she knew they said it. The same is true of Klaus von Bulow, the husband of the beautiful and very rich Sonny von Bulow. Even aquitted, as he was, he will never enter a room, or a restaurant, without someone whispering, "He's the man who was accused of trying to kill his wife." ' And he tells me now, waving his freckled hand dismissively, "Of course he did it."

But no one in fashionable society in New York was talking to him after *People Like Us*. He was *dropped*, my *dear*, by his fancy friends. Pronto. Persona non grata. Shunned. Rooms cleared when he entered. "I noticed, the day it came out, the fact that a coldness came from a certain group in New York—instantly." Privacy is the thing with the rich. Exclusivity. God forbid you should *laugh* at them. *People Like Us*, my personal favourite, is a satirical exposé of New York society and the ascent and crashing descent of the ridiculous, self-conscious, vulgar and grasping nouveau riche on a collision course with jail, scandal and financial ruin. Published in 1988, it was a prescient parable to say the least. "It is absolutely about the '80s. You know, I read what is absolutely my favourite novel by Anthony Trollope, called *The Way We Live Now*. It is one of the most fabulous books I have ever read. It is about the nouveau riche in London in 1860 and about a family that took over and how the old guard of everything got sucked into it because of the wealth and the kind of person they loathed but needed. My God, I thought, that is New York now, today, that is it. And that is what gave me the impetus to do that. I moved in those circles. If you are a well-known person and people read your books and everything, they just invite you to all those things. So I went to all those billionaire things. I was fascinated. You know, I thought, 'I can do this.'" So, of course, he betrayed them, as the writer must. "It got me into a lot of trouble. It was a very interesting learning experience. It scared me a bit at first and then I realised I don't care."

Because the writer, in the end, must be true to himself. Must find the truth and tell it. Cannot crave to be loved. Must be able to walk away. Dominick Dunne moves uncomfortably in his chair. "I have walked a narrow line ever since I started to write." Because he is not a ghost at the feast. He is not like the rest of us journalists, glimpsing a world we can never inhabit, our noses pressed against the glass, to look but never touch. He is one of them.

They are all over him in New York now. Well, he is, after all, more famous than them. Now. And just as rich. A celebrity himself. That took balls. Besides, he knows all the best gossip, darling. "As long as you play it the way you see it. The amazing thing is people are always saying, 'So and so will never speak to you again.' But it doesn't work out like that. Well, except the Kennedys. When *An Inconvenient Woman* came out, I mean people out here were just up in arms over it. But now they are all having me over to dinner. So who knows."

So he keeps writing about the swells; about the good, the bad and the tacky. About ageing showgirls dripping with jewels and memories; billionaires gone bung; fabulous houses, palaces and Arabian princesses; dubious dowager duchesses; the beautiful and rich Countess of Kenmare who was said to have killed all four of her husbands; the pretentious Australian heiress jilted at the altar by her ridiculous gay faux-count; Audrey Hepburn; looking for lost Lord Lucan. Residing in worlds so abundant and privileged that we, the demi-monde, can only rely on him to describe them. Chronicling their scandals and murders and eccentric behaviour: amused, outraged, wise. What is it with these rich people anyway? Is it the time or the money that makes them behave so badly? To behave scandalously requires, after all, the spare time to do it. Or is it simply that the consequences are merely inconvenient and never permanent?

A man who socialises in several stratospheres on several continents, sought after, listening and listened to, but in the end essentially alone. A writer. Lunching alone at the Waldorf Astoria. Talking every day to his ex-wife and sons Griffin, an actor, and Alex, a writer. Writing, always writing. Nearly 70, strong and vigorous. "I just keep taking notes down all the time of what I am going to use. Then I pull it all together. I get so many letters from people now. Journalism and fiction feed off each other. I keep notes on my computer. I love writing. I love it when I get back to Connecticut, I have a house in the country which I love. That is where I write now. I go upstate for long periods. I have this wonderful house. I am very happy there."

Happy in Connecticut, pondering the nature of evil. "I think there is a lot of evil around us, I truly do. I am not holding myself up as any bit of perfection because God knows I am not. I just believe in right and wrong. I truly do. It is getting all forgotten around us. Everything is corrupt everywhere. Ethics and morality seem to have gone out of our lives."

The phone is ringing as I leave to walk along the red swirling carpet in the hallways and out through the lobby of the Chateau Marmont, past the potted plants and back down south of Sunset to my own somewhat less salubrious quarters. "Really?" I hear him say as the door closes. "*Really!*"

And I, too, have other things to do. Things far less moral on my mind. I have a date with a famous former porn star. I have a dirty video to watch.

Down on Sunset near Hollywood and Vine are the shops of the sex trade, the fag end of the film industry. Porn. They've got it pretty much covered down here, everything except the bodies of the participants. Well, apart from the standard, stereotype wardrobe of suspenders and corsets. Gay, straight, black, white, anal, oral, tits, arse, group, leather, whip, discipline, slaves, masters, fantasies that would be comical if they were not sitting there in front of you on the shelf. Vast arrays of numbing and explicit pornographic magazines and videos. The dirty secret of an affluent society. Always have to take it that little bit further, and then further again, pervert it, twist it, reach through the dark cracks; always the flip side. The thrill ever bigger. More stimulation, harder, more, yes, yes, yes, no, more. More, more, more. Getting your rocks off is mandatory, at all costs. But how did it get so hard? All this for the brief satisfaction of the momentary muscle spasm in the genitals. Love, emotional connection, is another continent.

Women attempting to look alluring to camera while stretched, straddled, penetrated wherever possible or covered in cum. The actresses who never quite shone in auditions. So the core gets harder. The dreams wither and die. Unlike the penises, which seem to stay permanently upright and thrust in your face.

All the lonely people. All the ads in the papers. Singles ads with sad desperation, singles with college degrees, singles with children, 'bolder' women looking for younger men, couples wishing to swing, 'well hung' black men available and willing to pay attention for a price; encounter groups, therapy groups for those damaged in the skirmishes. I hit the phone one day. I heard straight phone sex, I heard bent phone sex, I heard 'nasty girls' phone sex. Now those girls knew how to talk dirty. They just said what they really felt.

A phone psychic told me that I was "fast, quick, intuitive" and, helpfully, that "I was doing what I was supposed to be doing". If only she knew. But then again, being a psychic, I suppose she did. She advised that I would have problems with my health in the near future. That night my face blew out like a football and the next day I had to get an impacted wisdom tooth removed, before, the dentist in Hollywood informed me, "the infection went to the brain".

I went down to the Tropicana one night, naively thinking 'Female Mud Wrestling' meant just that. Red lights run around the room at the Tropicana. It smells of antiseptic. It is the bucks' night special. The strippers slide up and down poles, strutting, wiggling, sashaying, shedding the merest suggestions of lace. They lap dance, they strut. For thirty bucks they will leap on you in a skimpy bathing suit and mud wrestle on a giant waterbed. The men drink beer and heckle. One drunk college boy pays his $50, starts taking the mud wrestling seriously, gets carried away, lays into the girl and has to be hauled off.

Where do they go, these beautiful silicone showgirls who never made it in the movies? Where do they wind up? Pornography? Prostitution?

Traci Lords is going the other way. From pornography to family television. This takes sheer, audacious willpower. It has taken weeks to organise this interview. Her 'people' are apologetic, week after week, fax after fax. She is just so busy.

Traci Lords is on a roll.

# Talking Dirty

You have to hand it to the Americans—they do love a bad girl. In spite of themselves. In spite of God and country and the Republican Party. Particularly, evidence would suggest, a bad blonde girl. Preferably with big tits. The Mae, the Lana, the Marilyn, the Madonna, the Sharon, the Courtney, the Drew, in a straight line of succession as icon. The painted, peroxide, pneumatic parody of female sexuality. The blonder, it seems, the better.

While a male public figure can crash his career overnight with a kamikaze blow job on Sunset Boulevard, a blonde not his wife in a boat, a harmless wank at the movies, playful persiflage with a prostitute, their slut goddesses flaunt their genitalia, their drug addictions, their scarlet lips, their pain, their dangerous carnality, their Attitude; they strut it in fishnet stockings and red satin pumps. They provoke, they tease, they sleep around, they stridently scream expletives; they inhale. They are experienced blondes. They have Pasts. And, honey, they *never* apologise.

Who can tell what lurks in the seams of the American psyche? In the blood-hot hearts of the silent majority? In the darker reaches of two car garage suburbia, in solitary hours in the wilder recesses of the cornbelt? But their bad blondes are revered—and they are forgiven.

Traci Lords's prurient past, however, leaves the rest of those flagrant faux-blondes for dead. Now, here is a reputation with a capital R. No. Make that all capitals. America gone wrong in the night. "I've done it all," she smiles sweetly.

She slides sideways to a showy stop in her souped-up sports car, spraying stones across summer lawn. Long legs; lean and lissom in jeans and leather jacket, she crunches across gravel, strides through the carved wooden doors of the old Hollywood Hills mansion, clicks across parquet floor, hand outstretched, flicker of a smile followed by a graceful folding into a chair. All muscular California girl.

**TRACI LORDS**

So. Here she is. In living colour. America's most famous Porn Queen. X-rated. The fornication fantasy of millions of furtive men. Fitfully tossing away, no doubt, beside the wife. A 26-year-old woman whose flawless porcelain beauty is so untrammelled, so fine, that it disguises at first the steel in the wide, flinty, speckled eyes. Eyes that can flash dangerously and without warning, like a suddenly angered cat.

She bought the ticket and took the ride. She gave 'the best orgasm in the business'. The voluptuous little girl who loved to fuck. Wild. "Come on, baby! Is that all you've got?" she snarled and screamed, legs spread wide, in *Beverly Hills Copulater*. "She was as cute as can be," says a fellow, er, actor from *Sex 5th Avenue*. "A nasty little girl who enjoyed being bad. I just wanted to fuck her." So did everybody else. She was the superstar of the sex business. She was hardcore. She was 16 years old.

She leans forward, elbows on the table, breasts perfectly round, lights a cigarette and blows. She is funny in the tough, edgy way that bitter experience can confer. But her past is there in the voice; the deep, creamy come-with-me-to-the-boudoir voice. A voice that promises to blow your mind. And it is there in the extraordinarily lascivious mouth: glistening, full, fat, pouting, carnivorous lips that are almost obscene against the dazzlingly white teeth. Pure raspberry sexuality set against pure ivory silk.

It was this devastating mixture of tensile strength, molten sexuality and pale angelic innocence that got her into trouble in the first place. Well, that and the fuck you bad girl who still lurks there, you can tell; mischievous and profane beneath the cool and beautiful revised patina. Talking dirty. "I'm not really bad," she smiles winningly. "I'm just strong." Talking dirty because she likes the feel and texture of the words on the tongue, talking dirty because she is defiant—"People tell me not to say 'fuck' in interviews, but too fucking bad"—talking dirty because she is not expecting clemency or pardon, because she has not been and never will be shamed, cowed or tamed. "I am not ashamed of who I am, not for one minute." She leans back in the chair with asperity, crossing one long leg over the other, rotating a cowboy boot, shrouded for a minute in cigarette smoke. "I have a fucking opinion."

Down below, through the French doors of the mansion office of her record company, the city of Los Angeles shimmers in a toxic haze. The city that took her apart and then reclaimed her. Down there is garish neon Sunset Strip, the twilight backdrop for the legend of Traci Lords. A famously fallen woman before she even left her teens. She certainly packed it in. Tackling the ticklish subject of her past, I gingerly feel my way, careful. I feel her start retreating, I am losing her. "It is just that there has been so much said. If there is something that people didn't get there is stacks that they can read. They can look at the fuck-up. I became extremely bored with all that," she shrugs, "but I can understand why people are fascinated by it." But then she squares up. Yep, she delivers, Traci Lords, always has. She slugs Coke, chainsmokes and tells her story with the kind of honesty that requires bracing herself and staring the past down. The kind of survivor honesty that requires guts. "I was fuckin' *there*," she once told *The Face*. "I remember every single minute of every single one, every cock, every guy, every chick. You can rise above it but you never really forget."

There is, you see, the old Traci and the new Traci. Two separate lives. A demarcation line painted in pain. The old Traci was a conspicuous fuck-up. A runaway child whose acting career was pretty much from the waist down, featuring her glistening and swollen vulva in high definition, and whose twisted and exploited journey through puberty was watched by solitary men wanking enthusiastically in ill-lit X-rated theatres. The new Traci is a class act. Smart as a whip. A young Hollywood actress and singer building a body of significant work. Day by day, inch by inch, pushing through. Tarnished icon, working actress. Striving. "I am very impatient. I want things to happen *now*."

The sad and sordid story of the old Traci started in Steubenville, Ohio, a poor and freezing Appalachian town on the banks of the Ohio River. The only things lower than the temperature in

Steubenville were the expectations from life. Nora Louise Kuzma was not, initially, destined for greatness. Her father was a Ukrainian-American Jew, a steelworker whose towering frustration and disappointment at what life had dealt him merged into violent alcoholism. Her mother, who had grown up in poverty and married at 20, was a doormat because she did not know any different. She worked, had babies, and suffered the raging, abusive, alcoholic scenes. That was the way it was in the white trash Appalachian Mountains. "I was a good wife, I kept my mouth shut," she once told a reporter. Frightened of her father, the household out of control, Nora's churning anxiety became a cleaning compulsion; an insecure child ducking the shouting and crashing, not knowing what was going to happen next, trying to clean away the ugliness, to put things into some kind of order. A lurching, drunk, bullying father, a timid, cowering mother. A textbook case for a disturbed child. Emotional damage inflicted while her sprouting body, by 10, was that of a 16-year-old. A lethal combination, as it would turn out. They gave her hell at school.

Finally her mother snapped. A classic American story. She caught the Greyhound bus out of hillbilly hicksville, her four daughters carrying their belongings in plastic bags. First they went to Ohio and real poverty and then they headed for California and the American dream. There, nubile Nora ran wild in the sun. Smoking dope in high heels and hot pants, taunting the boys. Like so many winsome girls from the prairies of Kansas or the share farms of Tennessee or the swamps of Louisiana who come to Los Angeles and find something else, something altogether less savoury, Nora Kuzma dreamed of being discovered and becoming a star like Marilyn Monroe. A naive, shy kid from the backwoods on roller skates in a bikini who wanted to be somebody. She was easy prey. "Older men prey on young girls desperate for love," she says, wincing. "I was an easy target. I would throw myself into any situation just for the thrill and the pain. I am an experience junkie." She learned fast how to use her conspicuous body to get money and drugs. Maybe even the love she so craved. "You think you are shit because your father doesn't love you. I thought if I was sexy everybody would love me." It was her only asset.

The slide was a routine urban story. Drugs, an abortion at 14, and then she ran away from home looking for the highlife in low places. A street kid walking on the wild side. Defenceless and broke. Underage sex in cheap motels with lowlife men who treated her like shit. And she was angry. "I was very destructive. I was passionately angry. I was very, very rebellious. I hated everybody and everything. Especially myself." Older men exploiting her fantasy of stardom. The seduction of money. It wasn't a huge stretch to posing for adult magazines using a fake ID and to the distorted underworld of pornography. In free-fall as a plump brunette Hollywood runaway, by 14 she was more than averagely acquainted with hard drugs. "I lost three years of my life free-basing cocaine. What does a 14-year-old know, what does a 13-year-old know? It is true that you are really naive and really susceptible to influences. They say that as you get older you become more interesting because you have lived your life. But it doesn't always work that way."

By a blonde and transformed 15, with a sleek, perfect body, she had become Traci Lords. Legend. Mobbed in Paris and Tokyo when she made public appearances; in the States, drooling men would line up for hours to get her autograph at adult video movie conferences. While other little girls were dreaming of becoming Homecoming Queen, Traci Lords was a full-blown porn queen. A phenomenon. Forget the hick from the mountains. She was somebody now. She was a fucking star. The biggest fucking star in a three billion dollar business. So fuck off.

Her badly lit, shoddily shot videos—heavy emphasis on the zoom lens heavily applied to the genitals—outsold those of other porn actresses 10 to one. Even dope-sick, as she was, violated and demeaned, her eyes glassy and glazed, she had on film a wicked savvy innocence. Those long, clean limbs. The softness of her baby skin. That mouth. A coltish, tough, platinum Lolita who was insolent and combative with the men she was fucking. Hateful, detached, screaming for more. Fucking with a vengeance. They got off on her Attitude. She was known for keeping going long after the cameras stopped rolling, like she had something to prove. "Call it temporary insanity," she says now, with a hollow laugh. "I wanted to get attention. I have never chosen the easy way. Even when I know I am doing things I shouldn't be doing. I think for some reason I needed to go through that. I was exorcising my demons. I liked sex but it was not about sex, it was about self-abuse." Another resigned shrug.

She made scores of explicit films. Every configuration of the sex act possible, every louche fantasy; every lowlife and sleazebag on the planet wanted a piece of Traci Lords. Some of these guys were heavy, nasty dudes.

But there is something about Traci Lords, as she sits talking at a long wooden table, surrounded by serious art, that demands respect. Something in the arched eyebrows and direct gaze. The shooting-from-the-hip lack of artifice or self-pity. Unveneered. She can't, after all, hide her past. It is for sale in sex shops. But there is something about her that is compelling, something about her presence, something seductive and powerful and vulnerable that makes you want to reach out to her and make it all right. Show her somehow that you do respect her. That you are on her side. If the things you did in your troubled adolescence made headlines, Jesus Christ, you wouldn't get off so lightly either.

What, I suddenly wonder, did I expect a former porn queen to be? Huge laquered hair, too much make-up, skimpy leopardskin slit to the thigh, stiletto heels, big jewellery, bad grammar? Did I expect her to be nice, with a rippling laugh and hair scraped back off her face? There is nothing stereotyped, cheap or trashy about Traci Lords. The linen blouse is snowy against her long neck.

By 18 it was all over for the world famous baby doll porn star. She was busted by the FBI for being under-age. Someone had tipped them off. But it wasn't Traci they were after, it was the porn purveyors, the exploiters of lost and unloved children. The US Attorney's Office moved in on anyone connected with her.

Pornographers ran for cover. In truly bad-girl style, it is rumoured that she did a deal and walked away, but not before sending a video distributor to jail for violating Federal child pornography laws and costing a lot of people a lot of money in legal fees, including herself, to stay out. They all claimed they didn't know she was under-age. She got out of every subpoena. The mob reportedly was so enraged at losing millions of dollars when hundreds of thousands of her videos were pulled from the shelves that they put a contract out on her. But the traitorous golden goose was ahead of them. She was checking out anyway. When the FBI burst dramatically into her apartment in May 1986 to take her into custody she was hardly in a position to put up a fight. She was a fragile and quivering cocaine wreck.

Coming back to consciousness, she faced the overwhelming revulsion of what her life had been, what she had done, how far out there she had gone—too far to ever come back, ineradicable in X-rated video distribution. She loathed herself. There was nowhere to run. One night she emptied a near-lethal syringe of cocaine into an open vein. "I was fucked up," she says, shrugging and blowing hard. "I was a mess. I couldn't stand to look at myself in the mirror. I did go through not wanting to live." When she woke up in hospital she was skeletal, washed up, ruined and not even 20.

But, hey, she was alive. So, like everybody else in America, she went into recovery. "It has taken me years to feel OK within myself. People go, 'Oh, you are an old soul,' and I go, 'No, I have been to hell and back.'"

Ambitious blonde starlets on the B-movie circuit are a dime a dozen in Hollywood. But when the reformed, rehabilitated, reborn Traci Lords set out to claw her way to the top she was coming from the wrong end of the alphabet. The X-movie circuit. Beyond the pale. And that is a long, long way away. Trying to integrate the past, the present and the future. You can't divorce yourself after all. But that old Traci, man, she was something else. "It doesn't really matter what other people think because I have found my peace, my reason. I don't feel so destructive now."

Perhaps it is a strangely contradictory country with a big heart that can forgive and embrace its children who have fallen by the wayside. Perhaps it is that Traci's story of family dysfunction, self-abuse, drug abuse, institutionalisation and rehabilitation is so utterly commonplace; perhaps it is because she has publicly confessed, you know, shared, or perhaps she is the embodiment, as it were, of American Success, and the extremes from which it springs: tragedy and survival. The guts to go on, to start over, to work hard, that is the American story, the dream. Or maybe she is merely a novelty, a curiosity, an exquisitely beautiful freak show. But today she is a mainstream, albeit tainted, icon. A celebrated bad blonde gone straight. She is cool. In the more mean-spirited places of the world she would never live it down. But Americans are generous to the wounded, and she is one of theirs. *Details* magazine even went so far as to refer to her as 'America's Sweetheart' on its cover—with, admittedly, a sexed-up photo that screamed 'buy me'. And she has got the drop on those other scheming Hollywood starlets. At least everyone knows who she is. How could they forget? And she certainly has the savvy and chutzpah to exploit her notoriety.

Male journalists writing long eulogising feature articles are fascinated by her. She plays them, it would appear, like a piano. Phoning them, befriending them, confiding, taking them for spins in her sports car. Oh, the giddy thrill of it, walking into swank bars on the arm of the gorgeous, leggy, scandalous blonde, her body sculpted in the gym, men salivating, women hissing. It reduces hardened journalists to helpless, enslaved admiration. They turn all warm and runny and protective. The envy, no doubt, of all their friends. Male friends of mine, I have to confess, made foolish and ridiculous offers for the tape of this interview. One even went down on his knees and begged. It was pathetic. It wasn't that I tortured them by telling them about her amazingly smouldering voice and hinted that she might have talked dirty or anything. Nuh. A normally highly civilised film writer blurted that he was one of the old Traci's most compulsively wanking fans and that he had had a lifelong fantasy about saving her and her marrying him in gratitude. She was the sole reason, he whispered—a tad feverishly, I felt—that he was heterosexual.

But now she has starred on *family* television. That is moving *right* along, right up to the F in the alphabet, and a respectable F this time. Hey everybody, Traci Lords is legit. "It is how far I have come that fascinates people. It is like, God, she was a mess back then. If I didn't have the exposure and the new life that I have got, the family TV, the album, no one would care. The thing that people miss, though, is that what is happening now is as bizarre as anything that happened then. But I am on my way." She brings her hand down onto the table to emphasise this and laughs. It takes dedication, I can't help but think, to have teeth that blindingly white when you chainsmoke.

Her techno-dance album 'A Thousand and One Fires' zoomed to number two in the charts in 1995. "I wanted to do, like, a really edgy dance record," she explains. "I grew up drinking beers in the back seat of the car singing really loud, loving music, all kinds of music, rock, country, pop, blues, all kinds of metal. I had three sisters with very different personalities who had records in the house so I was exposed to a lot. I found a lot of record companies that said, 'OK, we can exploit that you are an actress, you know, whatever, we will package you and put you in the studio with ten, like, cool songs. We will do a nice little top 40 pop record, or a rock record'. But I wanted to write some stuff. I wanted progressive techno. It was really hard to get anybody to take me seriously. So I just waited. I figured, if I never make a record, I never make a record. I held out. I wrote it in the second person. I made it in London. The sound that I wanted was there. I didn't have any friends there, it was very, very lonely, it made it very intense. I was really miserable at times, but at the same time I don't think I would have been quite as reflective or gone inside. The whole album is autobiographical. It is all about things that I think or things that I have been through. The song 'Control' is as much about being out of control as being in control. Everybody wants to be in control.

Everybody wants that power. It is about power play, walking the thin line."

There have been guest roles in 'Roseanne'. So, like, was she the psycho bitch from hell? "That is not something anyone wants to make up and have it exist as a lie. Like anyone else I am sure she is capable of being a monster, but I don't know her to be the kind of person who wakes up in the morning and goes, 'OK, I am rich and powerful and I am going to fuck with everyone today.' When she is a monster I am sure that it is for a reason. I am capable of being a monster and I am sure you are. When you are pushed and you stand your ground you are considered to be a monster, to be a bitch. Because she wants to preserve her creativity, then people say she is difficult, she is a cunt, she is this and she is that. She has a creative vision, so be it. It is better than having a project that is complete and you are looking at it and going, 'Oh, this is shit, I should have said something.' If you are outnumbered and you say, 'I really feel this is right' and you have got five people standing there you can end up backing down. Usually, when your gut says you are right you are spot on. You usually screw yourself when you start to second guess yourself and then allow yourself to be persuaded and manipulated." There was 'Married With Children', mini-series such as Stephen King's 'Tommyknockers', and the role in 'Melrose Place' that will not easily be forgotten.

When her 'Melrose Place' appearance screened in the US, ratings went through the roof. "I was the sweetest girl at first but then I turned into a monster," she says, her face lighting up. "I was involved in a cult. I was a cool card, but I could snap at the drop of a hat. I worked in a coffee shop, I was a kind of drifter, really lost. I wanted Sydney to become involved in the cult. I saw her becoming one of my new best friends and me giving her a life. I am this really nice, nurturing person, but when she crosses the line that I don't want her to cross I really go after her. I caused a lot of hell." Traci Lords is grinning with sheer pleasure.

The best part, though, was that she got the deeply satisfying task of trashing the bar. Ah, the sound of breaking glass. "I trashed

Shooters. It was brilliant. It took about two takes. I walked in that morning, I was really tired, I had been up all night and was really pissed off about something. They said, 'Are you going to do it or should we get a stunt person in here, Trace?' and I said, 'That won't be necessary, no, I can deal with this.' Talk about *venting*. There were bar stools flying across the room. I had a pool cue, I knocked the glasses off the shelf. I looked insane. When I watched it, it was like, *oh my God!*" Laughing and laughing. "I looked like a crazy person, it was great."

Years of acting classes and bad B-movies. "I studied with the Lee Strasberg theatre and now I study with Howard Fine. If you've got the training it opens you up to a whole new thing." It is the process, you see, getting out of herself. "You can find your reality in things that are not real, making things become your reality. It is an amazing mind-fuck. Because if you were ever in school and you sat in the back of the classroom and you wished you were the girl in the front of the classroom, the girl who was prettier than you or skinnier than you or had a better boyfriend than you did, you can be all those things."

'The answer is yes,' pronounced the *Hollywood Reporter* regally after her outing in Roger Corman's *Not of This Earth*, in 1988, which came complete with floating monsters, 'she can act.'

Traci comes alive when she talks about acting. She does the voices, the eyes flash, she is transformed. Yes, I can only echo, she can act, she acted for me. As she talks it becomes clear that she merely went down an unfortunate cul-de-sac with the porn stuff on the way to her true vocation. "*Not of This Earth* was my first legitimate film. It was a B-movie. It was made for $50,000. We shot it in a lumberyard down in Santa Monica. I was, like, 18 years old, I didn't have a fucking clue. It was great. I have done films and just, oh, fucking stupid films and gone 'oh, God'. But this was really cheesy, a cheesy bad movie, that was what it embraced. It was floating monsters and men from outer space. As bad as it was, it was really good. It was the first and last time I was topless in a legitimate movie. I was a sassy smartass, a fast talker with attitude all the way. I wasn't trying to be anything else. I like what I did in it."

A big break came finally with that connoisseur of the damaged and eccentric, John Waters, and his deliberately weird teenage movie *Cry Baby*, alongside Johnny Depp, in which she, admittedly, played a lacquered-haired sex-bomb teenage tramp, vamping it to the max. "He is one of my favourite directors," gushes his good friend Traci. "He is very specific. He will say if there is something in the script that he feels you are missing, or a joke that you are not getting, then he will go so far as to act it out for you and show you what he is talking about. He is very comical that way. He will sit in front of the video monitor and play out each scene. He would do my lines in front of Johnny Depp, then he would snap into Johnny's, then he would snap into Ricki Lake's. He looked insane when he was doing it. Personally it was the most fun I have ever had in a professional situation. He is someone I really admire and respect because he has paid his dues and he has come out way on top. This is a guy that started out in back alleys. People used to laugh at him in school. He was the nerd, the undesirable. He was never cool. John Waters was never cool. That is what made him cool. The fact that he was a dweeb at school. Tall, skinny and not too attractive. That is why he and Divine were friends to begin with. Everybody used to beat them up. They were such geeks and such freaks and so eccentric. That made them have a twisted view on life and that is what made his genius. He was forced to see things from other angles because he was never allowed to hang with the cool kids. He learned how to mock them and imitate them. *Cry Baby* had a lot to do with me making a record because it was a musical and the cast did sing in that movie. That is when I first started thinking, 'Yeah, I really dig this and I would really like to do something with it.'"

And then, oh God, breathless excitement, nearly getting the lead, the showgirl, in *Casino*. Scorsese wanted her. She went back again and again to test with the great man. She was the real article. She knew the pain. "I really wanted to work with him. I guess

I will never really know exactly what happened. But I know that he really liked me and he wanted to work with me and it was something that everyone thought was going to happen. It was even leaked to the papers," Lords says.

Alas, it went to that other bad blonde, Sharon Stone. "I understood why they did it. Sharon is big box office." And what a bravura performance Stone turned in, it was her role, no question about that. But Traci could have done it. Traci would have brought authenticity, Traci knows things beyond Sharon's worst nightmare. Actually, you get the feeling that Traci Lords could out-Sharon-Stone Sharon Stone in the strong blonde department any day of the week. You don't mess with Traci Lords. Understand that.

"Look, it is still really hard for me not to be defensive about my past. There are still times when, if I feel someone is being disrespectful or judgmental, I will just go, 'Fuck you'. It can still set me off. It is a real issue with me. Where people mess up, and it is really easy to do, is when they surround themselves with people who do not have their best interests at heart. There are plenty of people who do not have my best interests at heart, who are just out to make a quick buck. But I have learned that if you surrender yourself to sharks you are going to get eaten. I have had the same manager for the past three years, my manager is ace, I would be lost without her. I have really good people around me; they are totally with me and what I am about. It is not a matter of them bringing a script to me that is demeaning, or going, 'Oh, yeah, Traci, they want you to take your clothes off'; it never even gets to me. It is when you let idiots into your camp that you mess up."

But listening to this preternaturally wise young woman speak, the question still hangs tacit in the air: *How could that have happened to a child?* How could she have gone so *completely* off the rails? How could her sense of self been so distorted? How could a pubescent girl become a world famous sex queen? How could she slip through the cracks like that? Didn't anyone care about her? Her mother says she went to the police but they told her there were too many runaways on the streets.

Going to buy the only Traci Lords video still available—because it was made after she was 18—in the darker corners of Manhattan's Times Square, I got a glimpse of the nightmare world she had inhabited. Men hovered in the doorway of the sex shop, lurked watchfully in the aisles as I chose and paid for my dirty video. I was followed up the street by a group of them, ill-dressed lowlifes, reeking of desperation, pestering to buy me a drink. And there was no tenderness to be found in Traci's grand finale video, *Traci, I Love You*. Written and produced by her, in it she seemed uncomfortable, detached, all business. The first scene was a tacky office scene where Traci bent over, clutching her ankles, and was taken from behind. The next was a lesbian scenario where a supine Traci was licked, sucked and stroked by two other women. The third featured group sex. Here Traci was heavily made up, wearing only high heels, legs wide open. One woman feverishly attempted to suck four or five proffered penises at once. A middle-aged and flabby Frenchman acted as voyeur as Traci and several other women had sex with each other and some rather seedy men. Then he took her from behind and pumped hard. His excited, heavily-accented voice-over was more a violation than a celebration of the disdainful woman to whom he addressed his ardour. She rarely appeared to be enjoying the sex.

Even after years of therapy she still flinches at the flooding memories. Still tries to find the answers. She twirls her long, too-yellow hair. There had to be something more. Something that pushed her over the edge. And there was. The key to the unravelling of her life, she says, can be found on her record, 'A Thousand and One Fires'. On it is a song, 'Father's Field', sung in a plaintive, half-whispered, little-girl, come hither voice, about being raped at the age of ten by a boy who was six years older and knew exactly what he was doing. One line goes: 'I heard my clothes rip, his hands over my mouth.' Another: 'Don't say anything, don't tell anyone.'

Traci says softly now: "I put that track on my record because that experience really changed my life. It changed who I am forever. I took that song from journals I had kept. I talk about things on that record that I have never talked about before. I didn't understand until then that I was still really, really bitter about it. You have to face up to yourself to confront it. If I wasn't already at that place I wouldn't have been able to do it. You don't really know who you are until you get older. And with that and the move to California and the drugs and experimenting and being a teenager anyway . . . it was maddening. I think it was just a series of events. I thought I knew everything. I knew a lot and I missed a lot."

She used to write. She kept a diary when she was a kid. "My mother is an English major, so when I was growing words were a really big deal. A lot of things on the album I took from journals, from when I was young. It tripped me out that when I was writing the record I still felt the same way. I didn't do much of anything during the drug period. What I did do, you can't read. It was a big scrawl, oh God." She flinches and puts her face in her hands. "You are in a corner of a bar somewhere writing on a cocktail napkin, oh God."

She is picking herself up now and walking towards the door. A long, cool, Californian chick. We stand blinking in the sun. "I am sort of bored with playing strong, edgy women, to tell you the truth," she says, digging the gravel with the toe of her cowboy boot. "I have played a lot of them. I am like that myself, a strong, edgy woman, but it is getting a little old. That is why I am more into the laughs now. I would love to do a wacky comedy or something really romantic. You are either funny or you are not. I am. That is one thing that a lot of people really don't know about me. That is why I did 'Roseanne' three times. That is the one thing they can't teach you. Maybe I could even do a romantic story. Now *that* would be scary."

Way to go, girlfriend, I think as I totter off down the gravel driveway, impressed as hell, past the flowers bursting in the garden, and into the clear blue sky, way to go.

# The Shower Scene

Even Janet Leigh, who knew it was only the movies because she was in that damn shower for seven days, was so traumatised by the brutality of her death 35 years ago that she never willingly stepped into a shower again. "It is true that I don't take showers. If there is no other way to bathe, then I make sure all of the doors and windows in the house are locked, and I leave the bathroom door open and the shower curtain or stall door open so I have a perfect, clear view. I face the door no matter where the showerhead is.

"I realised how vulnerable and completely defenceless we are. When I saw the film edited and scored, I had the perpetual screaming meemies. I felt every thrust of that knife, screamed with every lunge; I was completely terrorised."

Ever since she was stabbed to death in the shower screaming, her flesh tearing, the killing knife stabbing and stabbing, slashing and plunging, over and over, her hand sliding down the wall, her blood running into water and whirling down the plughole, the drumming water washing the blood down her arms, taking the shower curtain down with her as she clung to it desperately, falling to the white tiles, her eyes wide open, ever since then Janet Leigh has been famous for the shower scene in *Psycho*. It was the impact, the shock of it, the nervy music, the Bates Motel, that made it an icon of cinema, a pop cultural artefact of its own. Her sudden, nude demise so early in the film stunned and confused audiences. It wasn't fair, they were just getting to know her.

At that universally traumatising moment it stopped being safe to go in the shower. There you are, naked and vulnerable, outside sound dimmed by gushing water, nowhere to hide, no weapon at hand; defenceless. There is an intruder, you can't see him in the steam, you haven't got a chance. Alfred Hitchcock expertly exploited our naked vulnerability.

I stand out in the steep road at Benedict Canyon for quite a long time trying to figure out how to alert Janet Leigh to my presence. Dogs bark inside but no one comes and I can't find any buzzer at the high security gate. Her house is a fortress. The passage of time has not wearied the weirdos that came with the territory of *Psycho*. Finally I resort to the time-honoured method of yelling. The dogs on the other side become hysterical and finally a Spanish maid comes to check out the commotion.

Janet Leigh ushers me in, laughing, apologetic, and seats me on a deep green sofa. "I have trouble with fans, yes. But unfortunately, in today's world, everyone needs security. You don't have to have made *Psycho* for that. You just need security. Period. I get a tremendous amount of mail, considering that I haven't done anything in 10 years. Everyone has a *Psycho* story. *Psycho* is part of everyone's life. They remember when they saw it, with whom they saw it. They all have a story about how it affected them."

Hers is a large family house, comfortable, immaculate, expensive oils on the walls, photographs and statues of dogs, flowers on the tables. A tiny, wiry woman in her late sixties, with large blue intelligent eyes, a gaunt face that is stretched smooth and fluffy yellow hair. A dignity too, and a lack of the kind of artifice and plastic you might expect from an ageing star. Janet Leigh has a sweet smile and a surprisingly loud voice.

Down across the deep valleys Hollywood is enveloped in smog. She looks out over the place where she was once reigning royalty. As she speaks, it is almost impossible to reconcile her with the doomed Marion Crane of *Psycho*. "I pictured her as Everywoman. I pictured her as coming from the town that I grew up in, Stockton, California. She went to the movies and to the church and probably sang in the choir."

Back then, Janet Leigh was a porcelain blonde with a full mouth, almond eyes and a tiny waist. "It devastated me to look at her," said her then husband Tony Curtis. "It is almost like looking at someone else," says she after recently watching *Psycho*.

Indeed, it is. It is almost surreal to see her sitting there in an elderly tracksuit and running shoes, on her sofa, her golden retriever's head thrust into my lap. Like looking at an old bromide photograph that has faded and distorted with time.

She and Tony Curtis were the most glamorous of Hollywood stars. Back in those days, a star was a Star. They made an effort to look the part. They dressed up. They lived the movie myth. They did not have attitude. They had an image to maintain. "When I went somewhere, I tried to look as good as I could—which I would do for me as a person, anyway. Just for my own self-esteem. We led a glamorous life, just because of the nature of our work and our friends. Actually, famous people are just human beings," says Leigh, smiling a tad sadly.

'There was such incredible publicity about us,' Curtis wrote in his autobiography. 'All those magazine layouts about Janet and me as the fabulous, ideal First Couple of Hollywood. There was no bigger pair. Debbie Reynolds and Eddie Fisher could've been our maid and butler by comparison.' I once interviewed Tony Curtis about his slide into cocaine addiction. "How," he asked rhetorically, "could a fabulous 35ft-high-screen guy like me have gotten so fucked up?" They were spoiled rotten, those stars. And unfortunately, Curtis and his curving pompadour still believed his old publicity. As far as he was concerned, he was still a Star, and he behaved in a suitably petulant manner. He hated my story so much that he threw the publicist who had arranged the interview out of the limo late at night in an outer suburb of Melbourne. No wonder Leigh divorced him. "I don't blame an industry or a place, Hollywood, for two people breaking up," she said. "It is people who break up. Not a profession and not a city."

But in the heady years of 1959 and 1960, he starred in the Oscar-winning *Some Like It Hot* and she was nominated for *Psycho*. "It has all changed now," Janet Leigh says sadly. "Now the studio system is not in evidence at all. It is run by businessmen now, by agencies. It is a shame. The studio is just a shell. It is not a living thing. It used to be that the studios were almost like cities and we were all alumni. Everyone was under contract, you worked with the same people a lot. There was just a very familial association. Today, you are on your own from the word go. There is no one to plan or to set you up, to guide your career or nurture you. To build a career. The make-believe world is very hard work. There is a lot of downside, rejection. You give up some privacy. There's a lot of pluses, but you have to really like it to want to do it."

Janet Leigh apologises profusely for not wearing make-up. For not being a Star today. She was busy doing other things and did not have time to get made up. She had only agreed to do the interview when I told her publicist I would not be bringing a photographer. You get the impression that it takes many hours and a concerted effort to transform herself into Janet Leigh, Star. "It just gets tiring putting on the make-up and getting your hair combed. They say that if you are over 50 in Hollywood, you might as well commit suicide. But I am way over 50. I do charity work and write books. I just sort of backed off when the quality wasn't there for people my age. I am just as productive as I have ever been. I have a very full life."

Janet Leigh has a piercing intelligence and there are glimpses, too, of the wicked sense of humour for which her daughter, actress Jamie Lee Curtis, is known. "Jamie looks like me from a three-quarter angle, especially when her hair is light. She looks a lot like me."

Her gushy book, *Psycho*, which features her as a corpse on the cover, was written, she says, because, since the demise of Hitchcock and Anthony Perkins, she is the only one left to tell the story. "Of all the books that have been written about Mr Hitchcock, none was ever done by someone who actually worked with him. He had a wonderful dry wit." So has Janet Leigh. I remark that Hitchcock was always formal, always wore a suit and tie. "Always," she says emphatically. "Nowadays, you're lucky if they wear clothes—no, I don't mean that."

Before shooting began, the man she still refers to formally as Mr Hitchcock invited her to his house in Beverly Hills and showed her the models for the film. Here, she saw the master of suspense at work, the planning it took to thoroughly scare people.

He said: "You are free to do whatever you wish with the role of Marion. But there is one rule on the set: my camera is absolute. I tell the story through that lens, so I need you to move when my camera moves, stop when my camera stops. I will not change the timing of my camera." There were 78 angles for the shower scene, each one lasting two to three seconds on the screen. That meant 78 set ups.

The timing, and the heightened use of shadows and mirrors, symbolism for the duality that lurks in us all, says Leigh, "is why he could build the suspense and create the tension and the hysteria. The scenes were built and primed with his economical use of the camera so that there wasn't a wasted shot. It all led up to the climax. Because of the censor, you had to build the suspense without ever having to show violence or sex. He showed us what can be done with a camera. Perhaps the most striking symbolism in *Psycho* is Hitchcock's repeated use of mirrors and windows. There are more than a dozen examples of double images, hammering into our subconscious again and again the duality of good and bad, the split personality that lives to some degree in us all."

While Leigh went on to star in many films, Tony Perkins, who played the psychopathic Norman, had his career stunted by the film. But Leigh says, "A very famous actor once said that if a performer can be remembered for one role in their career, they are indeed a very fortunate performer. That is how I feel and that is how Tony felt, too."

The shower scene was her moment. It was 17 seconds long.

# The Dead Redhead

The dead redhead lay on the side of the road. Her stocking looped loosely around her badly bruised neck. Blood smudged her lips and her nose. Her pearls were broken and scattered. Her fingernails bloody and clotted with skin. She had fought, wildly, to the death. His mother had loved liquor and men. "She majored in booze and minored in men," says writer James Ellroy. "There are times when I can feel her and I can smell her. I can smell the cigarettes that she smoked, the liquor on her breath, the perfume that she wore. I swear there are times when I can smell the contents of the purse I used to steal money from."

Her killer had sex with her in his Oldsmobile. Then he bought her a grilled cheese sandwich at Stan's Drive-In Car Hop. She was "quite high and chatting gaily", her breast spilling from her dress. The man drank coffee and "acted bored with her" said the waitress who witnessed the post-coital pall. Then he bashed her, pulled a cord tight around her neck and dumped her on the side of the road. Her coat covered her legs. The cord and the stocking looked like a scarf, jauntily tied.

His mother picked up her killer in a bar. "She liked cheap men—she married my father," Ellroy says with a laugh. Her murderer was white trash with a vengeance, who then vanished. Case unsolved.

"There are times when I can feel the killer very strongly and feel this early middle-aged, lonely, horny, alcoholic milieu that took her life," says Ellroy into the white-hot Los Angeles haze 38 years later.

*My mother made love with her killer.*

Years of nightmares and fear of the dark. "I have always been beset by fears." But James Ellroy had hated his mother, at 10, when she died. "My mother had been lousy to me in the weeks before she died. I would find her in bed with strange men. She drank

**JAMES ELLROY**

bourbon and got mawkish or hellaciously pissed-off." Running away from something, his mother moved out to El Monte. 'El Monte,' he later wrote, 'was a smoggy void. People parked on their lawns and hosed down their cars in their underwear. The sky was carcinogenic tan. I noticed a lot of evil-looking pachucos.'

His tears, he later wrote, were secretly 'an expression of hysterical relief' at being able to live with the surviving half of that failed, cheap couple: his father. A picaresque woman-chaser; a handsome loser and liar who spent his days sunbaking in boxer shorts listening to Dixieland music. "He had this gigantic wang that used to hang out of the left leg of his shorts." Ellroy lowers his voice confidentially, still slightly awed.

But his mother refused to go away. She drove him into darker and darker places. Self-destruction and skidsville. A dozen lost years drifting and homeless; stealing and drunk, always drunk. Smashed and breaking into houses to sniff women's knickers. "It was pathetic, fucking pathetic." Haunted James Ellroy. The jail got real familiar. Her son's life has turned ever after on the unsolved murder of Geneva Hilliker Ellroy, 1915–1958. Divorcee. Booze artist. Tramp. Lonely, lonely, lonely.

At 10, Ellroy learned fast about the savagery and hidden brutality in saccharine '50s America. 'America was never innocent. We popped our cherry on the boat over and looked back with no regrets,' he writes in the introduction to *American Tabloid*, a book about the machinations in the underworld leading up to the assassination of John F. Kennedy, the book that blasted him from cult status and on to the best-seller lists. At 10, disturbed and frightened, he began compulsively reading crime fiction; a psyche precipitously plunged into psycho-sex and swaggering lowlife barbarity. He shoplifted books. He roamed Los Angeles. He prowled the suburb of Hancock in the dark looking at the rich girls through the windows. "I liked to watch them putter in front of their mirrors. I was a thief and a voyeur; a geeky minor miscreant about town." He was obnoxious. He enrolled in a largely Jewish school and declared himself a Nazi. He turned friends over fast.

In his own forensic and brutal crime novels, he has been possessed by his mother, avenging her death in his own twisted way. Circling the defining catastrophe of his life. Beating himself up with images of her murder all through his work. Exploiting it to the max for book sales 'by a master self-promoter with a tight grip on pop-psych show and tell' as he himself has cynically noted. Sniffing it, picking at it like a scab. 'This Valediction in Blood' was the dedication to her in *The Black Dahlia*, a shattering novelisation of the famous unsolved murder of Elizabeth Short, whose gruesome killing in 1947 somehow merged in his distorted adolescent mind with that of his mother. He had transferred his love and grief and longing to the formerly young, pretty, promiscuous Elizabeth Short. "I had fantasies of going back to 1947 and saving her and, uh, enjoying sexual adventures with her." And so in Ellroy's fevered book, the empowered adult rewrites the script. The murder is solved and rough justice is done, naturally, with firepower and depravity to the max.

"I wept for the better part of a day when I had finished it. Writing that book was a tremendous catharsis. That story had been building inside me for close on 30 years."

James Ellroy is hunkered down in a hectic Hawaiian shirt, staring maniacally at the menu, as if he might suddenly pull out a gun and blow it away. I seriously hope there is nothing irritating on that menu. I imagine an Ellroy thug cursing, "Chicken salad, man, I hate chicken salad", and blasting away the menu, whacking a couple of waiters on the way out, then barrelling up 6th Street in a shriek of rubber and smoke on hot bitumen. I try to act nonchalant. James Ellroy is a huge and powerful man. It obviously takes sheer physical size to write books as tough as his. You need to be big and bad and mean to even think that stuff.

But James Ellroy is merely gossiping with the waiters. We are, after all, in Ellroy territory—downtown LA. Outside, in the smog and heat, the summer seems exhausted. Ellroy's old, wounded neighbourhood is crumbling in the white light. Desperate edges in the cheap apartments and toxic streets. 'I feel chills of doom

whenever I drive through it,' he wrote in *Brown's Requiem*, his
fairly ordinary first novel, written when he was a golf caddy getting sober. Down the road, drug-infested Lafayette Park conducts
its murderous business as usual.

We are eating in the Pacific Dining Car, a legend in its own
lunchtime, which, in its guest appearances in Ellroy's books, sees a
lot of action. All through the *LA Quartet*, set in the '40s and '50s,
corrupt cops congregate in its hulking wing-back chairs to chow
down and scheme. It was at a soirée here in *LA Confidential* that
District Attorney Bill McPherson, fighting a tight re-election campaign, got his martini spiked with chloral hydrate. When he woke
up he was in a hotel tryst situation with an underage black prostitute, with the Sheriff's department and the press looking on. He
got off the statutory rape charge but his job and his wife went
south. His arch rival, the foxy Ellis Loew, a major player in all four
books, acted all innocent, like he just got lucky, that's all.

And in *The Black Dahlia* the crazy cop Bucky Bleichert muses,
'My hopes for the Warrants job had waned to the point where I
would have sold them down the river for pork chops at the Pacific
Dining Car.' In all Ellroy's work fabrication collides loosely with
fact, emotional subtext and fragments of memory.

When James Ellroy's father used to bring him here as a boy, it
was an open-grill steakhouse. Now the Dining Car décor is strictly
lower Los Angeles: red velour walls, all pseudo-grandeur and
spangled faux-luxury. One clashing orange rose sits on the white
tablecloth between Ellroy and me. And Ellroy is staring with those
homicidal eyes, unblinking behind wire-rimmed spectacles. "I met
my wife in this restaurant," he says, pointing a massive finger
across the room. "Over there." I peer across, wondering if it is too
dark in that particular corner to recognise full-blown psychosis
when you see it. I am, after all, in a severely shook-up and nervy
condition from reading his books back-to-back. I probably need to
rest. Quietly.

Only this morning I was sickened by the corpse of the severely
mutilated Elizabeth Short, held and tortured for two days before

her death. Body cut in half, organs removed, breasts sliced off, bones broken, cigarette burns, rope burns, face bashed in, mouth slashed from ear to ear.

There are no boundaries of taste or morality in Ellroy's repellent but compelling landscapes of devastation. No limits. Clipped, terse staccato; warped humour and aggressively *noir* and fast, you just can't relax. Not when there are the extremes of the underbelly of life, necrophilia, bestiality, incest, murder, profanity, sleaze and savagery, waiting around every corner. It is ugly in there. And Ellroy takes you all the way into the madness. In there *everyone* is rotten to the core. "It is alienating," his New York publisher Sonny Mehta told me with a sinister smile. A stranger to the verb and the adjective, Ellroy doesn't stop to look at the scenery along the way. Graphic snapshots of violent images and the gloriously accurate slang of snitches, patsies, rogue cops, shakedown artists, teamsters and the underworld come together in intricate, labyrinthine plots. "I dig all forms of the pre-politically correct US colloquial language," he says.

His books linger in a time before his world turned on its axis, a time when he was still a safe little boy listening to moody jazz; a time when mothers always came home. "I know what I do in the work is transfer the violence of today to a statistically much less violent time. Today it is caused by psychic displacement, racism, poverty, a tremendous profusion of drugs. You have got a whole culture of people who are brought up to believe that they can be anything. They want to be doing something else, they want to be someone else."

And, hey, James Ellroy is a normal guy. He may write like a homicidal maniac, he may look like a serial killer, he may have done some awful things, he may have been seriously fucked up, he may be Mr Showbiz on the promotional circuit, but to hear it from him, just quietly, he is a pussycat. "The truth is that I am quite sane, quite rational, rather a reasonable human being. Easy to get along with," he smiles with strangely small teeth. Today he seems rational. He does not turn into the carefully cultivated strange and savage self-promoting James Ellroy persona. During our long conversation he will be gentle, amusing, cheerfully and obligingly confiding the sordid details of his life. "Colourful and media-exploitable," as he is the first to admit. Well, maybe an unhappy childhood helps. There is, reportedly, nothing he will not do to sell his books. He has been known to get down on his knees in bookshops, barking like a dog, biting old ladies on the bum and rounding people up to buy his novels.

James Ellroy's voice has dropped to an appalled whisper. He is talking about the bad phase, the bender years. For five years he lived outdoors, stealing, drinking and speeding on amphetamines. "I used to basically stumble around LA and defecate wherever I happened to find myself. I was in a blackout once and my buddy told me," Ellroy looks around furtively and scrunches up his mouth, "that I walked up to a black couple at a bus stop, whipped out my dick, urinated and said 'white is beautiful'. I was a pig, Susan. Yeah. A pig."

But in the end, it seems, a sick and twisted mind and a newly happy disposition have somehow been neatly reconciled in Ellroy. He is crazy in love with his second wife, Helen, a journalist and writer, whom he married at the age of 43 after his first marriage, at 40, failed. "I have been obsessed with women for a long, long time and now I am married to a woman who is easily the single most great human being I have ever met," he purrs, "and I've met a few."

No writer has grown more accomplished (or nastier) with each book than Ellroy. While each book has been more complex, darker, deeper, more personal, more ambitious and more powerful, *American Tabloid* is something else again. A broader canvas, a departure, a writer reaching his awesome peak. "The last long haul, the last four or five months of writing it, really kicked me around. I had more hair and darker hair a year ago," he says.

*American Tabloid* is a brilliant, bloody killing field. "And now there is no going back," he says, chomping with satisfaction on a large and tender steak. "Heh, heh."

Jack 'the Haircut' Kennedy was cruising to be whacked, according to Ellroy. In Ellroy's spin on the Kennedy years, he never had a chance. The game was always rigged. Ellroy's Jack Kennedy is a hollow, hapless and priapic man. ("Jack laughed. 'That goddamn book's eating up all your time. You should get a ghost writer. I did, and I won the Pulitzer Prize.'") Bobby got them both killed. "John Kennedy's death was basically the result of Bobby Kennedy's Oedipal drama. He had a strong moral side and I think he recognised his father for what he was and took his vengeance on organised crime, you know, vengeance once removed on his father. It was an amalgam of renegade CIA men, crazy Cuban exiles, right-wing fanatics and organised crime that killed off Jack. Everybody wanted him dead."

Ellroy tells his side of the story, of course, from his natural habitat; the underworld, the corrupted, the subversive, the cold-blooded killer. 'It is time to embrace bad men and the price they paid to secretly define their time,' he writes in the introduction. His portrayal of the unholy alliances behind the scenes in *American Tabloid* certainly demythologises American history as we know it. Of his main protagonists, double agents all, it is Big Pete Bondurant, a psychopath working for Howard Hughes and a hit man for Jimmy Hoffa, who most resembles Ellroy and for whom Ellroy clearly has great affection. "Yeah, I like Pete, but no, no, I am not like him," he protests. "Well, obviously there is the sympathetic attachment to women. Pete was based on a private eye to the stars called Freddy Otash. He was a shakedown artist supreme. He was the guy who hotwired Peter Lawford's beach pad at the behest of Jimmy Hoffa and the teamsters. I looked him up and we became friends. He was a legbreaker and an extortionist but I came to like the old guy." Pete Bondurant is one of the many characters who check in and out of other books. In *Tabloid* Pete even gets to fall in love. ('Big Pete wants a woman. Extortion experience preferred but not necessary.') "I will give you a little tip," smiles Ellroy. "They are going to stay together. What I want to show in the next books is bad men getting older. I want to show them coming to grips with their humanity. I especially want to show eroticism in the American male."

Why is it, I wonder, that the rare hot blasts of love in Ellroy's books are nearly always with curvaceous redheads? "Yeah, adolescent fantasy brought to life. Of course, my mother had red hair, we can get really Freudian about that," he laughs kindly.

Well, yes we can, actually. James Ellroy is still looking for his mother. "I think I have run from her for a long time. I resemble her more every day." Now the unhappy woman whose death shaped his life is closer and further away than ever. He has hired a detective and reopened her case. Homicide Detective Bill Stoner had been on the Jean Ellroy case and was now retired. 'Lividity had thickened her features. She did not look like anyone I had ever known,' he wrote of the shock of seeing the photos of her corpse on the police file.

"We're going over and over her file," Ellroy says. "We've found a number of the original witnesses. I had always thought she wasn't raped, it was as if I wanted to hide the fact from myself. We don't know if it was consensual sex or not. The killer wanted to ditch this desperate woman he had fucked and get on with his life. We had a live suspect for about five days. We found my landlady from the time of the killing. She told us that a man tried to rape her in 1953 and that she had always thought he was a suspect in my mother's killing. He had picked her up in a bar near the bar where my mother met the man. He took her into the boonies and threw her into the back seat and was clawing at her clothes, but ejaculated prematurely. He said, 'Hey, you are lucky' and drove her home."

Ellroy and the cop located the man living in a trailer park about 8 km from the Pacific Dining Car. "His trailer was plastered with *Playboy* playmates of the month," he recalls. "It was obvious he was an old-time pervert, but he just did not match the description of the man my mother was seen with. We said, 'Hey Joe, we heard you used to date-rape women 40 years ago.' He nearly shit a brick right there. It felt good, you know. This guy got away with all this stuff for all these years and all of a sudden, fate knocks on his door.

"But we are beginning to believe that the same man who killed my mother killed another woman several months later. We don't think he is a serial killer. It was probably two date rapes that went bad beyond the rape. My feeling is my mother was the first woman he killed, and then he laid low for a while. He was out there chasing women just for sex but then it went bad with the other woman and he ended up killing her in the same way," he says sadly in his surprisingly soft voice.

And so now he confronts the old, old pain head-on. Would facing the killer drive the demons away? Will Geneva Ellroy finally get to rest in peace? "People always ask me if I will be able to keep from strangling him if I meet him. Think about it. If it happened to you and you knocked on his door, I think you would feel awe more than anything." Ellroy slumps back in his chair. "But he is dead. He was 37 to 40 years old then. He was a hard-drinking, cigarette-smoking guy out of that era. They tend not to make 78, 80."

And lest a minute of his life not be cannibalised, he has turned the investigation into a harrowing memoir, *My Dark Places*, which came out some months after this interview took place. "I think I need to write a book that is shamelessly autobiographical, graphically and emotionally, discursive and digressive. I want to trace a sexual journey from my teens to my mother, through profligacy, to my life with Helen," he says.

He never did find out who killed the redhead. Her killer got away with it. But he found out a lot of other things. He found out about police procedure and about sex-murders, about other murdered Los Angelean women, case unsolved. Detective Bill Stoner was, like Ellroy, haunted by dead women. They come into their dreams like ghosts, these women who do not rest in peace. Girls who went on dates and never returned, their bodies dumped from cars, women who trusted men for the ride home that became their last ride, lonely divorcees like Jean Ellroy looking for warmth in the night but becoming disposable sex. And he found out that he loved his mother with a passion. With no other points of reference, her death was the defining moment in his life. That hers was a sex-murder was, I think, the thing that fucked him up. That was the snag, the worm in the 10-year-old's brain. Mommy, mommy, mommy. Sex and death devastated that boy. He was too young to understand the impact, but he has pursued sex and death vicariously ever since. The most terrifying thing about *My Dark Places*, though, is that it is not fiction. Ellroy did not make this stuff up. Los Angeles Sheriff's Department Homicide files are more depraved and heartbreaking than even Ellroy could imagine. *My Dark Places* is LA *noir* for real. He writes of his own monstrous adolescence like a sinner driven to confession, driven to confess the worst things he has done, the absolute worst. From the moment Jean Ellroy died in the passenger seat of the Oldsmobile he retreated to a whirling fantasy world. This book is that interior monologue.

Like mother, like son. But if her aching need to drown herself in liquor and sex got her killed, the same nearly happened to her son. His self-destruction too, was nearly total. "I became promiscuous after I got sober because I was too crazy and voluble and frightened and unattractive to women to be promiscuous while I was drinking and using drugs. I have never had a family and I have always transubstantiated that hunger into a lust for women."

His father was 60 when his son moved in. "He was sort of past it. I moved in with my non-housebroken Dad into this crummy apartment. The dog defecated all over the place. My father hung out in the backyard showing off his Greek god torso. He was this loser that probably should have been president of the United States but he didn't have the drive. When I was 13, I went home from school sick and found him engaged in sexual intercourse with my sixth grade teacher. He was tragic and seedy and charming. We didn't have any money, my father didn't have a car, today we would be homeless. We wouldn't have been able to keep a roof over our heads. As it was we were marginal. I learned to lie to myself very early on."

Ellroy is slurping now, with relish, a hot fudge sundae. He was

17 when his father died after a succession of strokes. Broke, frightened and alone. Kicked out of school, he joined the army. "Everything about the army scared me shitless. I developed a stammer and faked a nervous breakdown and got an unsuitability discharge. It was a bravura performance."

Then he hit skid row with a thud. Years of destruction. Self-esteem zero. Sick, sick, sick. "In 1975 I was tenuously sober; I was taking a drug that was given to alcoholics to prevent them from drinking. Under its influence you become violently ill and wish you were dead. I was sleeping on the roof of an apartment building. I woke up and had 75 cents and thought I would get some cigarettes. But I could not form the next thought. It was physiological brain malfunction. After a period of time trying to form one simple thought in my mind, I started to scream. They took me to hospital and put me in restraints. I was having visual and audio hallucinations.

"I woke up about 24 hours later, my wrists and my knuckles raw. Those hours before I was sedated and lost consciousness were the most horrifying hours of my life. I was definitely physiologically insane. I got sober in AA. I believe what they say about total abstinence. Basically alcohol is there to comfort and sooner or later it will shut down your gift and you will just retreat behind the illusion that alcohol gives you. When I got sober, in some way the shell was formed and I was ready to do something with my life. I'd always read and read; crime novels were my *raison d'être*. I'd always harboured dreams of being a great novelist." Salvation and redemption through the aesthetics of evil. The nightmare re-directed. Massive ambition and drive took over. "That kind of drive can be painful. I live chiefly within the work. My books are very meticulously conceived, everything is planned well in advance and fleshed out in minute detail. I don't deviate from the outline, I embellish within the characters. A lot of the art of writing fiction to me is expositing as much information in as limited space as possible. I never give up, I never relax, I don't quit. I wrote six books that got some nice reviews but pretty much went right into the sales toilet. I didn't have a hit until *The Black Dahlia* and things have taken off incrementally since then. I learned to live in the world and postpone the anointment of Ellroy."

James Ellroy stands outside in the hot, hot afternoon. He seems wildly happy, squinting into the sun. Rich and famous in decaying jeans and running shoes. He has beaten his past by folding it into his books, staring it down. "I top-loaded all the pain in the first 21 years of my life. I was very lucky that I was an alcoholic and a drug addict and I had an identifiable obstacle to overcome, a clinical one. My parents were both dead so I didn't have anyone to blame. I didn't go into the sober part of my life with a big neurotic load."

I tell him that only a brilliant criminal mind could plot the crimes and scams in his books. His housebreaking scenes are particularly chilling. He used to drink their booze, lie in their beds, steal their daughters' underwear. He was fucked up bad. "It is a thrill to break into somebody's house," he admits sheepishly. He rocks on his heels laughing. "I was an absolute loser as a criminal. Now I make up entire police procedures. And I am much too moral to ever go back to crime."

In a later telephone conversation with Ellroy at his home in Kansas, I ask him what has been happening lately. "I've shaved my head," he yells gaily down the phone. "I have decided to embrace my baldness. And I am looking forward to coming down to Australia. We're gonna shake it baby, yeah."

He arrived in Australia calling us "kangaroo fuckers". He was a hit, but he never looked happy. He was there to work and he went at it like a steam train. I saw him in Adelaide towards the end of the three-week tour. I saw the madness in his eyes, I saw it coming loose; he was tense, he looked like he might explode at any minute. It seemed to me that he was waging a war with himself to keep a lid on it. But he never did explode. We should be grateful, perhaps, that he never has exploded, never has acted on his dark fantasies, that Ellroy's towering violence has always remained confined to the page. Because if it hadn't there would have been a trail of sex-murders behind him.

# ■ Make It Atomic

Downtown Los Angeles. Rotting garbage, decaying buildings, graffiti. No sudden movements please. People round here are plenty pissed off. The drunk and the drugged lurching up the street in broad daylight, looking for trouble. And not picky about where they find it either. Poverty, crime, fear. An overlay of danger.

But up, up, up eight floors in a rickety elevator, in a grimy, abandoned warehouse, it is the summer of 1950 again. Dozens of men and women move up and down a corridor; fast, slow, fast, slow. Stiff permed hair, full flouncing skirts, thin stiletto heels, pert pointed breasts. Starched and clinched femininity. Square jaws underline fedora hats.

Through venetian blinds yellow light throws long, thin shadows across a room. Dust motes dance.

This is James Ellroy territory, *The Big Nowhere*, say, or *LA Confidential*, in this time and on these streets, cops and broads, fashionable, romantic, nostalgic. Guns bulge under jackets, braces stretch. Suits are strictly sartorial on swaggering men. You almost expect a saxophone to start torching a peel-off-your-silk-stockings-real-slow-baby, late-night lullaby.

But, sigh, it's only the movies.

Nick Nolte, a cop in double-breasted grey, looms large across the room, tiny eyes squinting, hat scrunched low. He doesn't so much talk as growl from deep in a nicotine-lined throat. He gets paid a lot of money for growling. Tough guys growl. Guys who have seen too much. Guys who don't give a damn any more.

There are people and cameras and lights everywhere here on the set of *Mulholland Falls*, wires tumbling out of boxes. It is a $40 million production, $18 million of it going to the stars, who have brought their own yapping entourages of minders and make-up artists.

But hold it. There seems to be something wrong. There is a discordant note among the cacophony of American noise. A loud, broad, flat New Zealand accent; words falling like lumps of wood. Vinegar running across treacle.

On the strength of one visceral, low-budget film, *Once Were Warriors*, Lee Tamahori has come to Hollywood. "I thought *Warriors* would be a quiet little worker on the film festival circuit and that was it." Now he is acting like he has been here all his life. I remember when I saw *Once Were Warriors* at a morning press screening. I was so shattered by it that I distractedly walked the several miles to my office crying like a crazy person. It took several days to recover my composure. *Once Were Warriors* was a violent and powerful film about the place I had grown up in. It was social realism writ large. The settings were the houses and streets I had known all too well. When I telephoned Tamahori in New Zealand to interview him an hour or so after my return to the office, he told me that he recommended journalists not interview him too soon after seeing the film because, like me, they were often rendered speechless. But for me it was more than that. It took me back to a dark and ugly place I preferred to forget. My past. The film was about alcoholism and domestic violence in a big, brawling, disenfranchised Maori family, about urban devastation. It exposed the violence and brutality underlying a country with a habit of burying it under a veneer of politeness. There was no alcohol in my middle-class family with its big house and ponies and music lessons. But there was violence. Violence no different for the bruised child than that of the unemployed Maori exploding with frustration. We were educated, we read books, we had manners, but we were no different or better. All the more reprehensible, in fact, because my stepfather was a lawyer who not only should have known better but did know better.

There was always something ugly crawling under the New Zealand skin, festering in those green fields, still lakes, those snowy mountains, all that prettiness; something hypocritical and cruel. Tamahori captured it and held it up for all the world to see. It was so real to me that film. Somehow he got inside it, he knew something, something about the closed fist slamming into the face, how it felt. About living in fear. About the unpredictability of violence. And he showed too that the man who is violent towards helpless women and children is, in the end, a pathetic creature.

After the film's release and its great shocking success, Tamahori brawled publicly with Maori writer Alan Duff, from whose book it came. That book is really something; stream-of-consciousness, it sings, it weeps, it demonises and humanises, it is verse and rhythm. It is, in the end, about the birth of spirituality from pain. Duff, a difficult man who had lived the life he described, who knew first hand about fighting, drinking and borstal, felt that Tamahori had trivialised and sensationalised his great work, changing its ending, missing the point. But Tamahori made them both rich and famous with his take on it and he wasn't backing down.

Today he moves among the famous actors giving direction with calm, humour and supreme confidence, cheerful, completely oblivious to all the hype and idolatry around him. The celebrity cult, actor worship, means absolutely nothing to a Maori from New Zealand. Sycophancy is not a feature of the warrior race.

And Tamahori seems to be a stranger to self-doubt. "I was never nervous because this was such a good script. I was always kind of salivating to make a film like this. I just want to make a good film and move on," he shrugs. Besides, he can walk away, go home, he is not of this place. "This is a litmus test. If this doesn't work I am back home and I am making movies there and the phone doesn't ring from here again. I am not worried." Worrying about tomorrow is not a feature of the Maori either.

Richard Zanuck, the producer, is worrying though. He is the kind of guy who worries, worries, worries, you can tell. And he has plans for Tamahori. Plans that don't include New Zealand. He is trying to talk to Tamahori about the deal for their next picture. Tamahori steadfastly eats his lunch, eyes on the plate, mind elsewhere. He is a hard guy to impress. Hollywood executives throwing money at him are clearly not giving him a hard-on. Zanuck disbelievingly resorts to other deals in other places on his mobile phone, speaking rapid-fire to someone who is obviously jumping at the other end.

Zanuck, second-generation Hollywood power broker, is tiny, leathery and shrivelled. He is big, however, where it counts. Big hair, long, white and leonine; and extremely big bank balance. He jitters alongside large and laconic Tamahori like a small but aggressive lapdog.

"This is a guy picture," says Tamahori, turning away from Zanuck and addressing me with relish, of a film that is about four detectives in an élite unit of the Los Angeles Police Department. "It is a real bunch picture. I've always loved those bunch pictures. And from the moment I read the screenplay I didn't see anyone other than Nick in it. They were throwing forward some really good actors. It was embarrassing. But no one else had the toughness and what I call the quintessential LAPD look of the '50s that Nick did. Put a hat on his head and he is twice as tough."

Tamahori talks so fast and with such ardour that he trips over his words and answers questions before they are asked. He is ultra friendly, no star trip here, no bullshit; easygoing, disarming. His own man. Pleased to be talking to someone from home, someone with similar points of reference. "Come and hang out," he invites me. He is energy personified, on fire. Enthusiasm is common to the New Zealander. Until the phone rang from Hollywood last year, he was back making commercials in New Zealand which had been his lucrative living before the money came through for *Warriors*, his only feature film. Within three months he was here on this set. Now he seems to see *Mulholland Falls* as a giant commercial. "When you work on commercials every day you are dealing with nervous agencies and nervous clients, everyone is hovering on a knife edge. When you come to this it is exactly the same. The studio is like a client." Zanuck self-consciously hovers, furtive glances loaded with meaning, still trying to get a word in. "A topline A-grade American film costs a lot," continues Tamahori, "and this is a union picture. These guys come with big packages, but it is all relative."

Tall, thin and handsome, with cropped silvery hair and fine features, Tamahori actually looks more like a movie star than any of his cast. He has an arresting presence, loping around on long legs, encased in jeans. His rapid adjustment to the big time comes with a certain amused savoir faire. "Hey," he nudges me with childlike glee, "look out the window." Across the street is the cause of the sultry yellow light. Rows of giant arc lights are lined up on the roof of an eight-storey residential building, glaring in through the venetian blinds. "If I wanted a crane they would dial one," he laughs to himself. Hollywood, heh, heh. Back home, budgets are so low they conjure films out of thin air.

Nick Nolte, Chazz Palminteri, Michael Madsen and Chris Penn are male bonding, establishing character. Doing jokey tough-guy stuff, over and over again on demand, at a table, playing cards and smoking. Nolte growls and growls on cue. Fleshy and intimidatingly large, with small close-together eyes, he is mischievous with Tamahori. "Good, very good," says the unfazable Maori, constantly moving around the table talking to the actors, giving direction.

Melanie Griffith, rumoured to be neurotic and difficult, who plays Nolte's wife, has gone home. In the finished film she will be beautiful and tragic, a dignified, humane performance. Melanie? Ha. No problem. "She comes in and has fun. She is playing her age too. She has finally jettisoned the sexy late-twenties thing. If you give actors room to move and don't nail them to the floor then you get the best out of them. This has become the coolest movie in town to be on. It is because of the script. We have major actors coming in to play one- and two-day parts. Rob Lowe is coming in tomorrow."

*Once Were Warriors* was uncompromisingly violent, terrifyingly so. Pub fights, glasses in faces, drunken beatings. Tamahori likes a bit of violence. Actually, he likes a lot of violence: it's that guy thing.

"Directing love scenes is harder than directing violence," he says with feeling. "My approach to it is that it is very fast, very explosive and very ugly. That is the way most violence is. It belongs in the movies and not on the street. But this film is about tough guys who don't need weapons. It is pre-civil rights and pre-drive-by-shootings. It is about physical intimidation and violence by other means. We are going into the seedier side of Los Angeles. We have got a very murderous story going on here. But it is not about body count. It is about power, corruption and death, in the detective genre. *Warriors* was cut very fast, it was paced to be tough and only 100 minutes long. This is more languid, it slowly builds. I have distinctly avoided film noir. That has become such a cliché. Even though this is a full-blown American genre movie, it actually has a distinct edge to it that is un-American. This film is about substance." Zanuck hovers away, across the room, far from Tamahori's excruciating lack of movie diplomacy.

Tamahori, a victim of the tyranny of geography, of lack of opportunity, came late to filmmaking. "I was a technician and then an assistant director. But there are only two films being made in New Zealand each year, and they weren't going to give me one. So I got sucked into making commercials. Commercials teach you to be very fast and sharp. If a generator breaks down then you shoot with no lights. Yesterday we were shooting a scene that wasn't working so we just rewrote it on the spot. To fall behind schedule would be very demoralising. I would have people all over me."

Indeed, Tamahori makes fast decisions, leaving people floundering in his wake. "If I didn't tell him to eat and drink," says an assistant, "he would forget. But he is very down to earth, he knows what he wants."

Despite the fact that he has meetings, meetings, meetings over development deals for the future, it seems unlikely that Tamahori will repose poolside in Hollywood doing deals on the mobile. "If I had to sit here and need this town then I would lose my edge. I never want to need this town.

"But," he confesses, suddenly, looking around the buzzing room, "I do love this, I really do."

Tamahori's advertising background was evident in the finished film, design elements were distractingly to the fore. It had been an ambitious project loaded with prodigious talent. It was stylish and beautiful and complex. It dealt with the invention of the atom bomb, with the ethics and morality and human cost of that. John Malkovich was elegantly doomed as one of the inventors of the bomb, dying from radiation poisoning, rationalising his invention and the fatal effects on those who have worked on it. "A 1,000 die so that 100,000 might live," he coughs painfully. Jennifer Connolly was stunningly beautiful and sensuous as the dead call-girl who has seen too much and is pushed from an airborne army plane; in love with Nolte, a client of Malkovich. It dealt with a particular time in American history, a turning point, the seams starting to pop. After that they were in the shadow of the mush-room cloud. It dealt with love and sex and betrayal. It failed.

Tamahori moved on, as promised. To the next film, the next deal. He has not, as yet, been sighted in New Zealand.

"America was never innocent." Ellroy's words echo, but back then just for a moment, it came close, it tried. Women were in the kitchen, values were strictly family. But the Los Angeles Police Department always knew different. They knew things that other people don't. They knew about the gruesome flip side of truth and justice in the American way. They saw it every day. Saw the blasted landscape. Saw the blood splattered on the wall of a murder scene. Saw lives devastated by murder and violence. The twilight world of LA noir. A world into which I longed to plunge. Call it curiosity. My sensibility had been severely altered lately. I was not myself. It took a lot of phone calls. Days on the phone. Ingratiating. Persuading. LAPD has enough problems without journalists hanging around. Journalists, in fact, make them decidedly uncomfortable. I laid it on with a trowel. And finally I was cruising through the dirty, bad Los Angeles night in a black-and-white patrol car and learning fast.

# Melvin Lights Up

Melvin Howard II has definitely had better evenings than this hot Friday night. Things were bad from the start. And as he drives like a crazy man along the freeway in his blue El Camino truck with Melvin Howard III chattering beside him, they are about to get a whole lot worse. Melvin Howard II's El Camino slides around on the road down by the junkyards. He is drugged and drunk. And mad as hell.

The city of Los Angeles is shrouded in a warm, dirty mist.

Sergeant Mario Muñoz is cruising the threadbare fibro Terence City Housing Projects, stopping the patrol car to rumble the gang kids in the street. Frisking them, hands on shaved heads, twitching legs apart, cruxifixes glinting. Thirteen years old and murderous, they are the scourge of South Los Angeles. Muñoz is looking for guns. Looking for drugs. They have shot cops down here in Terence Projects. "We work them a lot," says Muñoz. "If you leave them here, then more of them will be turning up and then there will be trouble."

Muñoz currently has five cases of police harassment against him. One time he thought he saw a suspect walking down the street at Marina Del Rey. He was wearing the same colour T-shirt as the suspect. He stopped the guy. The guy tried to run. Muñoz jumped him, bringing him to the ground, standing on his arm. The guy's arm broke in three places. Wrong guy. Muñoz shakes his head. The guy will probably win his case. The Los Angeles Police Department has got a bad reputation for jumping up and down on people. Indeed, public relations have not been good in recent years. The Rodney King beating and its aftermath did not help its notoriously racist repute, nor did the Mark Furhman tapes at the O. J. trial, nor did the sometimes stunning comments of former Police Chief Daryl Gates, who turned it into a quasi-military force in order to counter heavily armed drug gangs, and who once explained that so many young blacks had recently died in choke-holds put on them by police because "black people's arteries fail to open as fast as they do on normal people".

But tonight it's just another Friday night on the town for the infamous LAPD; those trigger-happy cowboys so mythologised in countless books and films. So demonised in the O. J. trial. "They wouldn't have been smart enough or fast enough to plant that evidence against O. J.," Muñoz said with a smile.

Down here the streets are no stylised Hollywood movie, no neat endings, no fade out, no forgiving girlfriend. It is messy. It smells of rotting garbage and urine. It is gang warfare, jagged, explosive violence. It is desperation, psychosis, it is heartbreak. It is drive-by shootings and vicious domestic violence. It is enforcement on the offensive. It is non-stop.

"Keep on walkin'," Muñoz tells the truculent kids of the Terence City Housing Projects. "Don't you be hangin' around tonight."

"They need money to go drinking," he says to me. "They gotta rob somebody. Things can turn real bad, real fast. The crimes around here are mainly committed by gang members. You gotta know how to talk to them, you gotta get their respect."

There is trouble going down tonight.

"It is cooking, it is starting to rock and roll, you can just smell it," says Sergeant David Ruvalcada on another night with the Wilshire patrol, a Latino ex-green beret in aviator glasses and an ornate pinkie ring. We idle past decaying buildings oozing sultry Spanish music, and groups of swaggering guys in the street, cradling AK47s under jackets. "The stage is set right now, all the actors for the scene are getting in place. There is a homicide going down. Which one is going to be the victim? Nobody knows. But the word is on the street. I don't know how many kids we have had laying here in these streets over the years." Ruvalcada is a hard, coiled-up man. A lieutenant colonel in the army reserves. He has been a cop for 26 years. He has seen pretty much everything. He is getting out in three weeks. "Oh, man," he says with a massive grin. "I'm gonna get out alive. I've been in more gunfights here than I had in Vietnam. It's a fast life."

Ruvalcada interviewed Rodney King when he was working for internal affairs. He knew Stacy Koon, the sergeant who was acquitted in the King beating and then wrote a damning book about LAPD. "He was an enigma, Stacy Koon," muses Ruvalcada, who has a master's degree in administration and who once sued the police department for discrimination.

Above us the choppers whirl and swoop across the city, their searchlights filtered in the mist. We cruise the streets looking for a girl who was a witness in a murder and is not showing up in court. Surprise, surprise. Through rarefied palm-lined Hanbury Park, with its mansions and chateaus and trimmed hedges, where an enchanted and disgusting pre-adolescent Ellroy once pressed against the windows at night, and down, down through the run-down suburbs going east. Endless flat indistinguishable streets. Blurring rows of fast food joints, countless service stations for a car culture, clubs where doormen run metal detectors over the patrons before letting them in. LAPD is where the rich and the poor, black and white, those different planets, come together in extremis.

*Three unknown male suspects shooting at passers-by, domestic violence, child abuse*, comes over the radio from another part of the precinct in what will become a constant refrain, a chorus of catastrophe.

Ruvalcada stops to squint at the graffiti on a wall, the intelligence of the 'gangbangers', trying to figure out who is going to be hit tonight. "When names are crossed out, that is the next victim. The worst thing you can do is go into somebody's territory and cross their name out." Every division of LAPD has a gang unit. Gang violence has proved an insoluble problem, in spite of Operation Hammer in which 1,000 cops were deployed by the city in an arrest frenzy in 1988.

The extortionist Korean Killers have gone quiet lately, says Muñoz. "We worked them hard, the gangs around here sell a lot of dope, the only way to get money is by narcotics. And there is a lot of shooting, carjacking, burglaries and robberies. Sometimes we get a spot where they can't see us and videotape them. The better evidence we get the better it is. But we put them in jail and then new players come and take over; all we can do is keep the status quo." The cops know what's going down. The Rolling 60s gang has a sophisticated bank robbery operation going. And the mad dog Mexican Mafia, who run narcotics and guns, took out someone from the Young Crowd gang yesterday. Retribution will be swift and deadly. Within 24 hours. It is written in blood. Always a payback. Today and tomorrow and tomorrow. Black against Hispanic, Asian against White, everyone against everyone else. The gangs are criminal organisations. "The drug operations are run like a business," says Muñoz. "It's very hard for a patrol car to operate. Someone will hold the money in one place, the dope will be held elsewhere, everyone will be armed." And it is strictly territorial. "When someone tries to take over someone else's territory, that is when the shooting starts," sighs Muñoz.

A thin young guy with a straggly beard in a wheelchair is wheeled across the road, survivor of a gunfight. "Gotta watch them," says Muñoz. "He is probably sitting on a gun." It is a badge of courage around here to take a bullet for the brotherhood, to have jagged knife wounds, to carry the scars of battle.

A kid down at a taco stand, the Ghost Town gang hangout, has taken a drive-by bullet in the guts, crazy on drugs, and fought off the paramedics, vanishing into the night. No cops, no way, man. "He could bleed to death," says the ambulance officer when we arrive, "but he wasn't sticking around till the cops arrived."

*Black male suspect has kidnapped child, driving blue El Camino, heading towards the freeway. Wanted for child stealing and battery.*

Melvin Howard II has bashed his on-off girlfriend and taken off with their five-year-old son. Muñoz squeals rubber, floating across four empty lanes in a U-turn. We are on the case. Thundering down the freeway. Fast.

The girlfriend lives in a basement apartment. Neighbours'

doors close as we arrive. Her mouth is bleeding. The TV jabbers. Stuffing spills out of the sofa. She doesn't cry. She smokes with long, red, lacquered nails. Her eight-year-old son eyes the cops defiantly, with liquid brown eyes. Her three-day-old baby squawks. She says she has full custody of Melvin but she has lost the papers.

Ruvalcada and Muñoz are both solid primal muscle, pumped up in the gym, tough as hell. They creak when they walk. Loaded down with hardware packed into leather, 25 lbs of weaponry. A 9-millimetre Beretta in the holster, a backup .38. They go in firing with two hands, when they go. The only time I have ever been physically protected by a man was when I went out with Mario Muñoz. He would only go to bars that he knew were cop hangouts. Even then he covered me, kept me under his shoulders, where he could protect me, he looked around constantly, looking out for me. I was both in danger and a liability. And he was a target for anyone he had put in jail or arrested or harassed. And he does harass people, trust me on that. Pissed off, they would almost certainly be carrying a gun. It is an isolating profession. "If you want to have a long life you have to have something outside your work," he told me one night in a bar. "You see a lot of bad people. Things can really drive you crazy."

*Child abuse, child abuse, child abuse, domestic violence, domestic violence* streams constantly across the car radio. Domestic violence is endemic. More people go to jail for domestic violence round here than anything else. "They are dangerous calls," says Ruvalcada. "We end up becoming the focus of the attack. We use up a lot of our resources dealing with it. We used to say, hey, get a divorce. But now, if we don't arrest them the way we are supposed to, we are guilty of a felon ourselves. They can take up to five hours of paperwork. There is too much paperwork now, it is burdensome."

Muñoz sees a blue El Camino. We chase it off the freeway, siren blaring. It pulls over. "Step out of the car, hands on the top of your head. Step over to the curb," he says, approaching with his gun ready. But the guy is blonde and white. Wrong guy. It scared the fuck out of him, though, you can see it in his face. LAPD has a bad history of shooting innocent people.

A shrieking black single mother of five children to five different fathers, welfare dependent in the poorest part of the projects, has pistol-whipped her teenage daughter. I see the desperation, the madness in her eyes. I see her daughter's frustration, rebellion. I see the hurting. It is familiar. I think of my own mother, widowed with five children at 32 and not coping. Not enough money, alone, frightened. Demented with grief at the death of her husband in a plane crash. I think of the fighting between her and me, her eldest child. I think of the random accident of geography, of circumstance. What if my mother had been born into a culture of crack cocaine and firearms? I shrink deep into my bulletproof vest. Seven out of 10 black children in this district will grow up without a father. "Kids get into the gangs and look at the gangs as family," says Muñoz.

Down in the Korean district a shaken Asian man has been bashed and robbed at knifepoint. He has a bleeding slash across his cheek. He describes his attackers. Muñoz thinks he knows them—"We know everyone around here." They could go to jail for seven years for stealing. Harsh laws, clogged jails, and still they are dying in the streets.

On the edge of bombed out Lafayette Park an outraged middle-aged Mexican in dirty, loose trousers is babbling in Spanish through missing teeth. A prostitute took his $100 then refused to have sex with him. Hardly surprising, given the filthy sight of him. Forget the money. He still wants the sex.

Hey, call the cops.

Muñoz shows me the scars on his hands from when he was undercover in the vice squad busting streetwalkers in Hollywood. Prostitution is illegal here and vigorously pursued. Back then he grew his hair long to look like a client. "This prostitute got in the car with me. They search you to see if you are a cop. If you use certain tactics they will know you are a cop. You have got to talk to them like you are some guy. My partner was following me. I had to signal my partner when it was time to arrest. She solicited me for sex, I had a violation and I badged her. My partner drove in too close, the window was open and he badged her. She reached down and grabbed a knife and started stabbing me in a frenzy. I grabbed the knife by the blade. She crawled out the window and ran." Round here hookers have a high mortality rate. "The street prostitutes are so conspicuous and blatant," says Muñoz, "people complain about them. They don't complain about spending $500 in a motel. Street prostitution is very dangerous. They gotta make the money to smoke rock cocaine or shoot up dope, they need $300 a night for their habits, so they will do things like get picked up by a guy who wants them to urinate or defecate on his face. These are not safe people. Then they overdose, or get AIDS or their pimps kill them."

"The strange thing is," Ruvalcada tells me as we take a dinner break in a gaudy Mexican restaurant, "a lot of them are in love with their pimps. It is an act of love for him. We get college kids down here for the weekend. Football players, jocks. They rent rooms in motels and their girlfriends turn tricks for money." Muñoz remembers busting a group of law students from the mid-west, turning tricks for thrills and money. Lives ruined overnight. No respectable law school or firm would take a woman with a conviction for prostitution. "Hollywood is the armpit of the world," says Ruvalcada. "The whole world going to hell in a hand-basket."

*Domestic violence, robbery, robbery, child abuse, car jacking, car jacking.* Every minute, all over this city, something bad is happening to somebody.

The chopper swoops down and hovers, streaming light.

Cop cars scream into a white Cadillac, cutting it off. It crunches into the curb, tearing metal. Carjacking is out of control. In LA, stealing a car is not merely a simple act of hot-wiring it when no one is looking. It is an armed hold-up. "Driver step out of the car. Hands on your head, legs apart." The Berettas are drawn. Four Dodge City Cribs face down on the road handcuffed.

On a one-way trip to a long stretch in jail. Nineteen years old. "They have problems at home," says Muñoz of the gangs. "They have no role models. You get little kids 10 years old who are too small to be in a gang. They are called taggers. They commit crimes to impress the big guys into letting them join. They look up to the gang members. If you are not in a gang when you go to jail you soon will be. They recruit in jail. You have to belong to a gang to get protection. Otherwise you are dead. When you get out you are given a mission. You are in the gang for life." Which may not be very long.

The underclass is a culture bred into the genes, nurtured by violence, coming of age with a death wish. For these kids there is no other way. They never had a chance.

The oil refinery is lit up in the industrial night. We drive past a laneway. "We had a murder there last week," says Ruvalcada. "A guy had been taped up with tape, handcuffed and had 11 rounds fired through his head. People saw the car pull up. The guy gets out of his vehicle, locks it and walks away. A week before, the guy he killed had tried to carjack him. He had been kidnapped and beaten up. They rub you out for your car."

A twenty-first birthday party in a church hall has gone flat. Some bad dudes carrying AKs tried to gatecrash. The young guests are milling around outside. "Stay inside," Ruvalcada tells the birthday boy. "They will come back and do a drive-by shooting." Happy birthday to you. Next door in the church a service is in progress.

A gang kid is under a truck in a parking lot firing shots. He won't come out. There are cops everywhere. They move closer to the truck, covering each other, guns drawn, tense. Overpowered, the kid finally comes out. He is swaying drunk. His friends hang out of the window in the apartment across the street, jeering at the cops. He waves and swaggers, mock macho. For his one moment of glory he will pay the price in jail.

*Black male has poured petrol over himself and is threatening to torch himself.*

We have found Melvin Howard II. We follow the fire engine up the narrow street. *Waa, waa, waa* go the sirens. Melvin Howard II is standing in the concrete driveway at his mother's house. Petrol runs down the concrete. Melvin lights a cigarette. A blue flare lights up the ground. The water from the fire hose hits Melvin. Melvin hits the ground. Melvin is saturated and reeking of petrol. But saved from self-immolation. He sits up and puts his face in his hands, a study in despair. His girl, he tells us, heartbroken, told him tonight that the baby is not his. She has another boyfriend. He didn't know, man. He loved that baby like a father. "I told him that girl was no good," says his mountainous mother, clutching his two other boys by two different mothers, "but Melvin was in love. My son has a lot of psychological build-up starting from his father's childhood. He is shook up. That girl is bad news." Melvin gets put in a psychiatric ward for 72 hours. A danger to himself and others. He is going to feel like shit tomorrow.

"Women," says Muñoz, twice divorced at 35, shaking his head.

The sun is coming up as we drive back to Wilshire police station.

"You learn how to read people," says Muñoz, accelerating behind a car that braked when the driver saw a police car, so imperceptibly I didn't even notice. "You know when something is not right about a car or a person."

The Schoolyard Cribs who live over the freeway from the police station routinely fire shots into the yard. "Last year they ambushed one of my guys," says Ruvalcada. "He took two rounds and got hit twice in the leg."

Going to jail is a way of life. Last month Ruvalcada arrested a guy for carjacking. He had been out of jail exactly three days. "At least in jail I can get my sex and my drugs," he told Ruvalcada, "and I don't have to hassle with anyone. It's crazy out here." His male sex partner had started crying and blabbing when they were arrested. "You can forget him," he told the cops disgustedly. "He's dead."

A homicide victim has staggered into his house and died. A

Mexican Mafia guy. The payback is complete and right on time. "Told you," says Ruvalcada resignedly. Then he rubs his eyes in the pink early morning light. He smiles. "You go running from homicide to homicide and then all of a sudden the sun comes up and it is a whole new day. Ain't that somethin'. Now we can go home and come back and do it all over again."

Not me. There would be other nights on the town with LAPD. But as the dusk gathered that night I was up at Newport Beach wrestling with a drunk divorcee in the dining room of the Sheraton hotel. She had a tanned and disappointed look about her when she slammed into the restaurant calling the waiters by name and badgering the guests. She was Southern California personified. Middle-aged and well maintained, her calf-muscles indicated tennis afternoons. Her short skirt, a pink tank top and high heeled shoes with ankle length socks were set off by expensively cut and coloured short too-blonde hair. She was celebrating, she told everyone within earshot, her divorce. She ordered elaborate cocktails with umbrellas. She was free now, she said fluttering long, manicured nails at two business-men at a table, and available. Judging by the heavy jewellery that flashed in the muted light, she was costing a lot in alimony. The busi-nessmen looked at each other knowingly. They had divorced this kind of woman themselves. Loud and high maintenance. Honey, she said, fastening on me, allow me to introduce myself. Then she got crying drunk, only rallying every now and then to disrupt the other diners. The ex, the bastard, had traded her in, it was turning out, for a 23-year-old version of the same species. And, well, I couldn't let a lady drink alone now could I? Besides, I had my own problems. Having had an argument with the male receptionist over my booking, I had slammed out the revolving door. Outside I realised my suitcase was too heavy to move, filled as it was with books, and that I had nowhere else to go. So I slammed back in again. Now I was stuck.

# ■ This Could Happen to You

The view from the mansion takes in the Pacific, glossy and rolling in the distance, then sweeps clear across the fried hills of Orange County, out here where the hot winds blow.

Flying down the freeway, palm trees flashing past, the amorphous mass of suburban Los Angeles had bunched and blurred into a frenzy of fast-food joints, then peeled away; swallowed by its own smog.

Out here in the land of the country club and easy living, things are a whole lot more rarefied than in those boiling suburbs back there. Out here your money won't let you down. No, sir.

As the butler silently places a gleaming silver coffee pot on the table, Dean Koontz pads across thick Persian rugs and closes the shutters against the vast blue morning outside. Dean Koontz likes the dark. Bad things happen in the dark. And somewhere here in this temperature-controlled mansion which discreetly hums with enterprise is where Dean Koontz gets in touch with his bad self.

Upstairs in a wood-panelled room is where he writes the books that scare the bejesus out of people. Books with catchy titles such as *Mr Murder, Strange Highways* and *Night Chills*, subtly embossed in gold foil on trembling covers that scream and drip with terror. Books often set in picturesque, family room, two-car garage, decent, wholesome, suburban America where it naturally comes as a terrible shock when evil comes a-calling. Wholesome, all-American families are terrorised and practically everyone dies in the harrowing, shuddering end. A world of prickly dread, preternatural predators and, occasionally, erotic pleasure in vicious killing. 'The pure pleasure in cutting people up,' explains the psychotic villain in *Strange Highways*.

Not that Dean Koontz kills off people in graphic and almost loving detail to get his own rocks off or anything. Hey, Dean Koontz is a sensitive guy. "There have been many occasions where

■ **DEAN KOONTZ**

I have had to kill a character for whom I am enormously sympathetic and it can bring me to tears while I am sitting there." He cries a heck of a lot then, judging by the average body count in his awful books. He must be permanently blubbering up there in his study as the royalty cheques come rolling home.

You certainly wouldn't think it to look at him, a moustachioed man in nerdsville maroon vest and grey slacks, but, just quietly, Dean Koontz is the living embodiment of the American Dream. The full cliché. The real thing. From the actual white trash, dirt-floor shack in the Appalachian Mountains to unimaginable wealth. The same place as Traci Lords, the same alcoholic, violent male culture. He has dreamed the dream, or in his case the nightmare, lived the work ethic and traversed the deep and wide mountains and ravines of extremes that are only possible in America. It is possible to be poorer than the poor in America, the third world for example, but there is nowhere else you start out as unimaginably poor and get as unimaginably rich as those who have made it, really made it, in America. You can do it in less than one lifetime. It can happen overnight. "I work very long hours; that is because I like to," he says, settling into a large, leather wing-back chair in the mahogany gloom of his mansion. On either side of him are bronze sculptures of spaniels, behind him leather-lined books in a bookcase and to one side a bar with high leather stools. This is, I think, what is known as The Den. Man at play. Though it does not look like much back-slapping masculine bonhomie goes on down here. The smell of freshly applied beeswax drifts from every polished surface and mingles with jasmine floating outside.

More than anyone, this mildest of men understands that in a culture of competing violent images, people demand bigger, nastier and more malevolent adrenaline shots to enliven banal reality. To know they are really alive. And by bringing his terrorfest, his killers and monsters close to home, by violating the ordinariness of everyday life, of daily interaction, to maximum effect, Koontz expertly mines the dark and nameless fear that sits in the collective psyche, the primal fear, the dread that triggers the silent screaming in us all, the terrors inherent in the shadows in the kitchen, in the whispers in the garden at night.

Halfway through *Intensity*, a particularly chilling and nasty little number, I suddenly felt the need to bolt myself into my apartment, to intricately plan my escape route should a crazed psychopath suddenly burst through the door. There was a gradual, sick realisation. *This could happen to me.*

Koontz, who brings new meaning to the words 'popular fiction', is not a writer—he is a phenomenon. I have never understood why people want to be scared shitless, indeed line up to do so, but they manifestly do. This is not reading, this is a cardio-vascular workout, this is Entertainment. He has sold about 160 million copies of his alarming books worldwide. Factor in film deals and a $26 million, three-book deal with Knopf's chief, Sonny Mehta, and think roughly in the region of the foreign debt. Every now and then Koontz will leap from his chair and, apologising profusely "excuse me, we have a major negotiation going on here at the moment", bolt up the stairs to take a call. The deal for the film rights on one of his books is closing, Hollywood is on the line and Koontz is getting richer by the nanosecond. "I like writing screenplays. I like it largely because when I start work on a novel I know I am anywhere from six months to nine months of long hours before I get the plot again. The screenplay is much quicker and it is so flexible, compared to a novel."

He rarely gives interviews ("I have avoided publicity; I don't really love the celebrity aspect of it, I have never done a book tour") and is seen as being far too low-rent to merit review or any kind of serious analysis—for example, why is it exactly that millions of people buy his books? And where do you get what he's on? The literary world, in fact, recoils in, er, horror from Koontz. But his sales figures certainly reflect what is actually going on out there beyond the sensitive guidance of the literary world and its white-knuckled grip on the culture. And that should tell them something. But what the heck, who needs literary pretensions. He has other more comforting friends, like the greater reading public. "I get

10,000 letters a year." That in itself is a kind of triumph of anti-literature.

And if living well is the best revenge, Koontz, like so many stories of American Success, writes books that refract a dreadful autobiography of suffering and prevailing. At an early age he learned the hard way about living in fear, about the presence of evil in your own house and about the shock of sudden violence. "What I do is therapy, I have since discovered. You work out all your stuff."

Evidently not satisfied with merely destroying the young Dean's childhood, his alcoholic, abusive, crazy father then tried to severely upset the equilibrium of the flourishing adult by trying to kill him several times. In a dramatic reversal of the Oedipus complex, he tried to stab his son in the heart with a switchblade. Fairly mean-spirited considering this same son had supported him for years. This is the sort of thing that happens in Dean Koontz's books. It appeared, in fact, in *Mr Murder*, as it happened. You can't make this stuff up. "The last time he tried to kill me he threw a tantrum and took a switchblade and turned on me. He had alcoholic degenerative syndrome and we had to put him in this retirement centre. He had to go on this medication and have it four times a day, always. You couldn't leave him alone because he wouldn't take his medication. For a year he was the best he ever was. But he had developed a tolerance for it and it had increased his aggression. One day he started throwing a tantrum and they asked me to come and calm him down. He had bought a fishing knife with a seven-inch blade and honed it very sharp. He had worked on the hinge and made it like a switchblade. He took the knife and turned on me and there it was. We had this very interesting struggle for a couple of minutes until I could get the knife off him. He could have killed me very, very easily. He was very close to stabbing me in the heart. I walked out into the hallway holding the knife, keeping an eye on my father. I said to them, 'Somebody call the paramedics'. They said somebody had called the police. The police responded so fast, around the corner came these two police officers. I was holding this knife and looking shaken. They pulled their guns and said, 'Drop the knife'. They were not friendly. They made me drop the knife and lie flat on the floor. I finally realised I was going to get shot. It was so humiliating."

It is hard to imagine anyone with less flair, less personal magnetism, less reckless flamboyance than the slightly etiolated Dean Koontz. No interestingly unstable behaviour, no signs of psychosis, no obvious neurosis, no drug problems, no wild parties, no tantrums, no personality; in fact, just the one wife, only the two mansions. All that liquid cash and no bad habits.

Well, for the truly bland zillionaire there is always that great Californian obsession—real estate. The bigger the better. "I haven't travelled, I don't do drugs, I have been married for 28 years, we have no children, we are very home orientated. I have got to spend the money on something." And so, in the great tradition of the newly rich, Koontz is building himself a monument to new money: mansion No 2, which sits in model form on a pool table with magnificently carved legs. Now here is a hell of a house. Pure Beverly Hills but bigger, bigger even than the fabled Spelling mansion. High concept. A vast, pink, many-columned Italian Renaissance extravaganza with three swimming pools (and a lap pool), which is taking a full-time staff five years to build.

It is hard to picture this quiet, humble, fried-chicken kind of guy sweeping down that curved marble staircase with the appropriate grandeur, somehow. Not in the grey slacks and the vest, anyhow. Or sitting languorously in the perfect golden light of those pretty rooms, or mustering the required grace and savoir-faire for the filigreed balconies. Koontz stands looking rather puzzled at the model as if he, too, is wondering whether he will be quite big enough for his own pink, purpose-built temple to the schlock-horror industry.

He sits back down in his mild, meticulous way. His eyes are warm and brown, his hair thinning; he is an angst-free zone. It seems absurd that in the leering recesses of his mind should live serial killers, psychopaths and the supernaturally undead, or that he could write with such relish about the pleasure of killing. "I am trying for my own satisfaction to really work out the nature of evil. Why people are capable of doing to other people the things they are capable of doing. Especially when you have experience of it growing up. It haunts you. I have come through a long process to realise that there is no explanation for evil, there are only excuses. Freudianism has become something destructive. People like the Menendez brothers can say they had abusive parents at the age of 25 when you don't have to live with them any more. I think people think they are not responsible for what they do because society may have abused them or mistreated them somewhere along the way. This has lead to, in this country, an inability to deal with it. It leads to sociopathic behaviour of one kind or another. Every trial is littered with psychiatrists."

A lot of Koontz's stories concern themselves with an unseen malevolent man going about scaring people and killing them with a kind of superior energy, and people trying to run away from bad, bad things that they don't understand and can't see. Often the reader knows what is going on, that evil is stalking, that two worlds are about to collide, but the innocent characters don't. Tension builds. Maw haw haw.

But although his books can be unrelenting in their awfulness, Koontz insists there is a moral dimension. Believable characters save him from the slasher category, characters so real to him that they sometimes seem to be in the room with us—a fairly unappealing prospect, it has to be said. "I don't write gory. I don't even like the word horror, I don't think it has got anything to do with what I do. If you write with enough force it doesn't have to be explicit. People sometimes think the violence has gone on for pages when in fact it is two sentences. What you want to convey is that it is awful. You don't want it to be entertaining. And you don't want the gore to be the part that is entertaining. That would be exploitative and I don't want to do that. But at the same time you don't want to write violence so that it has no impact, because you want to say how horrible violence is. For me fiction is a moral enterprise.

It shows why people succeed in life and why they don't in terms of their relationships with other people. My characters are always driven to the point where they have no choice but to use violence. And it is always made clear that it is only the bad guys who use it routinely. People say 'I love your sex scenes'. And I would say, outside a couple of books, 'What sex scenes?' Because I don't write sex scenes unless they are essential to the story. And they are not actually sex scenes. They are romantic scenes but we may simply draw the curtain. People visualise everything that you didn't write. It is trying to find the effect without being offensive. It is too easy to just do that."

And, of course, there is resolution: evil is always vanquished, although not generally until it has done a great deal of damage. "I always know when the bad guy is about to die. If he is bad enough, one of the cathartic things in this kind of fiction is seeing him get his just desserts. Life seems to be so chaotic and without meaning. What fiction does say is that life has meaning; it is not chaotic. There is something appealing about the idea that you can screw up your life and then get a chance to put it right again."

Koontz is backing his black BMW down the driveway of his mansion, leaving behind its flocks of dusting maids and officious secretaries. Everything just so. "I think my whole life has been determined on having a stable home life because there wasn't one when I was growing up," he admits, his gold Rolex catching the light.

In nearly all of his books, the bad guys, and some of the good guys, have had violent, traumatic childhoods. Like his. Like nearly all the Americans I interviewed who had achieved creative success. Pain is a primal motivator. Hideous scenes in his books come straight from his past. For the child of trauma the possibility of ever having a normal life has been removed, they have seen too much too soon, but they have found in their writing a way to express and discharge the demons that haunt them. Like the ghost of Ellroy's mother, Koontz's father walks through all his books. The devil incarnate. His mother just kind of gave up and expired.

"I am absolutely convinced it was because of what she had to endure. She was a wonderful person who shielded me as much as she could. But it was impossible when you are in a house where he smashes furniture and threatens to kill you. My father was a pathological liar and a schizophrenic with tendencies towards violence. He lost most of his jobs because he punched out his bosses, stuff like that, hysteria, drama. He ran around with women, we were very poor, he never worked. He was sociopathic, he had no conscience. It was a total lack of stability. We brought him out here in '77. It was a big decision for me. We had moved across the country and finally he wasn't a part of my life, except on the phone. I would always hear about the latest car accident or the latest person he beat up, he would be behind bars and he needed to be bailed out. Finally I realised I couldn't send him money because it would all be gone in one day. We brought him out here and we bought him an apartment and paid all of his bills. I said, 'You can drink anything you like but not around me. I put up with that all my childhood, all my adolescence and I am not going to put up with it any more.' The hysteria and the associated drama that comes with it.

"Then as he got older and older he got more and more difficult. He made two attempts on my life. I looked after him because I was never going to do to him what he had done to me. In other words there was never going to be a satisfaction for him. I was never going to be like him and that meant not treating people the way he treated them. So he had a very nice life in spite of all his carrying on. My mother died before I could do anything for her." Downcast pause. "You have to wonder. He lived to 81 and that was because he never cared about anything. He took all of his frustration and all of his aggression out on everybody else and then walked away from it. He never went to church, but when things got really bad he would pick up the Bible and read it around the clock and insist that you did too. In his personality type there is no conscience, it is almost sociopathic. I actually got the motivation to achieve from this, I never wanted to end up like him."

Koontz's words seem to resonate harshly across the smooth dappled lawns and splashing fountains of his exclusive neighbourhood. Then he lightens up guiltily and laughs. "And of course you do cannibalise your life."

Perhaps he is able to kill his father off in fiction, again and again, as the victimised child could never do. How deeply satisfying that must be. And frustrating too, because it is not, as it turns out, a resolution to the reality. The reality that as a little boy he had to depend on a person who hurt him. Time does not diminish truth. "It is terrible when you are a child because you are trapped and there is nowhere to go. I used to think there would be this moment where I would at least understand him or he would say he was sorry for all that he had done. That there would be this moment when I could relax. But I had to realise when he died that that was never going to happen, because he was incapable of that and he could only destroy everyone around him. You are told that you have to get past the anger. What I say to people is, yes you do have to get past the anger, but you don't have to forgive. It is all right to hate the son of a bitch. They have earned it. But you can't let it consume you. Because the hatred will not affect them."

Like so many unhappy children, Koontz escaped into books. "That was my way out. My way of coping. I had a rich sort of fantasy life without becoming mentally ill. On the other hand I may be insane. I just read huge amounts of material. I went to the library and just wiped out the whole fiction section. There were no books in our house except the Bible, my behaviour was considered abhorrent; my mother worried that I was not under cars with my cousins. She came from a dirt poor background. I was the first person in generations on any side of my family to go to college. I had to go to the cheapest college I could find and work my way through it. Books were for other people. My mother was a very gentle person who was very concerned that I would turn out like my father. She thought reading was goofing off. I had no interest in cars. She asked me one day, 'What are you going to do when you buy a car and it breaks down?' I said, 'I'll take it to a mechanic.' It was beyond her conception that I would earn enough money to afford a mechanic. What fiction did for me was show me that there are other ways, other worlds. As a kid you kind of think for a long time that it is like this for everybody. And then there comes a day when you realise that it isn't like this for everybody and you feel ashamed. Shame is a big thing with abused kids. I lied all the way through childhood. I always tried to make it appear to people that we had a wonderful loving family."

We are cruising along the freeway to a restaurant for lunch, the hot, dry southern Californian wind glazing the sea. Reflecting this car culture, a lot of the action in his books happens by car. Mobile fear. I remark that not liking the way your spouse drove should be grounds for divorce, since Californians spent the greater part of their lives sealed off in cars on the freeways. But Dean Koontz likes everything about his wife Gerda, a small eager woman who has darted in and out of the room during our interview, tilting upward toward her husband. "All the women in my books reflect my wife. We have been married for 28 years. My wife is a very strong person. She came from a poor family, an old-world Italian immigrant family. She was working two or three part-time jobs at the age of 13 to buy her own clothes." And as Koontz well knows, you never fuck with a Sicilian, not even a small one. "People often underestimate her because she is small and quiet and has a gentle face. I have been in situations where I have wanted to warn people not to underestimate her. When she has a point of view she has a point of view and it will get heard. And when somebody does something particularly vicious to me she goes berserk."

After cheap college, where he met her, he became a teacher briefly. But Gerda was clearly a woman with an eye for an investment. "Then Gerda said she would support me for five years and if I didn't make it as a writer in five years I never would. I seized that offer. For the first six months I made nothing. If you have any macho self-image it collapses. I spent so many years working without much success, but then gradually it happened. After about four years she quit her job to work for me. Now she jokes that she wishes she had kept her job because it was only 40 hours a week. Everything that has happened has been a team effort. If she hadn't been so supportive and the person that she is, I could never have had the time and the freedom to have advanced as far as I have. I would never have had the psychological support. It is tough. You spend a lot of time alone and I do like people. For a long time you don't know if you can do it. With every single book, even today, a quarter of the way into the book I become so overwhelmed with self-doubt, and right until the end it is a bitter, awful struggle. Even though I might be liking certain things, in my head is the feeling that this will be the one that will destroy my career. When *Midnight* went to number one on the best-seller list I was absolutely astounded. I was delirious. I never believed it possible. My agent told me that it was a fluke and that it would never happen again and not to get my hopes up. Well, we had five number ones in a row after that. We are continuing to sell more with each book. I never anticipated that it would become as large as it became. It was incremental."

Dean Koontz greets the restaurateur effusively. He relishes fine food, comes here a lot. Over lunch he will drink cabernet and get loose. Well, loose-ish. "I am not usually this forthcoming." He stops suddenly, surprised.

Other diners dart glances. Eyes slide towards Koontz; whispering behind hands. Strange and disturbed people come with his line of business. The frightening downside to fame in America. And still, everyone wants to be famous. But you have to wonder what kind of fans, exactly, would a horror writer have. "One woman sent me somewhere around 1200 letters. She sent paintings. She was a young, attractive and deeply disturbed person. She was convinced we were going to have a life together. For a while there is a kind of morbid fascination. You think, 'This is research.' You want to get a sense of how this mind works. But, of course, you can't respond. It can be very awkward when we go out to dinner. It is not uncommon during a dinner for people to come up to us three or four times. For years I kept my photo off the book jackets. And then, without asking my permission, a publisher took a photo and used it on a jacket flap. It was a two and a half million print run. After that it was impossible because people could see what I looked like."

Dean Koontz does have a personality, as it turns out. Maybe not as we know it, but the kind of quiet, modest power and humour that could come only from success, from being rich and famous beyond your wildest dreams. From appreciating your fabulously good fortune. From striving to deserve it. "The glory of it is the things you are able to do. We have nine nieces and nephews who have been able to go to college. They are all getting master's degrees. It is wonderful because this wouldn't have happened without all of this taking place." From scaring the shit out of people. "I just want to be happy," he says, raising his glass. "Cheers."

A two and a half million print run is a good place to start, Dean. Trust me on that. Maw haw haw.

Flying across America on my airpass, the place names resonate through my mind. I embrace them like old friends. They are places I have known all my life. Phoenix, Arizona; New York, New York; Tulsa, Wichita, Albuquerque, Chattanooga; place names that have texture in your mouth as you say them, places that trip mellifluously off the tongue, places that permeate the culture. Places where hearts get left. Or broken. Places where men go when they leave sleeping ladies by way of a note hanging on her door. Places heard on the radio between the races on a small town New Zealand Saturday afternoon, lawn mowers buzzing across recalcitrant suburban lawns outside. Seen on television at an impressionable age, places so exotic, so unimaginably glamorous, so far away. Places where hand-some strangers ride into town looking for the man who killed their brother. Travelling through these places, you have to marvel at the way they have built myth from out of the banality of everyday life, created poetry from the prosaic, animated the ordinary. From the endless repetition of diners and gas stations. It is a deeply romantic love affair that Americans have with their country. They write it in songs and odes, they glorify it, find excuses to say its names like lovers do, sing it to sleep every night. 'I left my heart in Brisbane' doesn't have quite the same ring. 'By the time I get to Swindon she'll be rising' doesn't do it either. 'Auckland, Auckland, it's a hell of a town' also lacks a certain *je ne c'est quoi* too, though these place may well be a riot on a fast night.

I was in a kind of hotel stupor in Seattle when I realised I could easily stay on the road and never stop. I could happily get stuck in an American song forever. Footloose, transient, taking my pleasure where I found it. Maybe, if I could possibly manage it, even breaking a heart here and there. Because, of course, I would always be leav-ing that man. No man could ever tie me down. I was born to wander, to be free, to walk the county line. I might even get thrown in jail from time to time for drinkin' and fightin', before I moved on.

Americans know something. They know that the key to human happiness is a king-size bed in a hotel room. Even the kind of hotels that I can afford. And here we are talking budget, sometimes even just this side of flea pit. Even your bargain hunters delight, even Norman Bates knows that a bed just has to be big. The English, alas, do not know this fundamental truth. This is what is wrong with the English. They never caught on. Never heard the subtext in the Gettysburg Address. An empire simply cannot be run from a single bed.

# ■ Still Life with Rain

It is raining in Seattle, suicide city, as we leave it. Not just any old rain. Hard, fast, merciless, Seattle rain. Rivers of rain, dumped from malevolent clouds.

Tom Robbins loves this mean black rain. "That is why I live here," he drawls. It stars, as a sniggering bad guy, in all his books. 'And it rained a sickness,' he wrote in *Another Roadside Attraction*. 'And it rained a fear. And it rained an odour. And it rained a murder. And it rained dangers and pale eggs of the beast . . . And it rained an omen.'

And it rains all down the freeway, so hard you can hardly see, turning forests of firs into liquid green. Then, sharply, it stops.

And there, in front of us, as if a curtain has been parted at the theatre, lies the Skagit Valley, basking and slumbering in the sudden sun; vibrating with every gradient of green. Norman Rockwell pastoral Americana; Tom Robbins territory.

We drive through wide-open flatlands, past rambling wooden farmhouses, bucolic barns, green rivers lined with weeping willows, church spires, tractors meandering across fields of flowers. It stretches out for miles and miles, muted shades of blue and green, carpets of tulip fields merging into ghostly hills in the distance, whirlwinds picking up ploughed fields and waltzing vertical across the landscape.

And huge three-dimensional cloud formations are putting on a show of their own. Wild horses are rearing and prancing across the sky. 'It is a poetic setting,' wrote Robbins in *Roadside Attraction*, not long after he arrived here in a Plymouth Valiant in 1962, 'one which suggests inner meanings and invisible connections. It is landscape in a minor key.'

We reach, finally, La Connor, Robbins's home, the merest suggestion of a town on an Indian reservation on a dead-end road on the banks of the Skagit River. Nowheresville, USA. "It is a long ways from here to any literary cocktail party," he says with some satisfaction.

In *Roadside Attraction*, Marx Marvelous learns not to cower in misery against the legendary Seattle rain, but to turn to it, to welcome it, to revel in it. "That is something I had to learn when I moved here," Robbins explains. "I really love it. The rain is very cosy, it has a tendency to turn people inward. There is an intimacy about it. It reduces temptation. It is the perfect climate for the romantic. I think my internal climate has always been raining. When I moved here, I simply matched up my internal weather with the external weather, so it was a perfect alchemical wedding."

Ah, yes, the alchemist.

Tom Robbins has rings on every long and narrow finger. Moons, snakes, skulls, silver stars. Symbols that catch the light and glitter meaningfully. The envoy from the mystical world. The magic man out here on the watery plain. His books invite us to improbable places of celestial light. Characters are possessed of ancient secrets. Beckoning toward enlightenment. Well, it was the '70s. The acid was incredible, man. I mean, like, *transcendental.* Talk about higher planes, man, talk about right out there.

Coming out of the drug culture, *Another Roadside Attraction*, a cosmic on-the-road tale about hippies, magicians, and the dastardly FBI, published in 1971, sold millions of copies almost exclusively by word of mouth. "I didn't know what I was doing when I was writing it. I never studied writing. There were some days I would think this is the biggest pile of crap I have ever seen in my life. I came very close to burning the manuscript. And there were other days when I would read it and think 'God, this is a work of genius'. It was first published in a very limited print run. It was real gradual; it was a seven-year period before it really hit its stride. It just hung in there by word of mouth. I like that because there is something pure about it. There was no hype involved."

It helped, of course, that his massive readership was stoned out of its collective brain at the time. Because Robbins was certainly coming in from his own dimension. And he was talking directly to them. The nation's youth was taking a trip and he became the tour guide. On the jacket of *Another Roadside Attraction* he went so far as to say he belonged to a cult that worshipped rainclouds. Bit embarrassing that, now. Now that the drugs have worn off. "Just a lot of nonsense. I was trying to keep myself as mysterious as possible." He stares at the Persian rug as if it might help him out here.

Following up with *Even Cowgirls Get the Blues*, Robbins was a counter-culture hero, whose own state was clearly severely altered. "Now I am reaping what I have sown," he says grimly, opening his fridge and reaching for a Diet Coke.

Full of misfits and indulgent extravagance, mixing it all up, throwing all kinds of cartoonish ephemera and metaphor into the plot, chucking in practically every passing interest, the books with the attention-seeking titles—*Still Life With Woodpecker, Jitterbug Perfume, Skinny Legs and All*—have since propelled him into a mega-selling mainstream zone all of his own. He had entered the American consciousness when it was altered, if not absent, and made himself right at home.

Today, though, at 59, he is earthbound, no question about that, as he slouches on the sofa, surrounded by early Warhols, and wearing sunglasses indoors, a suit, running shoes, Argyle socks and speaking in the seductive, if loud, southern drawl of the good ol' boy he was brought up to be.

Outside, the wind coming in from the cold, deep Puget Sound is turning malicious, full of sharp knives as it stabs at my clothes on the doorstep. Wind so fast and clean it burns your lungs. Blue paint peels back from the wooden cottage that was once his home but is now his office.

Solid and intense, serious and precise, he is certainly not the desiccated hippie or happening crazy dude one might expect from his playful prose and from a man who once worshipped rainclouds. You might have expected a few laughs, a joint even. But, no. No frivolity here. The chandeliers can rest easy today. Maybe even Tom Robbins gets the blues. "I don't laugh much externally," he admits, "but I am always laughing inside. My view of life tends

to be more comic than tragic. But I don't have that much stamina."
When the party ended Robbins, unlike Hunter Thompson or Keith
Richards, clearly went on home to bed. Went home and buried
himself in the beet fields of Skagit County. "I tried to write when
I was stoned but I got too interested in the way the ink was seep-
ing into the paper or the way the 't' was formed. Two hours later
I would have three words."

With reddish hair and sallow skin, going off into tangents
about Eastern religions and ancient philosophy—"I think we lost
something back there and we desperately need to go back and
retrieve it"—he is like some sort of eccentric genius who has zeroed
in, briefly, from some other, more interesting plane. Except that
there is an almost undetectable but mildly thrilling hint of psychosis about him. A strange fever underlying the Southern
manners. As if the brain is struggling with something that hasn't
been mentioned; something else again.

His eyes when he gets around to taking his sunglasses off are
red-rimmed. He has a small pointed beard, which gives him a devil-
ish quality. I mentally add two small horns to either side of his
head. They do not look amiss. Tom Robbins is, I realise suddenly
and with a jolt, a seriously bad boy. Mischievous. Not unlike, I also
realise, the mysterious Larry Diamond from *Half Asleep in Frog
Pyjamas*, who has a smile like 'a cat's scratch'. "Well, yes," he
allows, "there are some aspects of me in him."

Larry Diamond is just back from Timbuktu. Larry Diamond
used to be the hottest broker in the Pacific Northwest. Larry Diamond knows things. Things that other people don't necessarily
want to share. Things about astrology, Africa and aliens. Larry
Diamond makes cosmic connections. African rituals are connected
to Sirius the dog star and amphibians from outer space. Get the
drift? No? Yeah, well, this stuff is, admittedly, something of a
stretch sometimes. Robbins gets away with it though. Just. Because
finely balanced against the fantastical plot is satire; he sends it all
up. Sort of. And as in the book, like Larry Diamond, the question
is left dangling. Is he just a crazy old hippie, or is he a wise man,

a seer, who is trying to tell us something important? Is he merely a writer plundering his own imagination or does he actually believe this shit?

Tom Robbins, after all, is a man who, when writing *Still Life With Woodpecker*, sat in a room for weeks meditating on a packet of Camel cigarettes. During his personifying inanimate objects period he strained, it has to be said, credulity to the limit. Too cute, too self-consciously trying too hard, too tricksy. "I got interested at one point to find out what would happen if you allowed an inanimate object to function as a character, have a secret life of their own," he says doubtfully. "And I actually shut myself up in an empty room with a packet of Camel cigarettes. Somebody shoved some food under the door three times a day."

In fact *Frog Pyjamas* is the most normal of his books. In this comic novel set over a weekend in Seattle a ruthlessly ambitious and dishonest material-girl stockbroker, a real piece of work, who is in deep shit, having lost a lot of people a lot of money, is guided by Larry Diamond (and great sex) into the unmaterial delights of the cosmic. Even though on first meeting him she 'flinches as if you were a ripe tomato that's just heard the creak of the garden gate'. He imparts to her the real meaning of life, as well as her first orgasm—pretty much in tandem. God it's amazing the kind of trouble great sex can get a girl in. A morality tale if ever there was one. Or should I say cautionary? Yes, perhaps I should. She ends up in Timbuktu, for God's sake.

Or could it be that Tom Robbins moves with the times? Could writing about the stock market be a clever career move on the part of a cynical author, to successfully interpose the more enduring ideas of the '60s and deeper philosophical questions on those, more disastrous, of the late '80s? A hedge against going out of fashion. His readers, after all, are now more likely to be dabbling in the money markets than the occult. More concerned with school fees than the secrets of the universe. Or is it all just Tom Robbins's cosmic joke? "It is just the way it came out," he says innocently. "I try not to know too much about a book before I start it. I mean my books to be taken at face value, as a truth. But I do think they should be transformative for the writer and the reader. And I think it is important to frame the despair, ruination and suffering of the world in a context of amusement and charm. To me that is where wisdom starts to creep in."

Tom Robbins's own departure from the temporal world came many years ago when, as a journalist, he phoned his editor at the *Seattle Times* and said he would not be returning because he had "gotten well". Now this is one Tom Robbins idea, I think as I eye the green and fertile Skagit Valley on this frisky, dancing summer day, and his luxury car outside, that I can actually endorse. The green salt water sparkles in the sun, the clouds bunched up in the corner are still putting on a pantomime, the trees hiss in the wind, casting rippling dappled light across the grass. This is the well-spring of all his work. If this rural dream contains the meaning of life, hey, I am prepared to go along with it. Hand me the phone, pass me the gumboots, dust off the Kamasutra.

But Robbins recently in a, er, perky letter published in *New Yorker* magazine, strenuously objected to being viewed as "an old hippie". Certainly the scope of his material would indicate the grasp of the bigger picture, so big, in fact, as to be probing beyond the known universe, and would place him more in the realm of eclectic philosopher. The interfolding of the metaphysical world and modern absurdity, the ancient and the contemporary in daring construct, parallel plots, is the main business of all his books. Two worlds, two plots with nothing to do with each other slowly coming together. The two plots are often so disparate, in fact, that you can get to wondering how he is going to pull it off by the Big Finish. But collisions, according to Robbins, are transforming. Round the edges the books are full of intensely detailed minutiae. His interests and obsessions reflect a wide-ranging intellectual life, from quantum physics to the tsetse fly, from mushrooms to all the religions of the world and beyond that to pre-Christianity. His diatribes and philosophical workings through are those of a deep thinking, learned and reflective man. "I spend a lot of time reading and thinking." Thursday night is magazine night in his house. On Thursday nights he settles in with a fat cigar to read the many specialist magazines to which he subscribes, looking for bizarre ideas, and wrestles with the recondite. "I consider myself to be a very spiritual person. I detest organised religion, I think it is the most dangerous force in the world today. All of the mainstream religions, as deluded and corrupt as they are, still have grains of truth and grains of wisdom, but they are dwarfed by their atrocious dogma and the violence, they are mainly concerned with money and power. The Old Testament is very convenient for justifying acts of violence and aggression. A lot of it is genealogy in that so and so would smite so and so and they would smite somebody else and they would smite somebody else. It is just one smite after another, you know, for pages and pages. I have taken from Tantra, Zen, Sufi, Taoism and gnostic Christianity, all those non-mainstream religions that do intersect and I have rolled my own, so to speak. I have been interested in Eastern systems of liberation and philosophical systems for 25 years."

As he speaks an odd thing happens to this bulky man. The watery sun shines through the window and through his ears, turning them a glowing, carnal pink; his rings pick up the light in silver sprays. For a moment he is incandescent, almost radioactive, shimmering silver with bright pink ears that look as if they might start emitting signals any minute. As if he is transforming before my eyes. Ah, yes, the alchemist. The clouds outside are in collusion with this apparition, they are a chorus of ethereal dancers in 3-D; all we need now is the loud and dramatic soundtrack, Wagner perhaps. But then it all dissolves and he is covered in neat squares of light from the lattice windows. And I am wondering if I need to get a grip on myself. If the air is too fresh. If I have been reading too many Tom Robbins's books.

Tom Robbins's books positively reek of sex, it oozes off the pages. So does perfume in *Jitterbug Perfume*. So does food. They are aromatic books. The sensual man aroused by aroma, nostrils forever flaring. It was those beet fields being ploughed out there that inspired *Jitterbug Perfume*. "Part of it was the sense that smell is most connected to memory and I wanted to go back in time. And memory is, of course, applied to the notion of immortality and I wanted to explore that. And perfume has this amazing quality that it can evoke memory much more than sight or hearing. I was walking down a dirt road, I was trying to invent a perfume in my mind. I didn't know what to use for the base note. I knew it had to be something different that would make it stand out. I walked past the field where the beets had been left to go to seed and the smell was overwhelming. You have to wash your dog after it has been in the beet fields. It is extremely pungent. But if you take a tiny bit of it, it is actually sexy and sweet. So it was through the beet seed and palm that I got the idea." Quick with a vegetable metaphor, this is what he wrote about beets:

'The beet is the most intense of vegetables. The radish, admittedly, is more feverish, but the fire of the radish is a cold fire, the fire of discontent not of passion. Tomatoes are lusty enough, yet there runs through tomatoes an undercurrent of frivolity. Beets are deadly serious.

'Slavic peoples get their physical characteristics from potatoes, their smoldering inquietude from radishes, their seriousness from beets.

'The beet is the melancholy vegetable, the one most willing to suffer. You can't squeeze blood out of a *turnip*.

'The beet is the murderer returned to the scene of the crime. The beet was Rasputin's favourite vegetable. You could see it in his eyes.'

Aside from the vegetable thing, his books are profoundly female. "My family moved a lot when I was growing up and we always seemed to move next door to a family that had wonderful little girls. In the rural south of the United States there is a real macho weight on every little boy. If you are sensitive at all you need some outlet for your sensitivity; my outlet was always these little girls. As a little boy I could expose and reveal my sensitive side around them with impunity. If you were to do it around your male peers you would just get punched in the nose."

And he is a man who, if his books are anything to go by, has done exhaustive, er, hands-on research on the subject of sex. His characters have fabulous, life-wrecking, transcendental sex. "Outside of procreation," he smiles winningly, "that is the purpose of sex. To connect us to the mystery. The quickest, easiest and most familiar way of connection to the mystery is through the carnal embrace, where your ego dissolves. There is sex in all my books, but there is sex in every book, including the Bible. There is a great deal of sex in the Bible." This is a man who absolutely adores women. "You write about what you pay attention to," he says wryly, "and I have paid a lot of attention to women."

He gets right inside them. When Gwendolin meets Larry Diamond in *Frog Pyjamas* she feels 'his gaze in her uterus'. And when Amanda meets Ziller in *Roadside Attraction*, 'a telephone rings in her womb'.

Robbins's wife, his third, sounds like she was sent from central casting. Or somewhere higher up, perhaps, some other astral plane. Somewhat younger than he (about 30 years), she is an actress, a model and a psychic. Yep. And a tarot card reader. "She has true powers," he says proudly.

In his earlier books, women were often mortal goddesses, powerful, magical creatures, wise women. Or, in the case of *Cowgirls*, lesbian cowgirls in leather britches with enormous thumbs. He didn't think the film was *that* bad. He discovered the merits of the zip when he bound his own thumbs during the writing of this. He often writes in the first person female. Is this a turn-on, or something? "Oh, absolutely," he perks up. "If I don't get hot and bothered by it then I know it is not very good. Actually, writing from a female perspective can be a disadvantage because it is even more arousing. I don't think I put women on that much of a pedestal. The women in my books tend to be strong and independent, spunky, feisty. They have a sense of their own sexuality, and probably a certain mystical sense. Those are the kinds of women that I like to surround myself with. In *Frog Pyjamas*, of course, the female protagonist had all of those qualities but she was also greedy, manipulative, dishonest and just a thoroughgoing bitch. And I enjoyed working with her more than any of the female characters I have ever worked with because she was so frustrating. They become very vivid to me when I am working with them. I find if you give people freedom they will do those things in real life."

But the women he actually attracts can be something else again. The culture of celebrity. A society that identifies with fame. Worships it. Greets it with hyper adulation. "It always catches me by surprise," Robbins shakes his head modestly. "I don't know how to behave." You practically don't exist until you have been on television in America. Like Dean Koontz, Tom Robbins has been the uncomfortable object of the scary obsession. "I definitely attract the lunatics," he says with a shudder. "There was a woman in Seattle who would follow me around and write me letters about what I did that day. I didn't know what she looked like. She would write about how she would go out to the ocean and build a bonfire and sit and say my name into the fire all night long. And there was a woman in California who convinced my agent, who knows me pretty well, that she had been married to me and that we had two children. I think she was so convincing because she absolutely believed it herself."

Tom Robbins had a rich and varied imaginative life—well, OK, he was always weird—even as a kid growing up in North Carolina. His mother came from Virginian aristocracy, his father was a hillbilly from the Appalachian Mountains who started as a lineman climbing electrical poles for one of the largest electrical companies in America and worked his way up to vice-president. "I led a completely secret intellectual life and gave myself a completely secret education because the schools in the rural South were so terrible. If they could maintain order, they considered it a successful day. I would go out to the back of the house, where I thought I wasn't being watched, and I would make up stories or fantasise. As I was doing this I would beat the ground with a stick. I had a whole succession of sticks. My parents would refer to it as Tom's talking stick. They never asked about it, they were never condescending. I don't think they really wanted to know. It was kind of embarrassing. A skeleton in our family closet. As we moved a lot we left many houses with a bare patch where the grass was beaten down to bare earth. I continued this in high school, becoming more and more secretive because it would have been death if I had been caught by any of my peers. I was a very mischievous kid, I was always in trouble. I played sport a lot and chased cheerleaders. I was able to conceal all of my eccentricities. Although some of them managed to leap out. Even when I went to college, I would get excited by things. Of course you can't go around beating the ground with a stick on campus so I would beat the bed with a coathanger when I got excited about things. To this day, when stories start coming on I will pace the floor and slap my thighs."

The writer beating out the rhythm and cadence for his words. Indeed, you get the sense with his writing, sometimes, that he is like a child obediently playing the piano who suddenly raises his hands high and brings them down to bash the keys as loud as he can, just for the hell of it, for the sound and fury of it, to get the attention of those people in the other room, at the other end of town.

There is no question that when Tom Robbins is good he is very good, very wise, very funny. But when he goes off at a tangent, such as the inanimate object stuff, he can be just plain silly. And when he looks at you, dead straight, with those red eyes, he is coming from a long way away. He is cruising past mid-career now but still seeking alchemy and magic, the enthralling sublime creative moment, still shivering with the pleasure of the perfect, beautiful sentence. "The three themes that I deal with in all my books are transformation, liberation and celebration. The concept of crazy wisdom is absolutely essential to a critical, analytical understanding of my work. It is a Tibetan term. Not to understanding it as a reader but to an analyst. And there is no one in the New York literary establishment who would have a clue about crazy wisdom. I guess the people who tend to like my work are people with imagination and a sense of humour. And perhaps a sense of eroticism. They might have a spiritual bent. I guess what I have just described are the things that separate human beings from the so-called lower animals." He chuckles as if this has just occurred to him. "But to me writing is a form of enchantment," Robbins laughs, "it is a very pleasant way to spend one's life. That is not to say that it isn't hard work." Robbins's work is truly etched out, chiselled from stone. "I really only do one draft. But I revise as I go along. My method of working is to polish a sentence until it is as good as I think I can make it. It is very slow going. I set myself a goal of two sentences a day but I frequently don't make it. I don't recommend that as a way to work, it takes more than three years to write a book. I never know where it is going. I just do one sentence at a time. That makes it kind of terrifying. But it also gives you an edge and surrounds the act of writing with an aura of surprise and mystery which makes it a lot easier to go to work each day. I live for beautiful sentences. I don't mean beautiful in an airy fairy sort of a way, beauty can be just grabbing you by the lapels and pulling the hair off your head. There is rhythm too, part of it is language and part of it is positioning your noun or choosing a verb so that when it hits your noun it will yell 'surprise'.

"Writing is a tremendously parallel existence. When I have finished work for the day, if I have to go downtown for something, I will pass people I know in the street and not even see them. It takes me an hour to get back to this life. Often I have to go and lie down and take a nap. I am just totally drained. So often I am completely estranged. It requires such intensity and concentration. As the weeks go by and the months go by and the years go by, the time starts to shrink so that towards the very end of a book I probably work no more than an hour and a half a day. That is why I usually go off on some adventure trip when I have finished. You can develop post-partum psychosis. Mine manifests itself physically. I usually fall apart physically. I go to bed for three weeks. Everything goes wrong. Once that is over I usually head off for Africa to get me back in my body. Most writers tend to live in their intellect, which is not too healthy."

The clouds, shuffling across Skagit County, are kicking up a storm again. Literally. Over in the corner another dust storm picks up another ploughed paddock and whirls it away. Tom Robbins, tired from all the talking, is standing, in all his complexity, on stone steps that "started as a Zen garden". He has another, more tangible, obsession on his aching mind. Food. "It is a major interest. I just love to eat. I like to cook too, but my bride has gotten very interested in cooking. I have become very lazy about it, because she has gotten so good. She was horrendous when I first met her. She learned. My previous wife was a terrible cook, so we made a deal: I would cook and she would do the dishes, because I absolutely despise putting my hands in dishwater. I thought that was a very good trade-off. My speciality is leftovers. If you give me a refrigerator full of leftovers I will put them together and just make them sing."

Driving back across the chequered plain on this day that feels so truly alive, the clouds are turning into banshees and racing across the sky, turning black . And then the rain dumps down with a grudge. I turn and look back but the Skagit Valley is hidden by walls of water on the window. The curtain has come down.

New York City. Yes. And as the airport bus lurches loudly toward the island, heaving, agonised changes of gear, belching black fumes, as the great buildings rise from the steaming rock, the mighty bridges come slowly into focus—so too do the memories come flooding back. I lived here once and hoped never to leave. I had a husband here then, when I was young and in love and in New York City. A husband I seem to have mislaid somewhere in the '80s. Such a hectic decade, that. That brief and shining time of gold rush in New York, crazy and craven with lust and ambition. Man, what a city. What times we had.

It overwhelms, at first, the great metropolis. Layer upon layer of it. Turning in on itself. Eating its own vomit. Dazzling. Impressionistic. Vital. Carried along the street by the energy the minute you walk out the door. Music, music everywhere. I checked into the legendary Chelsea Hotel, former home to Arthur Miller, Bob Dylan, Robert Mapplethorpe. Arthur C. Clarke wrote *2001: A Space Odyssey* here; Andy Warhol made films, Sid killed Nancy, Dylan Thomas died drunk. Hardly surprising really, when you look around. The hotel seems to droop under the weight of its own reputation. Worn to the bone by the years of drug-addicted rock bands, spent, shattered, depressed. Through the threadbare foyer filled with the art of artists who could not pay the rent, up, up in a shuddering elevator with the residents and their small, spoiled dogs; my room, stinking of mould and rotting feet, the accumulated dirt of years of ceaseless human habitation. It creaks in the night. I did not linger long at the Chelsea.

But I went out into the blurred, surreal neon nights. The dirt and the dust tossed feverishly between the concrete canyons. Sat in the bars and talked to strangers, Frank crooning on the jukebox. Went to parties with my friend Deborah Leser, sat on stoops outside and got drunk. Stumbled upon sudden night gardens behind buildings with roses and stone paths, trellis and vegetables growing amid the grot and grime of lower Manhattan. Caught taxis home as night faded to morning and the city stretched and woke up.

I went back, too, to the old neighbourhood on West 72nd Street. It was like being in a dream. Time stands still. I remembered the Sundays of New York Times, smoked salmon and bagels, walking through the park to see the riches at the Metropolitan museum. Central Park was unnaturally green that day.

An old lady sits in Strawberry Fields feeding the pigeons. They mill around her, fluttering up onto her old, swollen knees. Through the trees the Dakota apartment building skulks and glowers in its gloom. John Lennon was shot when I lived here, at the gates of the Dakota. Going home. Midnight sharp. We heard it from over the road, the commotion. We saw the flashing lights and heard panicked sirens wail.

They gathered at the gates of the Dakota in the days that followed, bearing flowers. New Yorkers walked out of their apartments and came here in a spontaneous demonstration of grief. The street filled with pilgrims, police barriers went up, we could not get into our apartment. I remember the memorial service here in the park. The first thin snow of that winter drifting down onto several hundred thousand silent mourners, heads bowed, hot tears on frozen cheeks. I remember, I remember. The only sound the thwat, thwat, thwat of choppers circling overhead. And then they played 'Imagine'. Streaming across the island. The dreamer of peace who died by a violent hand. 'Imagine there's no countries/It isn't hard to do/Nothing to kill or die for/And no religion too./Imagine all the people/Living life in peace.' Imagination was not enough. And now a young Asian woman sits with the old lady, strumming her guitar and singing 'Imagine', leaves drifting into her hair.

# Start Spreading the News

Steve Dunleavy and I appear to have gone down behind enemy lines. Way down. Maybe all the way down. The sun seems to be coming up, the Manhattan night is gradually becoming a blurred royal blue and Dunleavy's steep descent from barstool to floor is nearly complete. As the street lights outside snap off one by one, our dangerous drinking companions—pimps, underworld heavies, shakedown artists and off-duty hookers, collected during the surreal night—twitch and slump into crazed babble.

But wait. Dunleavy decides on one last dance. One last lingering shimmer of the dwindling light fantastic. He takes his partner; gallant. He twirls her with a certain shaky savoir-faire. Always a bad mistake, that, to attempt such fancy moves so early in the morning. Even for Dunleavy. Feet hopelessly entangled, they both go down. And this time the redoubtable Dunleavy does not rise again soon. Not with that big blonde beached on top of him anyway.

Well, it has been a long, long night. Dunleavy probably needed to rest awhile. It is hard, dirty and desperate work being the King of Sleaze. Outside, the monolithic grey tombs of Manhattan slowly loom into sharp relief, the city begins to shriek and hum, and its Prince of Darkness will, in due course, shake himself off and blast out into the fluorescent light of the city desk at the *New York Post*, where he writes thunderous leaders for the paper. "I have to catch and kill my own," he says with a bloodthirsty grin.

"When I worked with him," says Gerald Stone, "I used to get into the office very early, and often I would find Steve asleep in a chair in his New York regulation overcoat, just snoring away. To him the city was his kingdom. Trying to keep a hold of him was like trying to pull a freight train to a stop. He is 100% pure dynamite. He would always come in with the stories all of New York was looking for."

**STEVE DUNLEAVY**

Indeed, ever since Steve Dunleavy and his immaculate Savile Row suit alighted on the stool beside me in a shabby bar under the Brooklyn Bridge—pausing only to flirt with the barmaid, cars streaming past the window, informing me he has checked me out in Sydney—I have been caught in the slipstream of the legend they call The Dog as he prowls the underbelly of his city.

They call Steve Dunleavy a legend because he manifestly is one. Possibly the last unreconstructed tabloid warrior. Tabloid journalism on legs. "Every ounce of him is purple prose," says Stone. Hard drinking, fighting, womanising, doing absolutely anything to get the story first, he has lived the life to the max, 24 hours a day. Still is. Nearly 60. It is living art. As we reel from bar to bar, shooting the breeze and throwing back vodka with his terrible contacts ("unfortunately, a lot of my contacts are either dead or in jail now"), he becomes a chameleon who talks like a Brooklyn wiseguy with mobsters, suddenly remembers his Irish roots with IRA killers, reverts to his native Australian when it becomes expedient to be neutral; ever the courtly gentleman with the ladies. "I never swear in front of women," he says with elaborate dignity, "and I have never ratted on anybody. I am never, ever vindictive."

"Steve, Steve, Steve," they call to the tall, sleek dandy as he struts the viscous sidewalks. Until he was axed Dunleavy, his melodramatic outrage, his suits and his hair unsettled 25 million viewers a night with his US edition of 'A Current Affair'. Especially his hair. Greying, upswept and carefully coiffed, it is a concrete monument of architectural suspension. Hairspray city, it deserves a programme of its own.

Like Hunter Thompson in print, on television Dunleavy did not so much inject himself into a story as blowtorch himself into it. Taking the high moral ground, the reactionary voice of the masses, he chucked out any notion of objectivity. Siding with the victim in heartrending displays of emotion, aggressively confronting the bad guy with righteous, righteous rage and a lurid, lurid script. It was pure, harrowing theatre. Often with a score of dramatic music and an artful re-enactment of the shocking crime, on the off-chance that any emotions might be left unmilked. "I am very conservative," he will allow. "I do firmly believe in God."

"He is a right-wing Catholic," says his old friend Mark Day. "It is ingrained."

"C'mon." Dunleavy is lighting a cigarette and briefly pondering the fact that he has been mythologised, mostly unkindly, in a number of movies. "We're journos and that is all we are ever going to be and that is all we want to be. We are comfortable in our agony. You can't get bitter and twisted out of someone making a billion dollars with a script about you in Hollywood." Dunleavy gets a faraway look on his face.

He wasn't quite so philosophical, however, when he first saw *Natural Born Killers*. Robert Downey Jnr spent time with Dunleavy then based his profane, crazed, killer-kissing television reporter on a characteristic Dunleavy interview which featured him reducing a death-row prisoner to tears.

"There is not a mass murderer I have been scared of," he says modestly. "They don't look any different to you or I. You could be a mass murderer. Mass murderers and serial killers almost fall into an identical category. It starts off like this: 'I know I am a nonentity and I know you wouldn't even look at me if I caused a traffic accident. But one of these days you'll look at me.' I spent 32 days in a cell with the Boston Strangler in 1972, the guy was a wimp."

Then there was Michael Keaton in *The Paper* (yes, it was Dunleavy as city editor at the *New York City Post* who was responsible for the headline 'Headless Body in Topless Bar'). "He stole my lines. Don't take my word for it, call up any journalist on the *Post* or at 'News'."

And William Hurt's crocodile tears during an interview in 'Broadcast News' came directly from a Dunleavy gem in which he interviewed the mother of a boy whose father had doused him with petrol and set him alight during a custody battle. "You can't believe how grotesquely mutilated this child is." His voice gets deep and sincere. "He had to keep having operations because he was physically growing out of his skin grafts. Being a normal, natural human being, I cried. Of course I didn't break down into a burst of tears, I thought I shouldn't do this, reporters are supposed to have no emotions. But I cried, I really did. Even now I get a bit choked." Dunleavy momentarily rearranges the vertical lines that flank the busted nose on his leathery face into caring mode. "He works for us now, I got him a job. He is now 19 with his little stumps and his grotesque face."

But it wasn't the actual crying that was in question. As we know from 'Broadcast News', crying is good. Crying is career building. But whether Dunleavy cried for the incinerated boy during the interview or self-interest after the interview depends on whether there were one or two cameras present. GQ magazine published an article saying there was one. Dunleavy lays a manicured hand with a glinting signet ring on my arm, looks into my eyes and speaks pure Australian in the deep and resonant voice of the masses. "It was a two camera shoot, GQ got it completely wrong. I take some relish in this."

It is an uncomfortable irony perhaps that Australia bred the men who sank American journalism to hitherto unplumbed depths. We unleashed these beasts on the world. The man who revved up the startled New York newspaper scene with sensationalism, sleaze, crime and chequebook journalism as Metro editor of the Post from 1980 to 1986 and who has been accused of forever debasing broadcast journalism by transferring these dubious talents to television with sex and gossip, was merely continuing as he had been trained at the Sydney Sun. "Since I was 14 as a copy boy at the Sun and later at 16 as a reporter on the Daily Mirror, I have never done anything different. Sydney journalism in the old days, you were brought up in terror. We didn't have tapes in those days, we had to have 110 words a minute shorthand. We were loud, of course we were, but I tell you what, we were freaking accurate."

And his savage ruthlessness in getting that story first is only continuing a family tradition. His father was a photographer on the Sun when Steve was doing police rounds for the Mirror. One night, chasing a story, he spotted a car from the Sun and, naturally, slashed its tyres. "I didn't know it was my father's car," he protests innocently all these years later. "I was brought up in a newspaper family. He never said a word until two years later. We both had a tip that the cops were going to arrest the Kingsgrove Slasher, but the old man didn't say a word. There were cops everywhere but I thought I was going to catch the guy single-handedly. *Au contraire mon frère*. I went into the laundry behind the house and suddenly I heard a deadbolt lock and all the cars racing away. My father had locked me in the bloody laundry, there was no window. I'm going 'Help, help!' It was hours before I got out. But there was much love between myself and my father, much love."

Such dedicated early conditioning has amply paid off for the adult Dunleavy. It was Dunleavy, after all, to whom David Karesch, shot in the stomach, his compound burning down, was chatting on the phone. "I called up directory assistance and got his number," Dunleavy says, raising both eyebrows. "He kept calling back even when he was soon going to meet the Lord. Steve Richards, his second in command, called six times in a period of about 18 hours. I had him on the phone for hours and hours. The David Karesch debacle has to be blamed on this government. Old David used to jog down to the coffee shop every day. If they wanted to pick him off they could have done it right there. But they decided to make a meal of it, with television cameras there. Go in like John Wayne and start shooting. There were a lot of innocent people killed by this madness. It was ridiculous and shocking."

And it was Dunleavy who paid Elvis's disgruntled bodyguard $50,000 for the sordid truth about the King, who wrote a book, *Elvis: What Happened*, the first exposé to say the blue suede shoes were not entirely pristine at Graceland, which came out two days before Elvis died and instantly sold six million copies. It was Dunleavy who tenderly romanced Mary Jo Kopechne's friend at Chappaquiddick with champagne and roses and got her exclusive story. It was Dunleavy who, after weeks and weeks of negotiation and cajoling, got an exclusive interview with the Boston Strangler, who then helpfully demonstrated for the photographer how he had strangled his victims. It was Dunleavy, too, who specialised in sexual exposés, who sat in the wardrobe with the Florida deputy-sheriff while he watched his wife have sex with other men, Dunleavy who got drunk with Fidel Castro, Dunleavy who paid big money to get a photo of Sonny von Bulow in a coma. And on and on it goes, scoop after scoop after scoop, lied for, cheated for, paid for; but got and got first.

"He is very cool," says Australian producer Melanie Morningstar, who was with Dunleavy and Gareth Harvey under fire in Bogota on a story about the drug baron Pablo Escobar (who put out a contract on Dunleavy). "There were bombs going off all over the place and death threats but he just stayed very, very cool. He finds out very quickly what the story is and just reports it. He got into a brothel run by the Medellin cartel and did interviews on how the drug barons spent their money. We had to hightail it out of town. He is just an old-school working journalist."

Dunleavy, however, shifts uneasily on his stool recalling that one and speaks in dramatic sound bites. "That was the only time I have ever made out a will. I have had six serious death threats in my life; Pablo Escobar was one. I have had threats from the Irish mob. But considering that covers 41 years, that's not too bad." He takes a deep drag on his cig. "And remember, I have never been sued. Touch wood. Colombia is like Cambodia."

"He has an unbelievable news sense," says Mike Munro. "He can smell a story before it happens. Sometimes he causes them. There was a guy who had a beef with the UN, buzzing the UN building in a plane in 1980. Dunleavy was talking to him from a phone box while he was doing it. He had put him up to it."

Dunleavy and I are hurtling uptown in a taxi and the night is getting very hazy indeed. We have just left a bar where a group of television reporters was having a drunken screamfest. Jumping up and down, shaking fingers at each other, screaming, no one listening to anyone else. Ah, New York, New York. Sitting back sagely, Dunleavy in conversation has a lot more going on under that bouffant than you might suspect.

The younger reporters are diffident, showing him tremendous respect, seeking his counsel on matters of crime, career and the heart; jostling to impress him.

"Stabbing hurts." The warrior is rubbing one of his many wounds. "When you get stabbed you feel on fire, you feel like you are being punched. I was stabbed by two Chinese in Hong Kong in 1963, I was stabbed by a Korean in 1961, I got stabbed in Yokohama by a crazy broad who thought I was cheating at cards. It hurts." More than when he got shot, even. "I was so drunk, I don't remember," snigger, "I was in a high state of relaxation." Even now, the man who once disarmed some people brandishing guns in his local, The Racing Club, has attitude, is still a fighting man, still likes a bit of a punch-up—"as long as I don't wreck my suit. Sure, I get scared, thank God I get scared. I won't take anyone pushing me around or pushing a lady around, or a gay guy." Dunleavy acts out being bumped. "And I will certainly suck a bit of dick but I won't put up with being shoved. I will go so far and then I get my reputation for a bar-room brawl. I have done wrong things, oh, God I have done wrong things, but I have never ever been unfair. I am not an arrogant thug and I will not be victim to an arrogant thug. Wise guys never swear in front of women."

He was on the run from gangsters in Tokyo when the man who never sleeps arrived in the city that never sleeps in 1967. It was the perfect marriage. "He has got to be where the action is happening," says Day. "He's just a junkie on it." Even more beautiful has been the marriage of Dunleavy and that other, less wild colonial boy, Rupert Murdoch—the Digger and the Dog—which has lasted for 30 sleaze-filled years and made many many millions of dollars. "When it comes to money," he admits, "I do not know how much I get paid each week. I got a raise because another show wanted me. I didn't know I got a raise, nor did my wife tell me."

The actor Max Cullen met Dunleavy in London when he was there to interview the prostitute who ensnared Fergie's philandering father "He is a very charming bloke. He told us he was once in a stake-out in a car when the guy sitting next to him got blasted.

The killer put his head in the window and said, 'You didn't see that Dunleavy. By the way, love your work.' We stayed up all night and then he went off to a 9 am interview with a major royal."

The Dog is still, er, resting on the dance floor as I grope unsteadily towards the hot light of day. It clearly is not going to be one of those rare occasions when he will actually make it home to the Spanish mansion on Long Island and the long-suffering Mrs Dunleavy of 22 years standing. In one of our taxi conversations he has admitted being a terrible father and a worse husband. The first Mrs Dunleavy was the short-suffering Yvonne Dunleavy, who wrote *The Happy Hooker* and books about sex scandals. Books for which Dunleavy has been known to take the credit. But it could be worse this morning. It could be a lot worse. It could be snowing. And everyone knows about the time Dunleavy and a female friend just could not wait to get acquainted and so were consummating their passion in the snow outside Elaine's when a snowplough came along and broke Dunleavy's leg in 17 places. "Apocryphal," Dunleavy always says slyly when the Snow Incident is mentioned.

This morning he may look like a dead man walking. But at least he is walking on two legs.

The *Sydney Morning Herald*'s office sits high above Times Square. The neon Sony sign goes round and round, proclaiming the never-ending latest news. Plane crashes, divorces, celebrity marriages, disaster, war, death. The news in virtual reality. Down on Broadway the streets are chaotic. Marquees shriek for your attention, the latest Broadway show. I sit with my almond coffee each morning as humanity in every incarnation flashes past and images rush at you. Those sudden, intense exchanges with strangers. I was having breakfast at the bar of a Broadway greasy spoon one morning when a pretty girl dressed up to the nines sat down beside me shaking. She had just been for a big Broadway audition. "I blew it," she lamented. "I blew it, I can't believe it." She banged her head on the counter. We had a consoling cigarette, me and her and the lady who was cooking the eggs. "So tell me, honey," said the short-order cook who had seen better times, "show me, I used to be a chorus girl myself." The girl stood up and high kicked, she sang, she va-voomed. We all stood up, everyone abandoned their eggs to give her an ovation. Bravo, we cried, truckers, bikers, businessmen, junkies. I wonder if she made it, that girl. She sure got us going.

Ah, the racket of the city in the summer, sirens wailing, cars honking, multinational obscenities, the air so thick it practically hums. 'The air was like chicken broth,' wrote Clive James once. 'Grease bubbles swam in it, and small bones.' Indeed, I turned up for appointments in the city my clothes melted to my body, perspiration pouring off my face in the dirty, hot days and hazy lost nights.

New York is like a large family where you have to yell to be heard. The streets full of promise somehow, in a city of outsize proportions. You can make it here, sure you can, it is written in those cracked sidewalks.

# Let Laughter Flee

The final destination for the New Yorker who has tired of life is an exhausted eight-storey building on the north-east corner of 30th Street and First Avenue. It is to this dusty, brown, uncherished building, built in 1960, that the recently dead are carted when they take their last ride. Worn linoleum and threadbare halls greet those sightless eyes. The interior has a disappointed, rundown quality, a sense of underfunded quiet desperation, the furnishings a feel of impermanence as if in sympathy with their daily business, the impermanence of life. It is the sort of place most New Yorkers wouldn't be seen dead in. But then, reluctant clients are hardly in a position to complain about the décor. All the medical equipment here is on the ceiling because the patients only ever lie down. The next stop is dust and bone.

They see it all here. After the event. Whatever you were doing before you came, it was fatal. And here they will not rest until they know what caused you to decease. All day, every day they discover anew what people can do to each other as they untie ligatures, search for needle punctures, human bites, semen stains, take X-rays to identify bullets, fragments of knives and fractures. "There are some amazing stories," says Ellen Borakove, director of public affairs, "really amazing." And Borakove is a hard woman to amaze. She works in the morgue in the city with the most homicides in America.

*Let conversations cease, let laughter flee, this is the place where death delights in helping the living.*

Let laughter flee. The creed on the wall made me want to flee. To flee outside and laugh at the deathless prose. But there is no place for loose laughter or gallows humour at the Office of the Chief Medical Examiner. I saw no hard evidence to support the wishful claim of death delights. Not when 30,000 deaths are reported here each year. The entire population of a largish Australian country town.

**CHIEF MEDICAL EXAMINER, CITY OF NEW YORK**

Perhaps it is the sheer volume passing through that gives New York's public buildings their stoically battered interiors, functioning but sighing and complaining; all right, already. Oddly, the dust in the foyer of the morgue flashed me back to my wedding at City Hall. My lasting image of that comically perfunctory nuptial ceremony performed by a celebrant in a cheap brown suit was that the plastic roses were covered in an insistent layer of dust. New York dust is serious dust; heavier, thicker, dust with attitude. Any other city would call it dirt.

There is only one way to avoid winding up at the Office of the Chief Medical Examiner. And that is to die unostentatiously of natural causes in the care of your doctor. To have a well-behaved death, uncontroversial. Go quietly. Then your mortal remains will be handed over to your dearly beloved without much further ado.

Unless, that is, you are the man who recently called to say he hadn't heard from his grandmother for a while. When he went over to Brooklyn to find out why, he discovered that she had died peacefully in her sleep, he said. "That one could have gone by us as a natural death," says Borakove, a crisp woman in a power suit. "But when we got the body the investigator was not happy. We found that the woman had a lacerated liver and multiple fractures on the ribs." Killing your own grandmother for money. Those are the kind of customers they get around here.

"One of the functions of the public examiner is to participate in the public health system as well as the criminal justice system," says the Public Health Examiner, Dr Charles Hirsch. "The determination of the cause of death is only part of our responsibility. The manner of death from a legal standpoint is even more important. Was the death from natural causes or from violent causes, and if violent was it an accident, a homicide or suicide? About 15,000 bodies are brought to our facilities each year. The rest are either certified or are brought to us only for cremation clearance."

Audio systems record all calls coming into the Chief Medical Examiner's building. Situational operation plans for 'large events', such as air disasters, have been in place since 1991. Indeed, if you have died from violent causes—suicide, criminal violence, accident, drugs, in jail, or anything that is not *au naturel*—you will find yourself the subject of an autopsy, on the slab, your internal organs removed, examined, put in a plastic bag and sewn back inside, or, if you are a really baffling case, put in a jar to be prodded and tested. Your skull will be sliced open like a boiled egg at breakfast and your brain will be removed. Questions will be asked. They will want to know why exactly you had that plastic bag over your head whilst wearing suspenders and high heels and dancing to Carmina Burana at full volume in your living room, or why you were in that motel room wearing nothing but a condom, with a dent in the pillow and an open window the only clue as to the identity of your companion for the big finish. Best to make it fashionable if you can possibly manage it. And be more discreet in future. Or try if you can to hide the evidence first.

I came to the morgue because I felt that finding out how people died would tell me something about the way they lived. And so it did. I found that this city is having an escalating outburst of non-violence. In 1996, for the first time in 20 years, the murder rate dropped to below 1000. Less than half that of 1991, which was 2250. An outbreak of peace? In the open arteries of New York City? A city whose reputation rests on danger. What the heck is going right? And has anyone told Dunleavy? "A good measure of this is from improved policing," says Dr Hirsch. "There is also a lot of talk about changing demographics and the fact that crack cocaine is not as prevalent as it once was. When the police are able to control and eliminate drug dealing, that will reduce violent crime. They now arrest people for quality-of-life offences, and when they do so find guns in their pockets and this sort of thing." Even the image of the sudden flash of violence, the serial stalker in the alleyway, the menacing mugger in the hooded sweatshirt, is a bad rep the city apparently no longer deserves. "New York has never been the most violent city in America," sniffs Dr Hirsch defensively. And just like an ordinary city, most of the homicides in NYC are domestic. The New Yorker is most at risk, says Hirsch, from his friends and relatives. Well, that would be former friends if you have come under the auspices of Dr Hirsch. "About three-quarters of the homicides that occur are by relatives and acquaintances." Out of the 500 children who are brought here each year, approximately 25 have died at the hands of someone who was supposed to be caring for them. Issues of race and class are of little use to a department that deals only in aftermath. "We are not judgmental," Borakove tells me, but it has been noted elsewhere that the sharpest decline in homicide statistics is among white victims.

"The frequency of positive findings of drugs in crime victims is about 30 to 40%," says Borakove. More people die, she says, from failing to complete a course of antibiotics. "People start the treatment programme then they start to feel better so they stop. Then they relapse. But their bodies have become resistant, multi-drug resistant to things like TB and hepatitis."

Dr Hirsch presides over a roiling and disruptive metropolis jurisdiction of seven and a half million people. All of whom could drop dead at any time. And do. Manhattan and the five boroughs deal with some hundred dead people a day. One hundred people shuffling off this mortal coil in dubious circumstances day in and day out. And as the Celsius soars outside in the killing summer heat, even more do. Holidays and long weekends, and business here booms. Hirsch estimates that there are another half a million potential customers who are undocumented non-citizens, illegal aliens, homeless. "A fair number of homeless people are homeless because they are alcoholic and drug dependent. Those are risk factors in circumstances that could bring you to the medical examiner. They often die outside the system and hospitals and so end up here."

If you are so alone and forgotten that no one comes to claim you they will hold you here, in this place, where no one has gotten around to removing the smudges and marks from the walls, for 14 days. Your final resting place will be another island, a less hectic island, and you will have what is reassuringly called a city burial. "Hart Island is only accessible by boat," says Borakove.

"The prisoners from Rikers Island do the burials. The Jesuits built a chapel there. A lot of people don't have the money for a burial. They don't have individual grave sites. But people can go and visit and feel more of a sense of completion."

They are on the case here and the case is never closed. "You can always amend a death certificate, it can always be changed," says Borakove. "Our findings are only as good as the evidence we get and the information that we base our findings on. We never close anything. It is not unusual to find skeletal remains. Anthropologists can tell you the age, race, what happened."

Thirteen percent of Dr Hirsch's customers will be HIV victims. In 1990 it was found that a number of mothers did not know that their deceased infant had been infected with HIV. That meant that they did not know of their own infection. They had to be located and counselled. A surprising number of people, in fact, have died completely unaware that they were infected with HIV. Their poor bloody partners had to be located. Of the 70 prison inmates who die in jail each year, the majority will die of HIV. And if that doesn't get you, the epidemic of drug-resistant tuberculosis within the prison population just might. A jail sentence in New York can be tantamount to a death sentence. "Everyone who comes in here is potentially infectious," says Borakove.

Of the approximately 500 suicides, jumping from a high place will be the most popular way to go—and there are plenty of high buildings to choose from—very messy, very messy indeed; followed by using a firearm. The head blown off is not a good look on the slab. Then overdose on solid or liquid substances, then drowning. Cutting and piercing with instruments, for instance wrist slashing, is less fashionable nowadays; so is hanging yourself. It is the jumpers you have to watch out for in Manhattan. Statistics do not show whether there are more bodies flying through the air in the financial district than anywhere else, but it is disconcerting to ponder the disarray in the mind of the person who stands on a sky-scraper, looks at the concrete far below onto which they will soon be splattered, and then takes the leap. Takes the fall, so to speak. Determination absolute.

A glance at the causes of natural death shows just how much we collude in our own demise. After cardiovascular disease, which is way in front of all the ways to die, around 8000 a year, come drug dependence, closely followed by cirrhosis of the liver. I ask Dr Hirsch if there are any new trends in death lately, new risk factors, new things to avoid now that sex and drugs are out. "No," he says with some satisfaction, "everything is decreasing."

But this and the statistics sit distinctly at odds with what Dunleavy and his ilk would have us believe. That we are all in mortal danger from evil as we stroll the glutinous streets. That it will rear up from the sewers of the city. New York, as Joan Didion wrote, is 'rapidly vanishing into the chasm between its actual life and its preferred narratives'. When something goes badly wrong New Yorkers like to sentimentalise, they love drama. It reminds them that they live in cramped apartments without direct sunlight or freshly cut grass underfoot because they are at the centre of the universe and it is crowded there. And Dunleavy is just the man to provide it. As Tom Wolfe pointed out with such amused contempt in *Bonfire of the Vanities*, a lot of people can profit from the misfortune of others. An untimely death, a shocking murder, a tragedy, can resuscitate a political career, make a journalist famous. Make everyone connected with it famous. Spawn a spate of splenetic editorials. Create issues. You can get to go on television. To the New Yorker it becomes another illustration of living in the city, it folds itself into the seams, further fuels the energy, the edge. And, as Dominick Dunne will tell you, the victim will be victimised all over again. Death is no defence.

No one at the office of the Chief Medical Examiner is famous, though, as they slice and dissect and saw a never-ending supply of people whose lives have been snatched away. As they examine for clues, faces shielded from fine bone dust with plastic masks, as they see up close and inside what most people are once removed from: the fact that humans can be so amazingly cruel. As they go beneath the immediate and the obvious and find another world in itself. "If someone drops dead in the street and we don't know their history, we will have to get it," explains Borakove. "So much depends on the scene investigation, lab test results, toxicology, forensic biology, histology, microscopic slides, police investigation, their recent past, witnesses. It is like a jigsaw puzzle. There are so many answers that you need. We look for injuries, injuries that are not consistent with what we are being told. With children we look for injuries that are in various stages of healing. If something doesn't look right you take a look. There is no step-by-step procedure, no preconceptions. Our people are looking at what they see. They are using their intelligence to go to the next step. We had a really interesting case recently. A woman was found in a freezer. We did her ID by working out on the computer a photographic superimposition. By manipulating the computer, you can see if the face fits the skull to get a positive ID. Sometimes it is like somebody speaking from the grave. One man who was murdered made a tape before he died."

The air chills and the smell of death gets stronger as we walk down the grey-tiled corridor to the fridges where the bodies are stored in drawers. Laughter has certainly fled from here. Men and women in gumboots are hosing down the floors. At four degrees the dishevelled bodies are naked and wrapped in plastic, neatly labelled and waxen like store mannequins. The human remains. The animated person that somebody loves has departed. The spirit has flown. The breath has gone from the lips. Conversation ceased.

Seize the day, Susan, I tell myself as I feel the sun on my face back with the living, in the churning street outside, seize the day.

I was on the loose in Manhattan, sailing out into the night, nowhere in particular to go. I stayed in hotels, lofts, all over the joint, trying to find the right place at the right price. And finally I found her. Jeanne. The actual social X-ray from *Bonfire of the Vanities*. She lived in a luxurious apartment on the upper east side, sealed hermetically from the reckless streets. She was blonde, with help, thin and recently beautiful. But the divorce, you know. Fallen on hard times. She had to take in lodgers while the divorce was going through. "I love you," she said in a wide Bronx accent, "you're never here. Some people, they want to cook, they want to sit around your living room, oh my God." And I heard the whole story. I knew it already from Tom Wolfe. Second wife. Wall Street husband, older. Traded up for a 25-year-old. And now she was middle-aged and fighting the son of a bitch for every dollar she could get her hands on. Just another discarded woman. Just another New York story.

# You Take What You Are Given

'The soul of the city was always my subject, and it was a roiling soul, twisting and turning over on itself, forming and re-forming, gathering into itself and opening up like a blown cloud,' wrote E. L. Doctorow revealingly in *The Waterworks*.

Doctorow is a child of this city. The real article. Immersed in it. Folded into its dark and glittering fabric; fascinated, absorbed. Enchanted. Adversorial. "New York is life," he will tell me. "It is one and the same."

The literary lion stands outside his apartment building buttoning his jacket, gazing heavenward, radiating eminence. As if on cue life incarnate lurches toward us, hand outstretched, a black man begging. But something strange is happening in the sky.

Against the cloudless blue, a hurtling aircraft is secreting a vertical vapour trail. Straight up and moving fast. Higher and higher, steeper and steeper. We stand there watching. We apply our minds. We can't figure out what is going on up there. The vapour trail starts to break up and dissolve. The vehicle vanishes. The beggar shrugs. "Beats me," he says, loping away, still staring skyward.

New York is life.

New York is happening in the streets all the time. New York is intensity. New York is brief and vivid encounters with strangers. Forming and re-forming. New York is a beggar, a journalist and a world famous novelist momentarily united by a vexatious higher matter. Why, indeed, write about anything else when you have all the populace of New York to play with? A disproportionate backdrop like Manhattan to appropriate.

Floating back to earth, we walk through Greenwich Village. Every step we take has a literary equivalent. Has appeared on a page somewhere. It is like a narcotic for a writer, this city. Everywhere you look there is something to see. Every square inch is filled in. I remember I once did a photographic course here.

Every time I looked through the viewfinder I found a picture, a tableau of humanity, eccentric, complete and fully formed in its composition. Each different from the last. New York is all centre. 'A city of souls whose excitements have always been reportable,' wrote Doctorow, much concerned with souls in *Waterworks*, 'who have always been given to that nervous, vocal, exhausted but inexhaustible combat that defines a New Yorker . . .'

He is a large, bulky man. Tall. Watchful. The literary gent subsides into a cane chair at his local street café. Temperature climbing, the day threatens to turn equatorial. He looks at me through small round glasses. I have the uncomfortable feeling of being sized up.

"How come you spend days with other writers and you think you can do me in an hour?" he enquires in a reedy Brooklyn whine. "You mentioned those other writers, you think *they* are great writers," he sniffs, offended, it seems, to be in the same company.

Momentarily stunned by what seems so petty for one so fêted, I am almost lost for words. Particularly since he had been so gracious in his replies to my faxes. And it was he, not I, who had stipulated the time. Ego and insecurity are more common among the mediocre, in my experience. Not in someone of Doctorow's stature. Mean-spiritedness is generally found in those who have ambition but lack larger talent. Those poor sods who wish to be famous for its own sake but lack the wherewithal. With success comes security, usually, and grace. Largesse. Nothing left to prove. The evidence of an artist's greatness laid before him, the attention it engenders, in my observation, is more often humbling than not. Fame feeds from itself. And Doctorow is, after all, talking to a journalist from a country of which most Americans are only dimly aware. But then again E. L. Doctorow is a New Yorker. Nervous, vocal, exhausted but inexhaustible combat. And in a city of obsessives obsessed with their city Doctorow has elevated it to high art. Made a career of examining the amorphous mass, like an engrossed botanist trudging through the field with a microscope. 'My New York,' he caresses and admonishes like the lover of a seductively dangerous woman in *Waterworks*, 'Oh my Manhattan!' And in *Loon Lake*: 'It had size, it had magnitude, it gave life magnitude, it was one of the great cities of the world. And it went on, it was colossal, miles of streets of grand famous stores . . .'

Ever since he was a small Jewish boy in Brooklyn he has gazed up at it, looked at it from every angle. Send me your huddled masses. E. L. Doctorow's is the classic huddled masses migrant story. All his work is shaped by the exposition of his own soul, aspects of autobiography. "You take what is given to you," he explains directly from the nasal cavity. Features of his childhood appear and reappear throughout his work, worked and reworked. The repeated figure of the father eking out a living from a music store is his own father. It was his father who named him Edgar after Edgar Allan Poe, his father who had Toscanini as a customer and a friend. In a marginal spin on the theme, the tragic Paul Isaacson in *The Book of Daniel* has a radio repair shop. "Yes, my father was a kind of radical who read all the newspapers at the kitchen table. And thought about things. And took a very critical look at his views of things, but," Doctorow snickers softly, "never did anything about anything. He was an entrepreneur. He was a man of contradictions. He had a very fine music shop which he kept going all the way through the Depression. So in that sense he was a bourgeoisie. It was fortunate that there were great differences of opinion among the adult family members. For instance, my grandparents came over here as children in the 1880s. They married here when they were teenagers. They both came from Russia. She was a very religious woman, thoroughly orthodox. My grandfather was a renegade. That old country stuff was just what he was trying to get away from. He saw religion as fraudulent. He was a socialist. He was a great student of socialism. So here I am seeing them at the end, still arguing, still disagreeing, the difference between a secular sensibility and a religious sensibility. To a certain extent my father being brought up by my grandfather and my mother who really was orthodox and more conservative and religious had that kind of irresolution. It sets the debate going and kicks it off."

Arguing already. The New York Jew. Inexhaustible combat. Inbuilt sadness. "Everybody in my family, my wife, my daughters, are people with strong opinions and clear ideas about things. My son is very strong minded."

Sirens wail in the street, drowning Doctorow. We silently chew our smoked salmon and bagel. This gives me time to ponder our tetchy start and the discomforting suspicion that perhaps I did not show sufficient reverence. Writers around here are celebrated, and perhaps a certain amount of fawning is required. Matey may not, I begin to feel, have been the best way to approach this interview. He is, after all, as his book jackets clearly state, twice recipient of the National Book Critics Circle Award, the National Book Award, the PEN/Faulkner Prize, the Guggenheim Fellowship, a medal from the American Academy of Arts and Letters, and he is a professor of American and English Letters at New York University. Holy shit. All that eminence. Credentials. Exhausting, exhausting. It may, admittedly, have been a mistake to mention Hunter Thompson quite so early in our acquaintance.

But as the begonias bloom pinkly in their pots, and the sun slants down through trellised vine leaves, I shift sheepishly in my chair. I begin to have the dawning realisation that E. L. Doctorow formed a low opinion of me, cast doubts on my credibility for quite another and more tangible reason. A nasty accident on the way here. I had stopped in a bar. Not to drink mind you, it is still only mid-morning and early even by my standards, but to assemble my thoughts and my notes and because it was air-conditioned. The barmaid had accidentally knocked a full bottle of Rolling Rock beer from the bar into my lap. Then, rushing to recover the situation, she had knocked over another one. No time to go and change. Now my still-moist linen trousers are catching the sun and sending thick fresh beer fumes across the table and straight into the sensitively quivering nostrils of E. L. Doctorow. He thinks I am a sot. On the job as well. And he may be right, but not today.

No, no, I tell him, you are wrong. It was a terrible accident. I have not come here from the early opener. He laughs. Tension deflates. High intelligence takes its place. Professorial. Gentle and amusing. You sort of want to sink into him, metaphorically, as you would an untidy comfortable sofa, and take in the conversation by osmosis. The whine, so peculiar to the native New Yorker, has vanished. But Brooklyn remains, ineradicable. You are looking at a scholarly literary gent and you are hearing Robert De Niro in *Taxi Driver.*

E. L. Doctorow is unique, however, in this book, for one reason at least. The past that drives his work was not savage and cruel, he is not a damaged human being finding redemption in art. His is not the autobiography of angst. There has been no central trauma to force him to reappraise the human condition in a rather more vigorous way than your average citizen. I went to a talk once, when I lived here, given by the esteemed editor Bob Gottlieb. "I had an unhappy childhood," he said of his literary success. "That helped." Doctorow had no such luck. "I was very fortunate in my parents because it was a very stable if tempestuous family life. But they didn't separate, they stayed together until he died. And our home was always filled with books and music. I saw myself as a writer at a very early age"—laughs—"long before I found it necessary to write anything."

The effect of a happy childhood on literature. Is pain essential for powerful prose? A mildly interesting question. One that might bear looking into one day. Another day. As Norman Mailer once said of Gore Vidal during their monumental battle of egos: "Vidal lacks the wound." Doctorow was Norman Mailer's publisher once when he headed up Dial Press, whittling away at his early novels at night. In lieu of the wound, Doctorow's leftist compassion and outrage against injustice comes from the times in which he has lived. He has a way of strategically pausing to consider when he speaks. "I was at a very tender, impressionable age when Hitler was this monstrous mythical figure. And what the Germans were doing, the extent of it was not really known, but everybody in New

York who was Jewish knew that things were terrible there for Jewish people, that all hell was breaking loose. What we were aware of was something called the concentration camps. The problem with the profound justification of democracy is that whatever excesses, whatever injustices, whatever imbalances your own society overpowers is not concentrated in one small grain, so there is a kind of diffusion of the madness and the evil. It is a more diluted and less purposeful malignity."

Doctorow is frequently attracted to the theme of childhood. To the innocent, the partial understanding of the protagonist of what is going on as a literary device. *Ragtime* is seen through the eyes of 15-year-old Billy. In the abrasive *The Book of Daniel*, his most famous novel, the trial of the Rosenbergs for espionage is all the more harrowing and indicting when told through their two children, abandoned when their parents are jailed and sent to the gas chamber, and the tormented adults that they become as a result. Such unassuageable grief. There is such authenticity in the way he writes about sad, lost children. "Somewhere along the line a sense of being orphaned was established in me. I don't know where it comes from, this sense of abandonment. I do know that when my elder brother went off to war, those were years when my parents weren't getting along very well and I would often have this feeling that if I wasn't there to keep them together things would fall apart. A psychiatrist would call that the corruptive, the triangular child who becomes a party to the marriage and whose burden it becomes to keep the marriage together. Somewhere along the way I conceived the idea that the way to be intimate with something and yet not to know what was going on was to be a child. This is a condition of childhood, which is to have experiences without knowing what is happening. You don't have a vote, you have no control and you find you are intimately connected with what is happening but you don't know why, you don't know the truth. So I don't like to disillusion you with my empathy for children, but there is a tactical advantage to being intimate with the story without knowing exactly what the truth is. The sense of the child's predicament, bewilderment, terror, that was easy to do. So somewhere in me there must be an abandoned child."

In *The Book of Daniel*, the daughter becomes suicidal and neurotic, breaking down as an adult, the son sadistic, depressed and cruel. Cursed by memory and intelligence. The passage that lingers for most people is a scene in a car where he forces his crying young wife to take off her trousers and kneel in the passenger seat, her genitals facing him and exposed, while he caresses them, then presses the cigarette lighter. Whether he applies it or not the reader will never know. Doctorow, in a minor literary conceit, refuses to divulge.

Doctorow wrote that book when his own children were little and obviously being observed by their father for literary purposes. You take what you are given. He has been married for 43 years. The mudbath of domesticity, the stability of that, has been critical for him and his work. He spends summers at Sag Harbour, has a house at New Rochelle and his modernist apartment here in the village. "Without realising it, that stability was important to everything that has happened. That is the way of the world, our lives. Many friends of mine, New Yorkers who are writers, cannot write in the city because there are too many distractions. Too many temptations. But I have never had any trouble working in the city. It may be that I am not terribly good company. I go to a dinner party but I am not sure that I listen. One of my kids said to my wife, 'Dad is always hiding in his book. Why does he do that?' To me that sense of preoccupation, of having two lives going on, is really a condition of this thing. I don't know if it is kind of controlled schizophrenia. When you have a book going you become a kind of magnetic field force and you are pulling from the actual life around you whatever it is you need just when you need it for the book. Whether it is something you see or something you hear. Everything circles around you, it is very hard to describe. You lose yourself when you write, you are not the self you usually are. It is a true fever. You feel your own potency. It is a very draining thing.

"When I finished *Daniel* we were living in California on the beach, um, where all the action was in 1970. I had left the manu-script for my wife to read. Californians are like Australians, they really know how to use the beach. I am walking along this Amer-ican scenery wondering if I had written a book that was any fucking good. I came back about three hours later and Helen was sitting in the same chair where I had left her, she had just read the last page and tears were coming down her face. When I saw her tears it was one of the happiest moments of my life."

E. L. Doctorow has a sudden and sweet smile. All the more so because it counter-balances, when it comes, the slight frown. His beard is grey and flecked. He folds his hands under his chin in a childlike gesture of listening, one that somehow reinforces the smile. The brewery coming from my person is radiating so strongly you can practically see the fumes rising. Soon, I fear, I will start slurring my words. And so will he.

His excavations of Manhattan plunge back and forward in time. With *Ragtime* he deals with the turn of the century and takes, as per usual, the liberty of toying with history. Freud, Houdini, Jung, Stanford White, Edith Nesbit, filthy immigrants, Pierpoint Morgan, Rockefeller, Henry Ford, all present and accounted for, all on the loose in the metropolis, all hammering their names into history. "Some of the best writings are connected with transgres-sions." Doctorow raises his voice against incessant car horns, the scream of the city, causing it to quaver: "When that book was pub-lished people were very upset. Wallace Shawn, later editor of the *New Yorker*, said I had gone too far. Now everybody writes novels using historical characters. No one even thinks about it. I always thought that is what novels did. It is a great big kitchen sink for one and all and anything goes, it is the intrigue, it is using every-thing. For *The Book of Daniel* I knew nothing about the people. I had never met them. The trial was going on when I was in the army in Germany. And yet many years later I start to write about this situation. This is one of the books that didn't start with the idea of investigating the nature of civil rights in the US. This was in the late '60s when all hell was breaking loose here. The anti-war movement and big marches, civil rights demonstrations, sort of spontaneously radical students inspired by people who were in fact anti-civil war for the most part and, um, there were no communists among them to speak of. And what I started to think of was that anti-intellectualism was very strong and the drugs of course and the new music as opposed to the old left which was dominated by European ideas, and this tracing of it just sort of became a fulcrum. It was a way to do 30 years of life in the US from the '30s to the '60s."

He stumbles on his words, trailing off, looking across the street at the grubby brownstone buildings, as if they might provide inspiration. In *Waterworks* he wrote, 'I am sensitive to architecture. It can inadvertently express the monstrousness of culture. As the complicit expression of the ideals of organised human life it can call forth horror. And then something happens to appropriate it, and maybe from its malign influence . . .'

In most of Doctorow's books there is a moment when the novel begins to turn, subtly, the ground shifts and another, more sinister picture starts to emerge, the subplot forms the larger picture and presents a stunning realisation for the reader. "I begin with a scene," he says as another homeless person stops at our table, palm open. "The truth of the matter is that when the book is working you are not conducting yourself as an intellectual, you are not saying to yourself 'I am going to do this so I can prove whatever I am going to prove.' You are operating at the same intuitive level as a person walking down the street and seeing all these impressions. What the light is like and who is walking toward you and your next appointment. All going simultaneously in the mind. The total being is engaged. The writer is not a stage director giving specific instructions to your actors. You are just living that moment. You are not yourself anymore, you are whoever it is. It is an extended act of concentration, which is why you have to be methodical and working every day, because the writing generates the writing. It takes years to understand. To be aware on a level of metaphorical understanding. I kind of see myself as a really observant person but that is not the sort of work I do. You realise things later. "

Do you ever sit there at your desk, I ask, and wonder what the hell you are doing? "Every day," he replies as cars screech around the corner. "All the time, every book." New Yorkers can't even drive quietly. We are being assaulted by noise. "But you have to trust the act of writing to tell you what to do. The book gives you references as you go along."

*Waterworks* is a wonderful book, complex, dark, sinister. Poetic. In it there are diabolical schemes, kidnapped orphans, swindled women, stolen fortunes, exhumation, high level corruption, slave trading, secret laboratories, dungeons, dastardly behaviour; Dickensian. 'A conspicuously self-satisfied class of new wealth and weak intellect was all aglitter in a setting of mass misery,' he writes, the parallels to the city a century later obvious. The narrator is a newspaper editor named McIlvaine. "Journalism is a philosophy rather than a trade," Doctorow yells above the traffic. Perhaps he should visit the newsroom of the *Sydney Morning Herald* sometime, I think on the quiet. Journalism can be a blood sport. Terror rules the life of the average journalist. Fear of being found out. It is a public activity, executed at speed, the journalist is judge, jury and judged all at the same time. Withstanding constant criticism requires a strong constitution.

Each of his books covers a certain period: *The Book of Daniel*, the cold war, *Ragtime*, the heady turn of the century, *World's Fair*, *Billy Bathgate* and *Loon Lake*, New York during the Depression, his own childhood, so deeply felt. Each is bathed in compassion. "The money really controls US politics," he is leaning forward now "all these guys like Newt Gingrich, waving the banners of fiscal responsibility and talking about revolution. It is only revolution if you don't remember Herbert Hoover. And while they're doing that they are selling out the country to the people who bankroll their elections. It is very simple, there is nothing complicated about it." We talk of the backlash of the militant right. "It really is quite extraordinary. It is the failure of the analysts. They knew to be mad at something but they haven't thought it through. If you live in one of those towns where a factory provides the economy and where everybody works and the people who own that plant can turn to Indonesia and pay 16 cents an hour and do, you are going to get your gun and walk over the hills and get mad at Washington. Then they take away their guns. There is a misalignment. A lot of the conservatives have tried to pin the right militia on the '60s and the left. Here the major difference is, when the left is up in arms, with the exception of just a margin of them, they were activists with ideas. They saw their function as publicising their ideas and listing debate. They had teach-ins and sit-ins and outrageous displays. The Yippies would form a ring around the Pentagon and try to levitate it and stuff flowers down rifles. There were alternatives to conformity in forms of descent to engage the nation in debate. These guys get upset and go right for their guns. There is nothing between their anger and their gun. They don't see any other alternative, they don't form conferences, they don't march in the streets, they don't have slogans. The conservative politicians cave in badly, they are really victimised because they are fighting with issues like abortion and guns and the real issues, the things that are really making lives miserable, they are not connecting with. It is the failure of the analyst. Whenever I am in Europe talking in this kind of situation, invariably they say 'why is America so violent?'. And you know there is astonishing violence here."

I remark that for the outsider America's own PR job is terrible. Misleading. For the American violence is drama. Violence is plot. What the outsider sees is violent films, television, books. Here violence is resolution. The nation was built on violent resolution. But the average citizen understands the remove between dramatic fiction and day to day life. Violence is not part of daily interaction. "It is the diffusion," says Doctorow. "Somebody in Moscow asked me why we are so violent. And I said, 'Well, yes, we are, but we have never produced a Stalin or a Hitler or a Mussolini. So I mean lets talk about the beautiful things.'"

But, alas, there is no time to talk about beautiful things or any other things. E. L. Doctorow stands tall in the sun and then slowly disappears down the sonorific streets of his city, the great metropolis; beckoned into it, beckoned into its huge, restless heart, where he, the insider, belongs.

Watching his retreating back I recall a wistful passage from *Waterworks*. 'Ever since this day I have dreamt sometimes . . . I, a street rat in my soul, dream even now . . . that if it were possible to lift this littered, paved Manhattan from the earth . . . and all its torn and dripping pipes and conduits and tunnels and tracks and cables—all of it, like a scab from new skin underneath—how seedlings would sprout, and freshets bubble up, and brush and grasses would grow over the rolling hills . . . entanglements of vines, and fields of wild blueberry . . . There would be oak trees for shade against the heat, and white birches and weeping willows . . . and in winter, snow would lie everlastingly white until it ran off as pure and glistening as spring water. A season or two of this and the mute, protesting culture buried for so many industrial years under the tenements and factories . . . would rise again . . . of the lean, religious Indians of the bounteous earth, who lived without money or lasting architecture, flat and close to the ground—hunting, trapping, fishing, growing their corn and praying . . . always praying in solemn thanksgiving for their clear and short life in this quiet universe. Such love I have for those savage polytheists of my mind . . . those friends of light and leaf . . . those free men and women . . . such envy for the inadequate stories they told each other, their taxonomies, cosmologies . . . their lovely dreams of the world they stood on and who was holding it up . . .'

But in the end, of course, you take what you are given.

The top of the Chrysler building was framed eye-level in the window, the sun glancing off its perfect steel arches and curves, a singular sight floating in the blue sky, the essence of the city. I sat in a small soundproofed room overwhelmed by music; attacked by sound, walls and splintering shards of it. The Bowie interview had come through. Soaring above the city, on the 42nd floor, reclining on the sofa in the office of his record company, I listened to his latest effort 'Outside'. Bowie had insisted that anyone interviewing him come here first and hear it on the finest sound system available. I peered out over the vertiginous skyscrapers of the city, taking it from the top. The streets below telescoped into miniature. Broadway blinking little fairy lights, tiny Tonka cars untidily arranged in the streets pressing forward, ever forward, what Doctorow described as 'the expanding, pulsating city pumping its energies outward furiously in every direction', way, way down there. Does the vaulting ambition of the New Yorker come from spending so much time in the sky, I wondered, the desire to rise above those pungent streets, to make it to the top, so that you might look down on it from a great, rarefied height?

The ambition, the magnitude of the music I was hearing seemed equal somehow to those tall icons of the industrial age embedded in the rock, solid in the haze with their deco trim, their Gothic garnishes. Bowie has burgeoned from the technological age but his vision of grandeur seemed somehow to underscore those men who built themselves towers and monuments from fortunes made in the contractions of the modern age. From brutish beginnings to marble and granite symbols of raw power. Men who knew how to make a mark. Men who understood sheer size. Suddenly Bowie is singing 'Thru These Architect's Eyes', as if he is standing here in the room facing the window, 'All the majesty of a city landscape / All the soaring days in our lives / All the concrete dreams in my mind's eye / All

167

the joy I see thru these architect's eyes / This winter bleeds on the girders of Babel / The rings of flesh and towers of iron.' When I staggered out of that room, still vibrating from the volume, I didn't know what to say to the record people, I didn't know what the hell I had heard, I only knew I had never heard anything like it before.

I took it to Central Park and put it in the Walkman. I walked and walked that day, across the sheep meadow, the buildings of upper Manhattan watching over it as if protective and curious, past the ponds and fountains, streaming with the people. It was there, walking among the rollerbladers as they whooped and dipped and danced and circled and showed-off, that I discovered 'Outside'. It knocked me out. The next day I was to fly to Los Angeles to meet the great man. That night the city softened and glowed before my eyes. As I left my office the yellow pink sunset bathed the streets, flashed off the Chrysler building, flickered across the upturned faces of the people lined up outside the theatres and down onto the asphalt. The sign in Times Square silently shouting the news went round and round and round.

California greeted me anew with its hard white light. Back at the Ramada, William the cook fixed me a special lunch and Larry the barman insisted on delivering me showily to the door of the Chateau Marmont in the two-tone Cadillac. "Sister," he said when he heard I was interviewing Bowie, "we're a team."

# Gone Out into the Snow

David Bowie has come at us from many places in his time, Mars merely being one of them. But after attempting to comprehend the literature thoughtfully provided with the nihilistic 'non-linear Gothic drama hyper-cycle', 'Outside', one may have been forgiven for wondering whether Major Tom had finally traversed the frontiers and shot out of the galaxy altogether. Gone outside all right. Gone where no man has gone before. Without a return ticket.

Earth to Bowie.

Los Angeles. He strides across the room extending a long, thin hand. David Bowie himself. In person. Oh my *God*. It's Him. Ziggy Stardust, Aladdin Sane, The Thin White Duke. The Diamond Dog. *The* personification of enigmatic cool. All morning I had been walking off nervous energy along the wide empty boulevards of West Hollywood. But playing the old songs—'Changes', 'Ziggy Stardust', 'Oh You Pretty Things', 'Space Oddity', 'All The Young Dudes'—on the Walkman had only served to resonate in the subconscious and heighten the build-up. The vast Italian palazzo lobby of the Chateau Marmont echoed and reverberated as I sat waiting in a wicker chair, not reading a magazine from the rack, wondering if the paralysis that seemed to be setting in was going to be total. The narrow, dark elevator had never moved so slowly. And now here he is. Standing on a thin rug. Laughing. Wolfish. Ebullient. The architect of some of the flightier moments of our fading youth. Lodged, remote and mythic, in our impressionable and fervent nascent consciousness. A man mythologised in some 45 books. Exhaustively analysed in countless articles. Every word hung on, every lyric scrutinised, every posture, every carefully staged move examined for meaning. And still, and still, he has remained mysterious, aloof.

"No," he will say, "no, no, no," throwing up his hands and actually physically recoiling from a large and serious anthology of writers scrutinising his work, earnest essays, which I have brought thinking we might go over some of the finer points of the Bowie mystique. The past is another country. Don't look back. The skin of the old must be shed to make way for the chrysalis of the new. I will elicit a similar response later when I misguidedly tell him I loved his 'All the Young Dudes' much more than Mott the Hoople's. He looks at me for a minute as if I have suddenly stood up, torn off my clothes and started singing 'Puff the Magic Dragon', then he waves his hand as if me and my observation are a piece of lint on a suit. "I can't really remember it, I'm afraid," he says as he fastidiously wipes the party anthem of my adolescence.

He is giving every appearance, though, of starring here today as Himself. Sitting, now, cross-legged in a leather armchair. Well, he looks normal to me, for an actual icon, up close. An icon who has gone into some rather dark and disturbing places lately. Black jeans, bovver boots, black shirt, single gold cross glinting on the neck. Wedding ring. No make-up. He is, naturally, really, really thin.

He is acting normal, too. Except that the fatigued finery of the Chateau Marmont seemed to shuffle and shrink as he strode across the room. The air seemed to evaporate. He is a hugely dominating presence; he takes up all the air. The normal-guy act is pervasive, I will discover too late, as unanswered questions flail defeated on the floor. This is the art of the interview as a friendly take-over bid. So expertly done, so animated and enthusiastic, that you are dispatched and gone long before you begin to realise that when you thought it was going really well—hey, he really likes me—he was saying exactly what he wanted to say and no more. Well, not much more. But even then you don't really mind because you have seen charisma in motion. The kind of staggering charisma that fills stadiums and sells millions of records. And no one has been more skilled at keeping an alluring distance, at dissembling, at manipulating the media. His career was built on it. Keeping us at a clinical remove by wearing masks, slipping away into painted personas. Elevated to such an art form that he remains forever fascinating, even when his records no longer sell in large quantities. No one, as far as I am aware, has applied the word has-been to David Bowie. 'Watching him tune it to just the right pitch of sincerity and parody was one of the most fascinating things I've ever seen in a studio,' noted Brian Eno in his published diary, *A Year With Swollen Appendices.*

From the window is that familiar view, palm trees rising to sulphur sky, square stucco buildings shimmering in riot-heat. Splashing down the window behind him are overblown, hyper-red bougainvillea and hibiscus, which fall like a Hockney painting to frame his famous face. His skin is surprisingly feminine: fine, baby-tender, the fashionable stubble a sparsely masculine smudge. No wonder he got confused about gender. And the eyes, those famously different-coloured eyes; the eyes that marked him, we thought, as untouchable, not of this earth, not one of us, glowing kindly now, beaming intelligence. This is one formidable mind. Make no mistake about that. High intelligence, I have to report, seems to be the secret. We sort of intuited that, I think, back there in Rotorua or Milwaukee or Dundee, even though he was wearing a plastic spacesuit, pancake make-up and vermilion nail polish at the time. Age has certainly not wearied him, nor custom staled his infinite variety. It is a bit of a worry though that he keeps referring to 'people our age'. I still had an 11 pm curfew when he was pack-ing them in at Madison Square Garden in a sparkling knitted one-legged jumpsuit. Mental note to immediately review extra-curricular activities.

It was he, after all, who showed us in our callow youth that image, darling, is *everything*. And he who also showed us that only he had the savoir-faire, and the haircut, to carry it off. He who, just as his acolytes were getting the hair and eye-shadow right, had moved on to another persona, leaving a lot of people floundering in his wake. Wearing, for example, tasteful thigh-high platform boots or a lightning bolt zig-zagging down the face, with empty bottles of henna cluttering the parental sink. As Tina Brown once put it in the *Sunday Times*: 'He was aped by a generation of teenyboppers. On his last American tour at the end of 1974 the concert halls were thronged with look-alikes of his last phase. They came expecting a Bowie who strutted and postured like a moon-age Liberace. They found him as cool as a mint julep in a white suit and side parting.'

Today, just for the record, the hair is a greasy quiff, streaked blond.

It can't be good for your mental health having acolytes, people constantly emulating you and poncing around dressed as a stage character you have made up. A tad unnerving to say the least. Worship, after all, has a bad history. It is not generally associated, for example, with a long life span. Mick Jagger has said that he believed his own mythology for about 15 years and then he stopped. And for Bowie, too, art and life began to intersect alarmingly when he started to actually believe he was Ziggy Stardust, the plastic pop superstar he had invented. Living out your own alter ego fantasy can only be isolating, since you presumably know somewhere deep inside that it is not real. Ziggy had made him excessively rich and famous, but he was meant to be *ironic*. It was a *concept* album. It was the drugs that did it. And it was out there, in Los Angeles in the mid '70s, that he came unstuck. In full rock star mode, surrounded by sycophants, in the grip of cocaine psychosis, he experienced a terrible dark night of the soul. Doing what his ex-wife Angie wrote was 'a gram of coke a night', becoming skeletal, paranoid, deep into the occult, locking himself into his darkened bedroom and refusing to come out for days at a time; at one point, having the swimming pool of his house exorcised because Satan was living in it.

"My experience was very bad in the '70s but it was the circumstances of my life." He looks uneasily out the window now. "LA just happened to be the city of choice. I was surrounded by people who indulged my ego, who treated me as Ziggy Stardust or one of my other characters. I was zonked out of my mind most of the time. You can do good things with drugs, but then comes the long decline. I was skeletal. I was destroying my body. I only come here for business now. I wouldn't live here. I find this the most intensely hostile, frenetic, agenda-filled city in the world in the guise of being laid-back."

We didn't always get it then, the multi-faceted stuff. The human morphing. But it was Art. High Art. With himself as the canvas. *Theatre*. It was Jacques Lecoq and Kabuki and opera and vaudeville. Plundered and projected into the future. "For me, that was the only way to do what I do and to do it well, that was the most comfortable, that is where I find I am the most productive. Like Kabuki, the rock and roll theatre is a really interesting idea. It has played itself out very successfully. The time of the signs. The signs at that time were for a society that was starting to fracture. It started in the '60s, I think, the idea of different levels, different stratas of cultural resonance, after the very linear, static, almost sterile world of the '50s. I have always loved contradictions. There are no absolutes, there is no one form for me, there never has been," he beams, working two ashtrays at once.

We didn't know a lot about art in Rotorua in the mid '70s. A big Friday night for us was drinking beer down by the lake in the back seat of a car. We just got off on the music, even though we had absolutely no idea what it meant.

And not all of us were getting it now, either, judging by the earnest, polarised and bewildered debate played out in the British press about 'Outside'. It was definitely murder—but was it art? This, then, is the question he was asking in the concept notes helpfully provided by the record company. In an 'art-ritual murder, a 14-year-old runaway girl is being neatly dissected, dismembered and displayed on a splayed web.' As Art. It is 1999. 'The pain must feel like snow.' An art detective is investigating her grisly murder by an artist or artists unknown.

Self-mutilation and castration are extremely limited edition performance art. Utter destruction is beauty. Art and death intersect.

It gets worse. In this sinister story he brought new meaning to the words 'cutting edge'. It was definitely art, but was it wankery?

That was the more pertinent question. Bowie's defiantly incomprehensible interviews in the British music press hardly clarified the situation. "There is nothin' better than a good debate," he jokes now in a mock-Cockney accent. The old master manipulator is reinventing even as I, watching helplessly, report back from the edge.

Art, you see, is his thing. His great, great passion. His own paintings and illustrations for 'Outside' cover the walls of the room. We look up at them. I grasp for an appropriate response. "Actually," he helps me out, waving at one of them, "that character is based on a real live person. Well, not any more. I have to be careful here, I'm not sure if he's alive or dead. But what I do know is that he was institutionalised in the mid '70s. He was an Austrian castrationist"—laughs long and loud—"he went right over the edge during a performance in Vienna and I am afraid he cut it all off and that sent him right over the edge. I wouldn't be surprised if half his audience went in with him." He is roaring with laughter now at this painful subject. "It was all very intense. That's the actual stuff he wore. That's not fantasy, that is real."

We move swiftly on to self-mutilation. "It has been clocked up throughout this century," he subsides. "Now it is gathering momentum again. André Breton in one of his manifestos suggested that a masterwork of art could be a man going out into the street with a revolver and shooting into the crowd. He suggested that in the '20s. In fact that had precedence in an article by the writer Thomas De Quincey on the idea of murder considered as a fine art. Mind you *he* was out of his head. Later on, of course, you had in Paris a kind of theatre that dealt with torture and killing and serial killings, a by-product of the revolution. That kind of really barbaric playing out, almost a gladiatorial spectacle, is inherently very important in our lives. It's almost a throwback to paganism. Here things are taken to such another level.

"I believe that the popular culture in America deals with the spectacle of sex and violence that can't be dealt with comfortably by the church. I mean the Judeo–Christian ethic is not equipped to embrace anything that investigates fear or exhilaration in sex and violence. I think that is the arena in which it is played out in popular culture. We have Stallone and Sharon Stone and all that goes with it. It seems to me to be a rational thing; I don't find it gratuitous, I just find it absolutely expected. I don't think there's any point in taking a moral high ground on these issues, it's very human to want to play these things out. One would imagine that the Western world would be in an even worse state of tragedy if these fictions weren't played out for us."

David Bowie, more than anyone, understands that the key to credible artistic survival is constant reinvention. He has always been a lurking presence on the underground club scene in the hipper cities of the world, watching out for the new. "That is just having a kind of understanding of what is in the air. Having the antenna of what the *Zeitgeist* is, it is not so much perceptive as it is receptive." But if he was ahead of us in the '70s, if he lost his way in the '80s, if he returned to his previous innovating form, and Brian Eno, in the '90s, he is way, way in front of us now. Brilliantly so, says this writer, wading into the argument.

"Like Rachmaninov on acid, don't you think?" he grins winningly of the return of Mike Garson, whose virtuoso piano often seems to go against the rest of the music, soars above and around it somehow on 'Outside'. "He played a phenomenal solo on an earlier album, 'Aladdin Sane'. I phoned him to see how things were and if he wanted to work with popular music rather than jazz, which he has been doing since 1975. He was delighted and threw himself into it. That was really the start, when I realised Mike was back in action again. He was just as eccentric in his style as he was before. He knows his style is inappropriate for rock music, but he makes it work. I have taken what would traditionally be the space for a lead guitar and I've put a piano in there, it really is very unusual. I can't think of many pianists who could give a hard rock lead guitar a run for their money."

Bowie's faltering in the '80s after 'Let's Dance' in 1983, his fall into following fashion rather than making it, seems to have been a humanising experience. Rejection can have that effect on a person. His persona today is manifestly that of a very human being. "I fell out with music in the mid '80s; I really felt out of sync. It seemed so muted and so about something else. There was virtually nothing going on in the musical world that had any interest. I started painting and sculpting almost full-time. I was that close to pulling out of music altogether, I was just not interested. But I am old enough and have lived long enough now to understand the ebbs and flows of an artistic career. Every artist has shallow periods where they really feel that they are beached, flapping around on the sand waiting for the sea to come back in, then the next wave comes in and the fish is swimming again. It comes with the territory.

"I don't think money has got anything to do with it. I produced some of my best work when I was absolutely flat broke and I worked incredibly against the grain to do it. After the absurdities and excesses of the early '70s, I had a total financial loss. I went to Berlin for a period of spiritual, emotional and financial recuperation, and during that period, when I was working against the grain, I made some wonderful albums that stand very strongly in light of today. But the '90s are really happening artistically, I think there is some tremendous stuff out there. I just feel back in sync again, I understand what is going on again.

"One thing that was a revelation was when I saw a clip of Kurt Cobain doing 'Man Who Sold the World'. I had always known that what I had been doing in my musical life had taken root quite deeply in Europe"—he hisses through his teeth—"but it never occurred to me that my music made any kind of dent or mark in America because it felt so European. I was thrilled that a major band was doing one of my songs. I could never have imagined Bruce Springsteen doing one of my songs. It seems almost ironic. Then I started reading articles and it suddenly became apparent to me that a lot of the stuff Brian and I were doing, like 'Diamond Dogs' and 'Scary Monsters', that clutch of albums really means something to those new bands. It is really great to know that you have made some kind of contribution, you know. I would be falsely modest to say that it didn't really do my ego good."

And now, after a long and circuitous journey, Bowie had gone back to the future, the place he is most comfortable. Utilising the rapidly moving technological revolution without, by and large, losing the melodic line. As a dedicated post-modernist he is in the unique position of having his own considerable oeuvre to plunder as he finds the way forward. David Bowie, with considerable grandeur, beauty and a soaring vision, had effectively deconstructed everything, including himself. With 'Earthling', the album that was the aftermath of the 'Outside' onslaught, he toned it down, got a grip on himself, though it was still instantly recognisable as the daring sound he had so recently pioneered.

Bowie has always had a way with a shining line. From 'Outside': 'Slinky secrets, hotter than the sun / No peachy prayers, no trendy réchauffé / All my violence raining tears upon the sheets'. But his lyrics are not generally a helpful map to whatever might be going on in his mind, they offer no revealing or glittering insights, since he coldly scrambles words in the computer to get them, a cut-up technique he learned from William Burroughs. "I just pile in all kinds of contradictory information, I can do it in a few seconds." He is getting overexcited again as he talks about the creative process. "Having typed in all the relevant and sometimes irrelevant information that I want to put on the album, the computer randomises that and then spews it back out again. I use that as the fodder for what I would make as my improvisation over the music. The first stuff is really out to lunch and then you start refining it."

Brian Eno documented the randomness of the Bowie creative process in his diary: 'David called (at 7.50 am) full of tangential ideas—the kind of ideas people usually have when their lyrics aren't ready. But no, these were genuine enthusiasms—a soundtrack for this, a title song for something else.' Then a week later, frustrated with the 'laissez-faireness of it all, the lack of rigour', he noted creative tension. 'Perhaps I should accept that he's the hunter to my pastoralist—he hangs around for a long time and then springs for the kill, whereas I get results by slower, semi-agricultural processes. It seems to work every time when we use these rules. Sometimes I wish he'd leave my side of things completely to me—that way we could end up with sharp, clear structures that could support the orgies of evocative chaos that he deals in so successfully.'

And Bowie on Eno to me: "Brian tends to take things from low art or street level and elevate them higher and I do precisely the opposite. I often take elements from the avant-garde or so-called high art places and reduce them or demean them"—he is roaring—"down to lower art. We kind of meet very comfortably in the middle. Not only that, but Brian tends to be a minimalist. He is happiest when he has four or five notes, and he rearranges four or five notes into interesting things for a long time. I like to layer and layer and build up huge textural pieces. And we somehow meet in the centre of these two points. And, as Brian put it to me in what I thought was a valuable allegory, the best part of being an artist is that it is like crashing a plane every time and knowing that you can walk away from it. So it gives you the advantage of pushing yourself to the extremes in an area that in real life would be extremely damaging. But in the arts it is at a metaphysical level, so it's something that you can immediately step back from. I think we are both typical examples of pluralistic artists who came out of the '70s. I think we really were products of the '70s in that we saw ambiguity in just about everything, in all systems and in the art forms. I believe we have a network of contradictions which weaves together the culture in which we live."

Bowie stretches a long, slim leg outward from time to time, as if using it as an exclamation mark, a physical reinforcement of what he is imparting. "I would give anything to repeat some of the things that happened to me creatively," he says, covering himself with cigarette ash as he gets louder and more excited and waves his arms about. "I mean, those, 'God, you should have been there' things. The first few days of working on 'Outside' were draining but magnificent. Just irreplaceable. It is very hard to pass on that exuberance to anyone else. I am at my happiest working in an area that I feel uneasy about, where I have not been before and I am out of my depth. Then I know it's going to be interesting work. If I feel I know how a song works and I feel safe in this area, then I can guarantee that it's going to become a bit of pudding."

Hey, guess what. David Bowie is not cool. He is churning with compressed energy as he flaps around in his armchair. He roars and shouts and hisses and laughs really loud. He gets red in the face. Smiling, smiling, smiling. And God, those choppers. Definitely new. Maybe even art. Huge and blinding. Snap, snap. They change his whole face. Remember the old snaggle teeth? Gone. And he talks and talks and talks. Fast. Straight over the top of the questions. "I am quite verbose," he pauses to fill me in, "I value discussion tremendously." That would be a discussion pretty much with himself today. This is a man, after all, who is used to commanding whole stadiums, who is accustomed to being heard. I know, I was out there in the dirt doing drugs with the red-eyed demi-monde when the show came to town. It was during the impossibly elegant pleated trousers period, if I recall, a look so cool that we out there in the dirt could never hope to emulate it. He was ice-cool, emotionless, bathed in light, thin, pale and fascinating, appearing to look down from a great height. My boyfriend of the time, what a dork, required being removed from the concert in an ambulance, he got that carried away.

But it seems a waste really to turn on the stadium-full-voltage for one journalist and some chintzy furniture at the Chateau Marmont. When David Bowie is on, man, he is *on*. "He always delivers," the rock promoter Paul Dainty once told me. Yesiree, David does not disappoint. I briefly consider a one-woman Mexican wave. I suddenly remember Ivor Davies, whose band Icehouse was once the support for Bowie on tour. "He had his own plane," Ivor told me, "and after the show he would just say 'Rev up the engines, Roger' to the pilot and off we would go to have dinner somewhere else."

I have a growing sense as I listen to him that he is a man who has found great personal happiness in maturity. A hunch that he has somehow come back into himself. From a long way away. Deconstructed and then reconstructed himself somehow. It practically comes off his skin. Pure happiness. Passion. The kind of infectious happiness that is attacked with vigour, savoured, appreciated all the more because of the tortured being, the extraordinary journey, that has preceded it. Where would we go, any of us, what strange highways would we travel if we could do and have anything we wanted? If we were idolised by several succeeding generations? Normality would probably, in the end, become an aspiration. All that *flattery*; you'd have to ask yourself after a while, wouldn't you?

"I think I produced the very best work I've probably done for maybe 15 years right now, without any drugs and without any booze and without anything at all," says Bowie. "I don't actually have many friends in the music world. My friends tend to be in painting or in the other art forms. It's nice to compare techniques. It's kind of interesting to find out how you do the same thing in another medium. What do you do if you have a blank or a block, or if you find such and such conflict, how do you get past that; I like those kinds of discussions."

'David, as usual very funny and enthusiastic,' noted Brian Eno in his diary after a phone call. And after a dinner: '. . . His delivery of lines like that is so perfect in tone and timing that I weep with laughter. It's interesting that he and Bono are both such remarkable comedians—but with David it's a side that is only recently beginning to be seen.'

The explanation for this may be found in Bowie's 1993 album, 'Black Tie White Noise', a lush, syrupy retro celebration of his marriage to the beautiful, regal, Somalian former supermodel Iman, who was described in *Vanity Fair* as having a neck like a 'black swan' and a 'dazzling smile'. 'You couldn't tell what was sincere and what was theatre,' reported Eno after the wedding, pretty much summing up David Bowie. 'It was very touching.'

Bowie is raising one eyebrow. "Marriage?" he smiles kindly as

I flounder in the astonishment of actually having managed to slip in a question. "In my case it is absolutely wonderful. We both knew straight away that it was right, but we thought we should wait awhile to be sure, so we waited three years and then got married." Children? "Absolutely." Proof perhaps that morning people should only marry morning people: "I get up at 6 o'clock every morning, so does Iman. That is one of the things I really appreciate about her. We both get up at extremely early hours."

His sexual predilection was always for black women, according to his ex-wife in her biography *Backstage Passes,* a gossipy inside look at the rock industry, breathily written, and a rundown on the Bowies' sex life, which was permissive, undiscriminating and prodigious, according to her. Well, it was the '70s and David Bowie was after all, single handedly, so to speak, blazing a public trail of androgeny. A task he had imposed on himself after thoughtfully informing the press of his bisexuality and causing an avalanche of publicity which kicked his career along no end.

I interviewed her once, Angie. David had described her as being like living with a blowtorch. I had to concur. The force of her personality practically blasted me off my chair. They must have been quite a duo, come to think of it; there isn't that much air space to go around. Small objects must have been constantly flying around the room with that kind of velocity combined. She was a strong woman, intelligent, complicated and somewhat sad, I felt, flogging a book about a long-dead marriage for money. Her time in the sun had ended with their marriage and she seemed never to have recovered, in spite of a brittle bravado. "I worked very hard promoting him for twelve years," she told me. He repaid her by keeping mistresses whom she would seduce in a game of sexual one-upmanship. "I thought it was a bit strong, yes, when David had two mistresses in flats in our neighbourhood . . . but it wasn't really a question of possessiveness, more a question of the time he spent with them. Time banditry is what made me jealous," she said in a conversation that was compromised by contradictions. In the ugly divorce, Bowie gained custody of their son Joe. "This is the high point of my life," he said, amply displaying the new teeth, when his son graduated from a midwestern university and announced his intention to go on to a doctorate. "I'll be able to say, 'my son the doctor'."

David Bowie was always far too intelligent to believe his own hype for too long. Asked by *Time Out* magazine whether he was hurt by being called a 'pretentious tosser', he took it as a compliment and calmly replied that he 'couldn't remember a time when it was never said'. And when the *Independent* newspaper asked just who his actual market was these days, he replied: 'I think probably there is a grumpy old post-modernist who lives in Notting Hill.'

He didn't care what they thought because he was lost and now he is found. Inventing again, the path ahead is clear. He knows in his heart that his latest work is good, maybe even great, and that his *garde* is *avant* once again. It is change that drives David Bowie: evolution, revolution, sloughing, regenerating, going outside and slamming the door. Modern art. "The 'Outside' album has no relevance to a rock audience at all; it doesn't lend itself to immediate assimilation. I would love it if it almost became a word-of-mouth thing," he admits, acting like the average experimental musician for whom an audience of more than three is a sell-out.

Not that he even has to consider his audience after his own audacious sell-out. He can do whatever he bloody well wants now. He's got $55 million in the bank. The first step was securing ownership of his own catalogue, touring with a greatest hits 'Sound and Vision' album and then perversely announcing he would never play those old songs again. Recently he offered investors a chance to profit from future sales of the back product, some of the classic Bowie albums that still sell around a million copies a year, in bonds that are expected to mature in about 2007 with a 7.9% yield. Once the bonds have been paid out, the royalties will revert to him. He has bought himself the freedom to stay outside in the snow, and he may be some time.

I ask him how he has changed in the past 10 years, given that he once routinely changed his whole persona for each album. There seems to be a kind of Zen-like calm. The kind of calm that is reached after a rough crossing. "I don't think I am that different. I think I've clarified my own existence a lot better. I just find my life easier because I have reduced what I've perceived as being problems; they are less complexities than just superficial issues. I really live from day to day now. It is about quality of life from day to day. I don't have much regard for the future, or the past."

Do you, I come back as sturdily as I can, knowing the horse is conversationally bolting when he begins a riff about the artist Julian Schnabel, do you, you know, with all these books and stuff written about you, feel pressure to be profound, to be a star, to be *interesting*? "No, no, no. I am totally indifferent to it. It's not required in my life. I don't see myself at all. I just carry on with my life. This magazine in Britain asked me to do my diary over 10 days. They have this thing called celebrity corner. I thought yes, well I'd like to do a diary but mine would be really boring because I was in the studio every single day and there is no variation on that. Not even the food changes."

Oh yes, he is definitely over himself now. Over that rock star stuff. But still, all those people out there adoring you, wanting to have sex with you, anything, anything; miss it, even just a tiny bit? "Nooo, it's not a turn-on. Not for me." Sucking in air. "I am not a performer"—laughter—"at heart. I mean I do it well. It's a way of having my songs heard, but something I could dearly do without. It's not a joy to go out and do a year on the road. It's the monotony of it, I find it vegetating. Sitting around, waiting for the hamburger to be sent upstairs. God, I hate that so much. Sitting around the hotel waiting for sound bloody check. Over the past few years my guitar player, Adrian Blue, who is also a nut about art, and I would get up early and go to all the great museums and art galleries. We'd get a little guide before we got there and be at the door at 9 o'clock in the morning. It was like, great, we are going to Bruges in Belgium now; we would know where the goodies were. It really made touring a joy, you know, seeing the artists, the products of other artists' minds."

He smiles wolfishly again and you just know he'll be back. In one form or another. You just can't keep an old post-modernist down. "I enjoyed it," he tells me as I leave. So did I David.

It was real.

# The Worst

When Keith Richards stepped up to the microphone to sing in a cracked voice his song 'The Worst', he did it with such shy, child-like offering, such humility, that it could have come only from a charred and wizened old heart.

*Well, I said from the first*
*I am the worst*
*Kind of guy for you to be around*
*You shouldn't stick with me*
*You trust me too much you see*
*Oh, put the blame on me*
*You ought to pass, you see . . .*

It was, without doubt, the wounded, bruised voice of experience. There was a time when being Keith Richards's girl was a good way to total your life. The road was once littered with broken, drug-sick, ruined women in the wake of the Rolling Stones. "It is not," he says of the song, "like you weren't warned."

Being Keith Richards, you see, has always been an extremely dangerous occupation. This is the man who parlayed bad behaviour, alcoholism and drug addiction into rock and roll chic. Made it fashionable to be nodding off on heroin in an Afghan coat. It helped, of course, to be photographed doing this in your latest mansion, artfully swathed in scarves handmade in Morocco, with your latest breathtaking blonde hovering in attendance. Many tried for this look, few succeeded. Tragedy is part of the legend. "People who got too close to the Stones got destroyed, baby," saxophonist Bobby Keys tells me. "The whole world was fucked up on drugs."

While he made debauchery look glamorous, so many, too many of Keith's contemporaries ended up on the slab. "Nobody should go to the same university as me," he chuckles, a deep, rolling, rusty, cigarette chuckle. "That is a definite no-no."

Even for Keith Richards, being Keith Richards is hard. He nearly killed himself, using his body as a drug repository, trying to live up to his own bad rep. Maintaining awesome Fuck You attitude. More than once. Much more than once. Routinely partying for nine days without sleep; totally wired. But never apparently losing his lawless, self-destructive cool.

"I saw myself as a laboratory and I was determined to experiment. The experiment went on a little too long, I'll give you that."

Being mythologised is bad for your health. And Richards got very sick being Keith Richards, strutting through the valley of death, giving himself completely to the macho rock ethos of his own creation. "The public imbue us with the mythical talismans. I am not saying anyone was spurring me on to self-destruction or anything, but you start to wonder: 'Am I playing this part or is it really me?' It was just part of life. But there is a difference between scratching your arse and ripping it to bits. To me drugs were, I'm 19 and I'm working in the States. We were doing three shows a day. I was travelling. It was the worst conditions possible. We were 19 years old and we were knackered. And these guys who had been doing it for 20-odd years—40 was old to us then—black bands, country bands, used to say if you are knackered take one of these. In a way, when I grew up in this business it was like a backstage secret. You didn't turn the audience on to it. It was like an industrial secret. Part of growing up with the gig was that you just learned from the other guys. They are hitting three shows a day, no problem, and we are just like crawling on the floor. You get the message. After that it just became an in thing. We were all very disappointed when everyone else started to get high."

Going to meet Keith Richards is a surreal experience in itself. And I don't mind telling you I was packing it on this one. The *Sydney Morning Herald* was flying me to Tokyo at no small expense for a rare Rolling Stones interview. As we were leaving I was told that the Stones gave interviews for 15 minutes and 15 minutes only. Great, I thought, attempting to calculate how many thousand dollars a minute this was going to cost, absolutely fucking wonderful. A journalist on overseas assignment has to get the story and that is that. You deliver, no excuses. Deliver what, I wondered: hello, how's your father, goodbye? It was nerve-wracking enough going to interview a Rolling Stone. Before we had even left the tarmac it was acting like the assignment from hell. But, added the publicist brightly, even though Mick watches the clock and finishes on the dot, Keith might keep talking if he is having a good time. And is drunk enough, she might have added.

And now we were stopping and starting in thick traffic, moving down the wide colourless Tokyo streets on a cold, darkening, late afternoon. Twisted bare trees black against the sky; huge, square, characterless concrete buildings. Maximum security, a flock of guards speaking into microphones at the gate.

Down, down, down into the freezing concrete bowels of the Tokyo Dome. It is like the catacombs down here. Harsh fluorescent lights in the bare grey-walled ante-room I have been placed in and left, I begin to suspect after quite some time has passed, to die in. Macabre posters peeling from the walls. Suddenly the opening chords of 'Angie' rip through the building from somewhere out there, sound check shaking the walls of my isolation chamber. Well, I guess Keith Richards is in the building.

In the reverberating aftershock a publicist appears wearing, chillingly, a stopwatch around her neck.

Up we go in an elevator. Down corridors, through doors, down more corridors, emerging finally into a warm room, lighted by dozens of flickering candles. The inner sanctum of the Rolling Stones machine. A cavernous space atmospherically draped and canopied, incense burning, flowers strewn everywhere. So this is it. The beating heart of the monster. The Rolling Stones on tour.

It takes 300 people to keep this show on the road. It is a highly efficient mobile corporation, with separate department heads and, I am told on the quiet, byzantine internal politics. The nature of the entourage has clearly changed somewhat since the days when everywhere Keith went so did a retinue of drug dealers and, at one time, a person whose job it was to roll the joints. As the early evening cranks towards show time, bottles of good merlot sit decorked next to shining silver tureens, small children run and shriek across the room, there is a lot of raucous laughter.

And I am waiting, waiting, waiting for the man. The main offender.

My colleague from the Melbourne *Age*, Peter Wilmoth, a veteran rock journalist, looks as pale and jittery as I do. "It's the *Stones*," he says grimly, rewriting his questions as I nod in tacit agreement. *Fuck*. But Wilmoth has a worse problem. He's got Mick.

Fifteen minutes, baby. Tick, tick, tick.

Finally I am ushered down another corridor. Knock, knock. We stand outside the door. I almost forget to breathe. We wait. Suddenly a conversation I once had flashes through my mind. A prostitute described to me once what it was like to go to a hotel room and knock on the door, what it felt like in those moments before the door opened, the sharp shock of breathless fear as she lifted her hand to knock, not knowing what was on the other side but knowing she was going to have sex with him. After interviewing a few rock legends I now understand that rush of anticipation and dread outside the closed door.

The door in this case opens onto a vast dressing room. Keith and Ronnie Wood are jamming close together on a sofa in the corner, a cigarette dangling from Richards's lips. They look like two old washerwomen. Soft leather sofas, candles, flowers, bottles of vodka and cranberry juice. Packets of cigarettes piled high on the coffee table. Richards glances up. Here is the battered, puffy face of rock and roll. I almost want to laugh. It is surely a parody of an old rocker I see before me. Stiff, greying, perpendicular hair. Skin shrinking from the bones. A hollow, collapsed face whose deep lines, vertical and horizontal, tell the story. No, this is it. The original. But the eyes, they are something else. Almost black, they are bright and beaming.

"'Ello darlin'."

He leaps up, somehow managing to deposit the guitar, shake

hands and swig from his glass, all in one animal movement. Wood politely excuses himself. Richards hurls a parting insult, making himself laugh and cough. Oh yes indeed, it is still testosterone city around here, even after all these years. Bad boy stuff still, well, bad boys of a certain age. Bad boy grandfathers now.

But chain drinking and smoking Keith Richards is turning out to be a sweetheart. Or so it seems to me when 15 minutes pass and he keeps on talking, and talking, with no end in sight. Unlike David Bowie, Keith Richards is unreconstructed on every front. He has never deviated from rhythm and blues. It is his religion. Waving his arms around, dropping ash, his skull-head ring catching the candlelight, he keeps calling me "baby". Baby, baby, baby. I know it's only rock and roll. But I like it.

The accent is pure working class. You could be down at an East End pub having a beer, doing a bit of business on the side. You almost expect him to whip out the form guide and circle the 3.30 at Doncaster.

The tidewater mark on that bottle of vodka is dropping fast. He is a topper, habitually freshening his drink, topping it up. He speaks slurringly and the brain appears to miss a cog from time to time, but he is lucid. But then again, I have seen old politicians do this too. Drink all day and stay lucid because they have said it all so many times before. Autopilot.

Keith Richards is warm, amusing, unpretentious, rambling around the conversation, open. No secrets with the soul survivor. There is always a kind of searing honesty in the reformed substance abuser. If you have fallen down drunk enough times, in enough places, there is no longer any point in caring what anyone thinks. If you are going to be that abandoned and uninhibited you probably didn't give a shit to start with. And it is, of course, a bit hard to lie about it when you can't remember what you did. "There were so many times in French nightclubs lying on the bar, and people were dancing around me and I was throwing up, waiting for the man, you know," he says, shuddering at the desperate memory. Keith Richards appears beyond ego. He has been so very famous for so long. And anyway, he is doing the only thing he has ever wanted to do. He is being a rock star.

Well, maybe not *that* reformed. Is that a deep sniffing sound I recognise? A familiar way of putting thumb and forefinger to the nose and breathing backwards? A suspicious drip in the nostril area? Even now there are nights when the minders have to help him onto the stage. "Over here mate, no, no, over here" sort of thing.

He was completely off his face of course in those early days of guitar glory when he and Mick wrote a string of rock anthems, in the mid '60s. "I learned a lot while I was on that stuff, including music. And I got turned on to other different kinds of music that maybe I wouldn't have. I dunno, life takes its course." Life, he is fond of saying, is about beautiful fuck-ups and beautiful recoveries. "Yeah," he nods when I say this, "it is. And it happens every night. I have relied on accidents all my life. Everything I have ever planned has never worked out. I am just somebody accidents happen to. Some of them are good, some of them bad. But the bad ones ain't killed me yet."

His subconscious seems to have been on the case with 'Satisfaction'. The famous opening riff came to him in his sleep. He picked up his guitar and played it and then resumed snoring. "I love it when they come like 'Satisfaction'. There are only two or three in my life that I have ever dreamt and just woken up and there's a tape recorder by my bed, I've put it in and just gone back to sleep. I only played it back because I noticed the tape had gone to the end in the night. Most of it was my snoring."

For Richards, writing songs appears to be a religious experience, divine intervention. "When I hear guys on MTV talking about writer's block, I think: 'Do me a favour, old son.' If you are anything you are an antenna. If you turn it on something will beam it on to you. Then you work on it, reorganise it and transmit it. To think that you created it is the height of egotistical big-headedness. I don't create these songs, they are everybody's. I know I am blessed, but by what and by whom is another thing.

You are working with four or five guys and suddenly you are three feet off the ground and you know what is going to happen. Before it does you look at your fingers and think 'I can't play this' and suddenly you do. Those are the things you go for, yeah. You feel like God, in touch with higher beings. There is a definite lift. If you do it by yourself maybe you are jerking off, but when you look around the room and all the guys are nearly three feet off the ground . . ." He closes his black eyes for a moment in what could only be described as guitar hero ecstasy.

Drug etiquette and rock etiquette are very important to the Richards world view. It was he, after all, who made the rules. "I've never turned blue in anyone else's bathroom," he was once thrillingly quoted as saying. "I think that is the height of bad manners." Lingering working-class pride, perhaps. "I have never done anything that has made me cringe."

His raddled face is like a flaunted badge of honour. He is a bluesman, an ancient being, a cool cat. You have to live it. You have to walk it, baby. You gotta know pain and despair. Man, oh, man. "It is about researching it," he is saying. "You don't want to be masochistic. There is the high but at the same time there is always the price to pay and you know it. In a way you kind of say, well, for that I trade that. You take the pain. As usual I thought I was indestructible and it turns out I was right"—phlegmatic chuckle. "That's why nobody should emulate it. It's not for everybody. I look at Muddy Waters, that is the example, gentleman all the way. Never slackened his pace. He was just as good the day he died as he was when he first cut a record. I guess if you want a role model that's it. Hey, we're just getting the hang of it now. "

It is about honour among outlaws, says the red-faced and blustering Texan Bobby Keys. Keith Richards is known for lifelong loyalty to his blues friends. An old Richards cohort and drug sidekick who had played with Buddy Holly, Keys first joined the Stones horn section in 1969. "We have shared some adventures, but right now we are not in any trouble," he says, grinning hugely. "His massive celebrity just bounces off him, he is pretty sure in his own

self who he is. That stuff about having his blood changed, total
jive. He was joking. It is not medically possible, for one thing.
Keith is the most honest person I have ever met in my life. He
doesn't bullshit you, he doesn't jive you, he is a stand-up guy. He
hasn't changed a lick, he is still the original package. I had a problem I had to solve. Keith helped me, he paid for the clinic. He is
probably the most intense person I have ever met."

Indeed, Richards's level of, er, intensity would kill most people.
There's the sleep thing for a start. He apparently does not require
it. Like Hunter Thompson. An inexhaustible subversive life force.
"An unintense life does not appeal to me"—his eyes are glittering
now—"the thing about it is that it is what you are here to do and
if you are not doing that then you are not doing your job. There
is a sense that if you are going to keep it together for this long then
you are very intense about what you do and, of course, if you are
intense about one part of your life then you are intense about all
the others."

It is a long free fall from the rarefied stratosphere of celebrity
to street junkie, as Marianne Faithfull discovered when she went
to the wall. Richards survived in style because he was protected by
stupendous wealth, a working-class boy with too much money. He
lived in fabulous houses, hired the best French chefs, bought the
best wines, entertained harems of beautiful women and got stoned.
Because Mick took care of business, Richards was completely cush-
ioned from the usual reality of junkie desperation. There were
cures in expensive Swiss clinics when necessary before touring.
Wherever he was, high-grade drugs were delivered in awesome
quantities every week. He could afford to support a retinue of up
to 30 lowlife drug fiends resident in the villa of the moment at any
given time. He could buy his way out of trouble most of the time,
paying off whoever needed paying off. He squandered a great deal
of his fortune on drugs and the law cases against him. Or getting
Anita Pallenberg out of trouble.

But things could get heavy nevertheless. Scoring in Manhattan
in the '70s, he would carry a Smith and Wesson to shoot the lights

out and run because the dealer would have buddies waiting to rob him on the way out.

And Richards does pride himself on street cred, on being a low-life aficionado; the street is, after all, man, where the vibe is; the music, man; the blues; the life blood. "Maybe it was another way of trying to stay in the gutter," he says with a hacking laugh. "It is like, don't put me up here on a pedestal and leave me up here, for Christ sakes. There is that weird feeling that you are being isolated from the mainstream of life. Some people revel in that, flying above it all in the jetstream, but to me that would be like cutting my heart out. Mostly I have no problems in Manhattan. I could be mayor. If it is raining, garbage guys or the police will give me a lift. It is my adopted mother city. Walking about, people say, 'How you doing, Keith?' It's cool. And then you turn a corner and there is a crocodile of schoolkids. You think, I'm too old for them to be interested. Then they break ranks and go 'It's him!' and suddenly you get deluged. You never know. I didn't do all this just to become a hermit and hide behind walls."

During our conversation, harassed people fly in and out of the room. Without taking his focus from me he rearranges the songs for tonight to an assistant with a clipboard. "No, 'Brown Sugar' then 'Jumpin' Jack Flash', let's chop and change it, fine," he tells the assistant, "cool". And then to me, "That's Jo Wood's eldest son but he is working for us, so I can tell him to fuck off." More wheezing laughter.

Still talking he walks across the room, absently pulling his clothes from the rack. In 1983, in full evening dress and blue suede shoes, he married the golden *Vogue* cover girl from Staten Island, Patti Hansen. His notorious relationship with Anita Pallenberg had become diabolical. They had destroyed themselves and each other with drugs. Hansen, who gave up her career to become a rock wife and mother, is credited with sorting him out and getting him off hard drugs. "I do like a good girl to come home to," he has said, "and we are a great couple."

Hansen must be a true rock wife. Richards plays music at full volume 24 hours a day. "I do have a big house so I can play shit loud. Ronnie is worse than me. He and I recently turned into Elvis freaks for an evening. My wife is one of the girls, know what I mean? Every now and then I get, 'Can't you turn that down a bit?' I go, 'Sorry darling, it's stuck'."

His relationship with Jagger has outlasted their marriages, their differences, the drugs, all the huge complications. It has endured. They have known each other for nearly 50 years, since their first days in primary school in Dartford, Kent. Marianne Faithfull is not the only person to have observed that Keith has always been Mick's great love. But in the '80s, musical differences and lifestyle differences drove them apart. Theirs was a very public divorce. Jagger had always looked after Richards, covering for him, taking care of business when he was in his "condition, my long, long pregnancy".

"That was difficult, the late '70s, early to middle '80s. You were the Rolling Stones and nothing else. You worked 18 months to two years and then did nothing for three. It is death for a band. Basically we had to resurrect it. Now in retrospect it happened quite naturally. We had come to a big crunch. 'We cannot go on like this.' Probably one of the problems was when I got my act together and came back ready to shoulder some of the burden, he didn't want to share it any more. Mick and I were going head to head. We couldn't have a little squabble without it becoming a major battle. It actually lasted longer than World War II. We were letting journalists wind us up. They would say, 'Did you hear what Mick said about you?' and I would go, 'Aaargh'."

The schism, naturally, was not without theatre. Charlie Watts, after many years of standing in the background, finally lost it and decked Mick one night in Amsterdam. Jagger landed in a plate of salmon and was rapidly heading out the window into a canal when Richards lurched forward and grabbed his leg. This was not friendship.

"The only reason I grabbed him," he says, rubbing his chin and laughing, "was that he was wearing my wedding jacket. I had loaned it to him for the night. At first I said, 'Well done, Charlie,' and then, 'Shit, the wife's going to kill me, he's going to go out the window into the canal'. It was a funny night. It was '84 and that was where we were at. We had nobody left to fight except each other. We were in a vacuum. The Stones were all we were and we didn't know quite what to do. It was frustration."

By a 1982 tour Jagger was forced to vacate the stage when Keith did his solo number because it was written into the contract. At a show in Scandinavia Richards hijacked the cherry-picker that Mick used to fly over the crowd for 'You Can't Always Get What You Want', and which Richards despised for turning the show into a 'circus', to perform a 20-minute guitar solo. Helpless and furious, Jagger dispatched Wood to coax him back down. But Keith refused.

But when Jagger decided to pursue a solo career, Richards was devastated. The Rolling Stones is his whole life. It forced him to find a new band, the X-Pensive Winos, and make two records, 'Talk Is Cheap' and 'Main Offender', both of which received better notices than Jagger's solo efforts. Richards was vindicated. "Everybody went off and did their own things and then came back and put it back together again. Now it all makes sense, but at the time it was hard. At the same time it is like family. You are always going to hit rough patches except we had to carry it out in the limelight. I loved it because it all healed up again. But going through it was a weird sensation. To me one great band in a lifetime is a miracle. Two, forget about it. As it happened, they made me put together another one. The Winos are a hell of a band."

But it was obvious, really. At a meeting in Barbados in 1989, Jagger and Richards screamed at each other for a few hours and ended up rolling on the floor laughing about the terrible things they had been quoted as saying about each other. "We will never break the bone in the same place again. Hey, this band is too good to lose." The chemistry between Jagger and Richards was always irreducible and indefinable. Not to mention staggeringly lucrative. What is it exactly? "If we could work it out we could bottle it,"

Richards says. "Very expensively. I dunno, that has been asked—not just by other people. Everybody in the band asks themselves that I'm sure. Quite often. You get to the point where first off it is impossible to find out and then maybe you don't want to anyway. There is a sense of curiosity about it and at the same time some things are better veiled because if you knew the exact ingredients you might not any longer be able to make them work together. It really is a matter of trust between each other."

Keith Richards is rocking back in his chair, laughing. I have just confessed I got sent to boarding school because I ran away from home in 1973 and hitch-hiked to the daunting metropolis of Auckland to see my idols, The Rolling Stones. Another casualty. "That's right," he says, "blame it on the Stones." Then he arches an eyebrow suggestively. "So. What are you going to do this time?"

In her breathtakingly honest and harrowing autobiography, Marianne Faithfull describes the young Keith Richards thus: 'He was ice cool, always. He hasn't changed at all, he's become more strange-looking and developed this grand desperado carapace, but inside, Keith is not unlike his 22-year-old self.'

"I haven't changed," quips Richards, "especially the socks. I love Marianne. We've always been good friends. She is a strong girl, absolutely." Marianne loves Keith too. Boy does she love Keith. When I met her in Dublin several months later she talked about him a tad obsessively, I felt. She had just spent a night with him in Paris, he was playing his guitar and singing to her. "He didn't even smoke a cigarette and we were up until 8:30. I made him a vodka and tonic, but our relationship is non-verbal. We were so into each other, we don't get to see each other much. It was without wives, girlfriends, he didn't put the guitar down for 12 hours. If Keith Richards wants you to stay with him all night and he wants to sing to you, you don't say 'I've got to go to bed' and we just didn't. I just thought I was going to vaporise with the intensity of it. He is an old lush, I must say. It doesn't change him, it never does. Where we all came from, we came from a very strong place. Do you know Keith hugs his trees when he goes back to

Redlands? I must say when I came out from that night with Keith, I thought, this man is really something."

It was Keith she first fell for back in the '60s, seeing him as a romantic figure, an outlaw. But after a night of hot sex and LSD he told her Mick was in love with her and was never to know they had slept together. So that was the end of that. "It was just a one night stand," she said with some regret. "Sexually it was a very good one. We do love each other, a very, very real love. He let me see it this last time. I do love him, I admit it. Much as I love him though, he does want his wife there and dancing attendance. Mick is like that too. But looking back now I think that with Keith I could have managed it. I guess I have romanticised Keith and he has romanticised me, when we see each other we are 18 again, we never went through the pain of being together, the friendship never got tarnished. It will always be perfect. I still think he is the sexiest man I have ever met. There is something very attractive about Keith, he has got a fantastic body."

The corporation that is the Rolling Stones is getting ready to take to the stage, to play before 60,000 reverential Japanese. "I know it's only lock and loll," they will chorus, coming right back at them. Another night. Another spectacle. Keith Richards will, as he has done so many times before, live out every air guitarist's fantasy of rock idol. Guitar hero. So I asked the question for the guys. Asked the man who has lived the life. To the hilt. What's it like?

"It is difficult to describe," he says. "Basically you are 23 feet off the ground. What you understand eventually is that it is really a transfer of energy. That adrenalin that passes through crowds. It passes over onto the stage. The more they give us the more we give back. Everything is opposite, except that we have got 30 feet. You are elevated and so there is this whole primeval thing. It is like opening a cage and letting the tigers out. When people are looking up at you it is almost sacrificial. You would have to be really bad to go out there and blow it."

"'ere we go, then," says Jagger, as four honky-tonk English geezers and their back-up performers move down the long corridors and into the cheering stadium, the blinding, glittering lights, and onto the huge metal industrial landscape of stage. Slowly Richards begins to uncoil and turn into Keith Richards; he poses, he sweats, he sneers, he gets down on his knees, he leaps, a war dance, a savage attack on the instrument he once said "you have to caress, not squeeze"—until finally he is bare-torsoed, surprisingly sinewy, riding the riff, seeming to absorb the waves of sound from his guitar, steaming up the chill Tokyo night. 'What can a poor boy do, but play in a rock and roll band?' Quite amusing really, watching the consummate guitar hero, to recall that more than one person watching from the wings has noted that Keith's fingers do not *always* manage to actually connect with the strings on his constantly changing guitars. The night ends with the old rockers, arms wrapped around each other, smiles creasing leathery faces, flowers, the full treatment. "I do it for the glory, darlin', the glory," he told me with a certain sardonic smile on the way out there.

One after another the songs come, a call from another time. They are his children. "I love 'em all," he has told me. "The weird thing is that they keep changing on me. It's not really that set in concrete. It would be like cursing one of my babies if I kicked one out. I'm still nurturing them."

And it was always about sex. Always and forever. Talking dirty. "There is sex," he smiles lopsidedly, "and there is how you feel about it and what you are going to do about it. There is nothing that makes a good song work more than getting laid to it."

And so to England. The reassuring chuckle of the black London taxi. And all the relentless green. And it is high summer. And it's a heatwave. One of those days in England. London has turned itself on. It shines, it glitters. Ornate London, with all its flourishes and cornices. Its detail. Its elegantly proportioned buildings and its bereft housing estates. Its rain-stained statues of its warmongering dukes and lords. War hero with sword, war hero with hand on chest and scroll in hand, war hero on rearing charger, war hero with sabre, war hero surely unable to sire heirs after what appears to be the nasty riding incident sculpted in bronze in the Strand. Sweeping and curved rows of cake-icing terraces. Flowers cascading down buildings, gardens drenched with fragrant flora. Geraniums red in every pot. And the heat, it envelopes you like a glutinous layer of skin. And the density. Layer upon layer of history until the past and present converge and move towards the future.

I went to stay with my sleek and beautiful friend Susan Haynes for a couple of nights while I got myself sorted, my suitcase so laden with books that it took three of us to get it up the stairs, and wound up lingering for months in her chic Notting Hill apartment, her daughter Clare calmly viewing the ensuing antics with a certain amused tolerance. Talk about laugh.

Oh, yes the heatwave was burnin' in my heart. A tree brought back from the Antipodes by an enterprising botanist got confused by the heat and suddenly sprouted breadfruit after 200 barren years in cold Kew gardens. It obviously thought it was back home sunning itself on a pale gold beach in sunglasses with a drink garnished with a paper umbrella in its hand.

Cruising down Portobello Road the day I arrived I was confronted by a large black man wearing a short floral dress. "I'm reviewing the situation," he sang to me as he tap danced off the kerb. He would later be one of two dramatic transvestites in the rental frock shop who kitted me out spectacularly for a frightfully formal ball to which I had been misguidedly invited by a man who was desperately and fruitlessly courting the ravishing Susan. The old get-the-friend-on-side trick. Unfortunately, the friend was me.

By then the large man had clearly finished reviewing the situation; his hair was now a towering blue wig which matched his lipstick and the dress was gold lamé, which matched the rings through his nose. His own ensemble, I suppose, should have raised the question of taste at the outset. But he paled next to his partner who was in plat-form shoes and an off the shoulder green taffeta evening gown with feather boa, reminiscent of Princess Margaret, early '70s. They fussed, they clicked their tongues, they whirled around the shop car-rying rustling confections of satin, taffeta and lace. "No, no, no, darling, too severe, here try this little fuck me frou frou. You shall go to the ball," they cried. They consulted, they teased, they primped, they painted, they tut tutted, until finally they stood solemnly satis-fied with their creation and a hushed silence descended on the shop.

For when I emerged like Barbarella into the lamplight of Portobello Road, my diamantes glistening cheaply, my hair hugely concrete, my sequins spraying light, my gloved arms waving, admittedly, like a Vegas showgirl, my legs unaccountably strutting, I was Ivana Trump incarnate. Now I know why she is always photographed reclining on those leopardskin sofas. You can hardly bloody stand up. That hair-style defies gravity. And when it crashes down it takes everything with it, including the face.

Even Susan's ardent suitor retreated to a safe distance. You don't have to worry about safe sex when you've got a friend like me. They go screaming into the night.

And the good times rolled. Roses in the parks visibly shrank from the sun as the cricket balls thwacked across the parched grass. The only time the sky seemed to darken that summer was when the Concorde flew in like a vast bird of prey descending for the kill and taking up all the sky.

"The thing about England," Bryan Ferry told me, rightly, "is that it is full of contrasts. I love history but I hate the class structure. And yet at the same time I love reading Evelyn Waugh or even Wodehouse. It is extraordinary the love–hate thing one can have. You get these incredible contrasts and tension."

I once wrote to Steven Berkoff that going home to Sydney was like putting on a comfortable old shoe. London, he wrote back, was like 'an old boot with a nail sticking through the sole'.

# High Noon on a Lonely Road

The English crime novel is, of course, quite different from its American counterpart. The body count is lower for a start. The traditional English crime novel is a puzzle, civilised, relying on clues and guesswork. "I am *very* fond of doing those puzzles in newspapers," confesses Ruth Rendell conspiratorially. It is the novel of quiet suspense. They like your classic detective story, the English, with your maverick detective neatly tying everything up at the end by using his or her brain. In his spare time he might listen to classical music or write poetry. This is not the sort of leisure activity you might reasonably expect of a man who deals in mindless depravity, who routinely blows everyone away. Nup, that sort of guy turns to liquor and women to help get through the night. Owing to gun control, and apart from the odd regrettable hunting accident, the English do not generally resort to resolution by firearm. That really brings out the weirdos. Your quietly determined psychopath grimly burying the bodies under the family home. You have to go to quite a lot of trouble, in England, to murder somebody. It doesn't just go off in your hand. You have to really want to do it.

Which brings us to Ruth Rendell. Hugely successful crime novelist of some 42 books and creator of Chief Inspector Reg Wexford, of television fame. But it doesn't necessarily bring Ruth Rendell to us. First you have to find her. This is definitely a job for Adam Dalgliesh. Except that Detective Dalgliesh is probably busy at home polishing off a bloody poem.

The train clacks and sways through fields of freshly cut hay. From the British Rail bar coach, crackerbox houses give way to marble-smooth green commons. And then to wheat, rippling yellow. And sudden fragrant fields of blooming roses. Such intensity of colour on such an English summer day. Church spires rise against the green to reassure that God is in his heaven. We

RUTH RENDELL

reach the Stour valley where the painter Constable found art 'under every hedge' as he painted the inner essence of these flat meadows and quiet rivers, of this summer tranquillity.

Her house is hidden in a tangle of trees. A large and creaking house that seems to whisper and hint at unquiet antique secrets. It is a house so hidden in fact, down such a narrow, twisted, overgrown dirt track, that I fail to find it.

Hollyhocks line the walls of quaintly named stone cottages in her Suffolk village. Ducks paddle through the tendrils of weeping willows that float like chiffon sleeves and outstretched fingers on the silver-green pond. I was going all right until I got to the pub. Having got the train to Colchester and then a taxi, I was early. Fresh off the plane, I naturally nicked into the pub for a thin beer and a ploughman's lunch. Should I have been suspicious that I was the only customer hunkered down beside the horse brass?

The complicated instructions had stopped at her village so I figured she must live here. So call me stupid. Still with time to spare, I found the post office—with some difficulty—down a narrow path, behind a row of houses, and asked where she lived. "Down the road," said the woman behind the counter, jerking a thumb over her shoulder. Taxi? "He's out."

Could we get him back then please?

"Dunno," she replied with thin, tight lips. "Dunno where he is."

Oh to be in England. Defeated by the obdurate attitude in the post office, I struck out on foot. Well, high heeled boots actually. The sun climbed in the sky. The neatly trimmed hedges of the village wilted in the heat. Unlike John Constable, who found such harmony and truth in this redolent landscape, Ruth Rendell finds something else altogether. She finds dead bodies under those hedges. She finds murderers roaming the panelled hallways of these crenellated manor houses. She sees evil incarnate in these cutsie wootsie villages.

On *her* rambles, her constitutionals taken after lunch, the innocent English countryside offers imminent catastrophe, grasping, murderous greed, dirty secrets, duplicity, naughty, naughty people. "I work on place," she says, "because it is very important to people. You need to be able to see it and feel it, to taste the food and walk through the rooms. I walk for miles and miles along the Suffolk coast and think about things tremendously. If you try to sit down in a chair and think like that you will go to sleep."

Pretty soon I am deep in the country. The golden wheat stretches away on either side of the road. My father used to lose us in the wheat when we were small blonde children on a farm and the wheat was higher than we were. The post office lady whose vague instructions I am following drives past with a cruel smile. I have long passed the heavily disguised driveway to Ruth Rendell's sixteenth-century manse. Our boys died on the beaches for you bastards, I scream after her disappearing car. My voice echoes in the empty afternoon. And now I am lost. And late, very late. A lone journalist on an empty road. In high heels. Are those the beating wings of vultures I hear? If I just press on will I make Scotland by nightfall? The sun is high when I finally teeter across a parched field towards the only building on the horizon, a farmhouse. The farmer views this apparition impassively. He perks up, however, when I get out my wallet. Hey, I was a desperate woman. By the time I am delivered to her door and the sum of five pounds handed over, my hair is sticking to my head and I am soaked in sweat. Standing on her doorstep she looks so *cool,* so composed.

"You went to *that pub,*" she repeats several times incredulously, "for *lunch*?" Her kind husband, Don, who is reviving me with tea, seems equally amazed. "You mustn't interrupt, darling," she shoos him away. An unnaturally large ginger cat slinks off with him.

She is a crisp woman, efficient. Precise. Strict. Her wide blue eyes and arched eyebrows give her a look of permanent surprise. As if she has just received some startling news. News that does not please her. I get the unnerving feeling that she is going to tell me off, give me a detention for being late.

But no. She only curls up on her sofa, cup of tea poised midway to her mouth, and talks, with a certain relish, about murder. And fear. Her particular line of inquiry. "We make a mistake if we think that people are always thinking and dwelling in their minds on what they ought to do. The fact that man is a moral being. He is not. Often he is just a creature of impulse. He doesn't think of the consequences. You are driven beyond control or else you are so off-balance that thought or motive doesn't really come into it. You have a gun, you pick it up and you kill somebody. It doesn't happen here though because the gun laws are so strict. It happens in America. It always happens. I think you can quite easily put yourself in someone else's shoes and think about what it would be like to do that. I can. It is remarkable what a lot of motives there are for killing. There is no accounting for them. We all know what it is like to be deprived of something and to need it very, very much. Somebody wants twenty pounds to finance part of his addiction so he shoots somebody for that money. Or he walks into a shop and the till is open so he sticks a knife into the person standing by the till. I used to think that the human race had improved but I don't think so now."

I tell her I am always astonished in reporting crime for my newspaper at how quickly people start covering their tracks. No matter how unpremeditated, how much a crime of passion or a tragic mistake, it is a human impulse to hide the evidence, to put immediate plans for self-preservation in place. Ruth Rendell sips at her tea, her eyes glint. "Exactly," she says with feeling. "In most of the Wexfords somebody has simply yielded to an impulse of the moment and covered their tracks afterwards, but not at the time. There is the disposing of the body and that is always what people want to do. Probably a lot of people do it very successfully. A lot of that happens in the Wexfords. The person didn't really mean to kill the girl but then they have to get rid of the body. I don't have any elaborate plotting. I have had, but not for 30 years really." She laughs a deeply private laugh.

The English have the advantage of their long and violent history for mystery and suspense, of architecture for mood, of early Norman arches and gothic turrets to set a scene. P. D. James's classic *A Taste for Death* is all the more shocking because the corpses are found slit from ear to ear in the vestry of the church by a 65-year-old spinster flower arranger, in the very first chapter. In such a mannered society, with its rituals and codes of behaviour, it is just not good manners, dear chap, just not cricket to go around doing chaps in. In the soothing, peaceful countryside where life continues in its meditative way for generation after generation, a murder is a serious disruption of the natural order.

"I don't know if England affects me as a writer, it is a question I can't answer because I have always lived in this country." The eyebrows are having a different conversation from Rendell. Houses affect her though, they are inherently mysterious. Houses layered with time, with lives lived, with lovers' secrets, with youth and age and death, and families gone, with daily dramas, and disappointments, the detritus of generations, old houses are one of the great literary devices. The house as dramatis personae, stories lurking in all its recesses. "I am very fond of houses," she says. "I am always exploring them. I like nothing better than when I go to see somebody and they say, 'would you like to see the house?'. I do like to live in an old house in a remote place. This house is 400 years old. I am very aware of that."

Ruth Rendell's house is enigmatic, like the houses in her books. A pink manor house; the sort of house, you sense, that has seen reckless romance. "I have owned a lot of houses," she says. "I love moving. I have a house in Regents Park in London, I spend so much time in the park that I could draw a map of it. I have another house by the sea. Nobody knows I am there and none of the newspapers have that number. I work right through there, break at teatime and stop for a few hours and then break again in the late evening. But just knowing people who live in interesting houses in interesting parts of the country is wonderful. Although I have almost done it to death. I don't think in the future I will be particularly writing about houses."

Outside the open lattice window there is a kind of arcadian

bliss, the trees seem to hiss, the flowers growing around the window shuffle, butterflies float in slow motion.

Ruth Rendell drums her perfectly manicured fingernails on the arm of the large green sofa. "I don't really kill people," she is saying. "That is old-fashioned now. People ask me if I have ever met a murderer or ever been in a prison. No. My imagination will do it for me. I have read a lot of psychology and I just put myself in people's shoes and then I know why they do what they do."

In all of Rendell's novels there is a point at which the tension starts to build and things are no longer what they originally appeared. "There are ways of achieving that sort of thing," she says with a certain tolerance. "I know quite a lot about creating suspense. The best novels have suspense in them. It is partly by underwriting, by understatement, by toning down. You create suspense and indeed terror and fear by very simple underwriting. I don't mean sensational bloodiness. I mean awakening in the reader a curiosity to know what happened."

Indeed, even working in three different genres—the phenomenally successful Inspector Wexford detective novels, the Ruth Rendells, which are psychological suspense, and the Barbara Vine books which are serious novels—Rendell's books have always been driven by character, plot and plain economy of style rather than showy displays of lush writing. "I am drawn to suspense, not to violence and sensationalism, but the novel of suspense," she says softly. "I am drawn to the mystery that has to be discovered and solved. When I come away from the writing I need time to unwind from it. It takes me about 20 minutes. I would rather nobody spoke to me in that time. Then I will go out for a long walk and think about it. Think about the next bit of the book. I know that a lot of it happens for me when I am not writing, when I am walking."

"Thank you, darling." She pauses as her husband, Don, a retired journalist whom she met at an inquest and whom she has married twice, hovers with more tea, followed by three more fat cats. Ruth Rendell has a big smile. When she smiles. Ruth Rendell was a journalist once herself. One who had problems sticking to the facts. "I always wanted to improve on reality." I'm with you on that Ruth, baby. Now at 65 she is a one-woman industry. Rich, rich, rich. Now Ruth, if I could just get a few tips . . .

"Would you like to see where I work?" she asks. "Ah, yes, I rather thought you might," she notes my reaction. The room where she writes looks out onto lawn and fir trees. It is a bare room, uncluttered. A computer sits on a wooden desk.

I nerve myself to tell her what I think of George Baker as Inspector Wexford, about whom she has written 17 books. A bit, you know, *bloodless*. Clumping about the countryside like that. Inspector Morse is, well, more romantic. "I like him," she leaps to Baker's defence. "I think he is very good, but he is not how I saw him. George has made Wexford but he is not the man that I intended."

Don presents me with a bag of cherries from the garden. "This is cherry country," he says shyly. They are sensuous, shining, red-pink cherries, overt cherries.

"Nonsense," she then says to me. I feel another detention coming on. I have remarked, unwisely it appears, that it has been said, and often, that women make better crime writers than men because they are more likely to notice the telling detail, the mud on the shoe, the cheap perfume on the tweed. "That old theory about women noticing all the details is always a corollary for men having the spacious long view. I do think men and women are different but I don't think they are different in that sort of way. Women are supposed to write crime fiction so well; I don't think we are any better than men."

Are murders by women more likely to be premeditated? The woman plotting and planning and silently hating for years before she acts? The old arsenic in the sherry trick? "Whatever they say about poison being a woman's method, the newspapers are full of stories about people who use poison, usually a man who is on trial for an attempted murder of his wife by giving her a noxious poison, and they always make a mess of it."

But not Ruth Rendell. She never makes a mess of anything. And my clothes are drying quite nicely now.

To say you are an Australian journalist in certain London circles is to understand what it is to be a pariah. Rooms clear. Polite expressions of interest turn glacial. People run for cover. Remove their hand from the gusset of the Hon. Arabella's knickers sharpish. Peel themselves off Petronella. Go home to the wife. Furtively check to make sure the frilly suspenders and silk stockings are not showing under the pin-striped suit. Hide the schoolgirl outfit. If you are an Australian journalist you must be a grubby Fleet Street hack. You are probably carrying a concealed camera. Ergo it is time to leave. I said now, Jeremy.

Like Steve Dunleavy in New York, Australians have tended to distinguish themselves in the lower reaches of English journalism. The glorious gutter press. This is somewhat ironic since overzealous libel laws prevent the same kind of ribald reporting in their own country. Besides which, the average Australian politician is generally too dull and prosaic to do anything as excitingly creative as dress up in stockings and high heels, accessorise by stuffing an orange in his mouth, complete the ensemble with a plastic bag over his head to asphixiate himself whilst attempting to reach orgasm, as one Tory MP obligingly crowned his career and thus wrote himself into tabloid history.

Australians take the long view that what you do in or on your or somebody else's bedroom, bathroom, dining room table, floor, shrubbery, car seat, or ski slope, is, as long as you are consenting adults, nobody's business except yours and possibly the neighbours'. It should not be taken into consideration in judging the way you run the country. Of course the fact that the only way he can reach orgasm is in a threesome on the cabinet room table, or that he always has a wild wife-swapping party after parliament closes, is just not something the average Australian considers more important than, what? Tax incentives, lower interest rates, post-structuralist theory, the new boat, name your subject. And if they had one of those lacquered Liberal Party wives they would want to swap her too. Perfectly understandable. I'll just take this curvaceous stripper mate and you can have the wife. No worries. We'll sort out the school fees later.

In fact, confessing to an extracurricular affair can be a vote catcher. Just ask Bob Hawke. Onya mate, lucky bastard.

Journalists all know that Canberra, the nation's capital, is just one big crazy pornographic petrol-sniffing sex-orgy party town, but we leave them to it, mostly, unless they really had it coming, because the thought of the average, and by average I do mean average, Australian politician at play is just too unattractive to even contemplate.

The English on the other hand love a sex scandal. A sizzling love nest. Other people's sex lives are a national preoccupation. They want to see the wet spot on the front page of their newspapers. Or so it would appear. In screeching, scandalised headlines every morning. *LOVE RAT. CAUGHT WITH PANTS DOWN. THREE IN A BED.* There is nothing so satisfying as catching a hypocrite in *flagrante delicto*, which is where tumid Tory ministers and errant aristocrats have always been so obligingly helpful in providing the laughs.

It is hardly surprising then that the Australian journalist who has shown such gentlemanly restraint gets dizzy with it all when he arrives in London and plunges headlong into the gutter. Or is it something more sinister? A secret weapon sent to undermine the Establishment. Those fetishistic naughty boys who just can't stay away from prostitutes, who just have to be spanked by dominatrix in leather. Flash, flash go the bulbs outside. For Gallipoli we give you Rupert Murdoch. For the common market we give you, put your hands together now, David Banks. Germaine, that exquisite torturer, we chucked in as a bonus for the sake of standards.

One of the great pleasures of being in London is the quality papers. Informed, considered debate. Wit. Fine fearless writing.

But the tabloids define the word persecution. They hunt in packs. They stalk. It is a blood sport, adrenaline pumping. They have cameras so small they can fit in the eye of a teddy bear and sound equipment so sophisticated they can hear the rustle of the extra-marital sheets from Scotland in a blizzard. They set people up. They vigorously destroy lives. In the *News of the World* people don't say things, they 'leer', women are 'busty'. In the tabloids you don't have sex, you have 'sex romps'. Everyone in Britain, it seems, is involved in a three-in-bed love tryst.

The front pages are routinely splashed with minor soap stars, singers and game show hosts leaving the love nest of the latest lust object after a night of passion. The next day the reaction of the dis-traught wife and children will be faithfully recorded along with outraged editorial that takes the high moral ground at the lowest possible level. BASTARD is popularly succinct, caringly taking the side of the wronged wife whose life they have just demolished. The world is full of love rats in love nests, it seems. And it is the job of the tabloids to track them down, photograph them in their rats' nests and punish them, in the public interest, of course, in a full-scale public flogging. Just ask Will Carling, or Chris de Burgh. They seize on calamity with glee. Send out posses of highly trained hacks to plumb the excitingly dire depths.

In his fine novel *fullalove*, a book about Fleet Street, Gordon Burn based one character on someone he knows. "'Clit' Carson is thirty-two or three, blond, studiedly understated in his appearance . . . At a guess, you would say he was in advertising or poetry, or a popular form master in a fashionable prep school." Clit earns six figures a year, drives a Saab 900 and runs a serviced flat in Kensington for his job—which entails sleeping with the female family members of noto-rious sickos and psychopaths and sometimes those of the victims as well. His job is to 'relieve them of all visual material in every medium for a minimal outlay' and to take them out of circulation. 'The coun-try house hotel is ideally suited to this purpose' so that the opposition can't get to them. Clit is an 'editorial consultant', known to his colleagues as a 'snatchman', and doing a kindness to a distressed woman will never show up in the records. Such are the lengths to which they are prepared to go to bring to you, dear reader, the follies of the famous, the infamous and the soon-to-be completely fucked over.

I was sitting in the office of the *Sydney Morning Herald* one morning, perusing the, er, tabloids, when my friend Elizabeth rang. Elizabeth is, like me, an enthusiastic New Zealander who had, like me, plunged headlong into all the sizzling love nests she could get her hands on. "I have met the most wonderful man," she enthused. "Kind, intelligent, gentlemanly, generous . . . villa in the South of France . . . chalet in Verbier . . . riding to hounds on weekends at country house in Gloucester. And he is a judge." As she filled me in on this paragon of virtue she happened to mention his name. "Say it again." I was suddenly alert and peering at the front page of the *Sun*. She repeated a double-barrelled surname, a name that carried the weight of exalted ancestry, the end result of generations of careful breeding. "Um, Elizabeth," I had to tell her, "your new friend is on the front page of the *Sun*, kneeling at the feet of a prostitute who is astride him wearing his wig and gown, making it abundantly clear she has nothing on underneath. Your friend, I am afraid, has been rather comprehensively sprung as a kerb crawler." Set up and publicly pilloried.

Loyal to the last, Elizabeth later lost her friend late one night in a cheap Chinese restaurant in the back streets of Covent Garden. She nicked out to get a newspaper to choose a movie, ran into another friend, went round the corner to a pub for a drink, and then couldn't for the life of her find that Chinese restaurant again. He may still be sitting there for all we know. It's not like he had anything else pressing, now that he was ostracised.

Why Tory MPs and judges constantly, daily, put themselves in situations, expose themselves so to speak, trawl the kerbs, bend over for the whip, romance the rent boy, compulsively impregnate their secretaries, consort with rapacious bimbos, where the woman, or man, involved can command huge sums from the tabloids for 'tell alls' is a masochistic feature of English life I will never understand. Their helpful complicity is like the journalistic equivalent of S & M. Surely they can't be stupid enough to be expect anonymity. Is the danger part of the erotic appeal? Is it sexual inadequacy? Or is it plain old desperation? And what does it tell us about their thin-lipped high-born wives?

Prurience is what lies at the heart of this once great nation. Smut.

No one, however, has been more persecuted, more thoroughly, over more time, than Paula Yates. When Paula checks into a hotel so does a flock of Fleet Street photographers. When Paula wakes up and looks out her kitchen window she sees not sky and trees, she sees journalists and snappers. If we are to believe the papers, Paula is a kind of louche fluffy blonde witch. A rock star accessory. She symbolises something in the English psyche, something shamefully desirable and morbidly fascinating.

# The Sizzling Love Nest

Paula Yates's full satin skirt whirls angrily as she strides across her bedroom on dangerously high heels and collapses dramatically onto the sequin-encrusted bed beside me. We are in the sizzling love nest itself.

The actual hotbed of iniquity. The supposedly natural habitat of the notoriously scarlet woman. She is recklessly throwing back, um, tea. "Well," she says with bitter sarcasm, "you can see that it reeks of sex and power games, can't you?"

Well, yes, actually. A bit. And no. It is all the contradictions that Paula Yates would seem to be. The contradictions that have kept the tabloids in a feeding frenzy for years. That have driven them to new heights of invective, to daily vivisection, since she wantonly ditched Bob Geldof for Michael Hutchence, incomprehensibly stealing him away from a supermodel, Helena Christensen. Tailor-made for the tabloids, it had everything: sex, money, rock stars, models, glamour, a spurned saint. It was rock shock scandal of Everest proportions. "It is a national obsession," she says. "It has reached the point of Princess Di and I doing alternate weeks. It is like being in the middle of some hideous nightmare."

PAULA'S 4-IN-BED SEX ROMP teased one; SHE LOOKS LIKE A GRANNY trumpeted another when she arrived at a Scottish bookshop to sign her book. She was constantly referred to, witheringly, in all the tabloids as the '35-year-old mother of three'. Yup, when the 35-year-old mother of three left her overbearing husband because she was unhappy she really got them going. She was flayed alive.

The perils of Paula may be, however, that she has simply become the victim of her own creation: herself.

In her boudoir, the cartoonish, pouting, sex-bomb, public Paula is evidenced by neat piles of seriously sex-bomb lingerie on the floor, frilly knickers, red teddies, and a row of at least 10 pairs of identical, extraordinary baby-doll slippers along the wall. Plastic, fluffy stiletto mules in many colours—a veritable rainbow of vamping. The overt sexuality, the wardrobe that is her Monroesque idea of glamour. Her loud and questionable taste has always irritated the English.

And, of course, there are the infamous, much photographed, va-voom breasts. Which I can report, somewhat wistfully, are spectacular and which she keeps adjusting; constantly rearranging her plunging neckline as if she cannot quite believe them herself.

The devoted mother Paula, who wrote books about babies and family values (now shattered, a bit embarrassing that), is evidenced by the train set on the floor and the artistic endeavours and clutter everywhere of her daughters, for whom she has a fierce, strong and sensual mother love. Left to her own devices she would talk endlessly about her children. "I love them so much." She cosies up and shows me photos. "Peaches isn't allowed out of the house, she is too dreadful. She is brilliant, she is the best girl in the world, but she looks like me and acts like me, which is why we don't let her out. She is such a wild little thing, she is going to be trouble. She is our special member of the family who is kept inside."

The disciplined, working mother Paula, award-winning television presenter and writer, is evidenced by the office that is whirring away in the next room. She has written 14 books and has a deal with a publisher to write four novels. "I'm just going to write and get through it. I have always been up-front about being more interested in being at home with the kids, but I always needed money and I still do, for my children whom I support," she says. "They say that I am a crap mother and that I am ugly. My daughter Fifi is appalled. She said to me the other day, 'I can't stand for them to lie and say that you have not been a great mother just because you are sexy.' She said, 'I love it that you smell nice and that you wear those *ridiculous* clothes. If you want to wear hot pants I don't care because you are the best mother I could ever have had.'" This is, I think, where the confusion lies. The bad girl in spray-on dresses, who is also an earth mother and an intellect all in one, is clearly a hard concept to grasp. The British public would presumably forgive her (and forget her) if she dressed in appropriately 35-year-old-mother-of-three clothes, a nice tweed skirt perhaps and those quilted green jackets. That would pretty much eliminate the rock star element too.

She languishes miserably on the bed next to me and we, thrillingly, do girl stuff. Since she is famous for having been one of the few women to have actually mastered the art of taming and domesticating the rock star, I am, naturally, paying close attention. On the off chance. She is much prettier than you might expect, with a tiny waist, peachy glowing skin and bare, perfect legs. She has a surprisingly deep voice and moves around in a rush of edgy energy. I have caught her at a vulnerable, tremulous moment yet she seeks to befriend. Not a lot left to hide, I guess, when photographers camp in your street. During the Band Aid period they rented houses on the other side of the street to keep up surveillance. "When it first happens it is really great because it is such a novelty and it is really glamorous. It is shallow, but it is thrilling. Then they start to pull you down and it ceases to be fun. Then you find yourself becoming what they expect of you because you are so antagonised. I am so tired of it now, I am so bloody tired of it."

But somehow through it all, through revelation after revelation, her fecundity never falters, she just keeps on writing books and having babies.

With her hair, violently strawberry today, scraped firmly back, she is having an extremely bad hair day. But not as bad a day as the rest of her is having. She is having the extremely bad day of the savagely persecuted. "You sort of become like a Jew to a German. I am no longer human."

In fact, Paula Yates is a wreck. As she sits cross-legged on the bed attempting to paint her nails purple, her hands are shaking so badly she has to give it up. "The hand-shaking is awful; it started in the last three weeks and has gotten worse since," she confides, her bottom lip trembling. This is the second time I have interviewed Paula and she is a greatly changed woman, she has a gravitas now that wasn't there before. Pain can do that to a girl. But I liked her then and I like her now. I have interviewed Bob Geldof too, at length. He slouched insubordinate, almost horizontal in his chair throughout, and I found him to be one of the most intelligent and articulate people I have ever met.

Paula too is clever; funny and eccentric. She says fuck a lot. I hate to tell you this but she is nothing like the tawdry homewrecker of the tabloids or the fluffy sex-bomb who did flirtatious television interviews from a bed, playing her platinum image to the hilt. Let us not forget that both her parents were entertainers. It seemed obvious to me back then, watching her on 'The Tube', that the carefully constructed Hollywood starlet circa 1950s image was tongue in cheek. She was *joking*. And that interviewing celebrities snuggled up in bed was done, like any working girl, for the money. "Absolutely," she brightens. "There were so many jokes and it always got so much more out of people. It made people say things that you wouldn't expect. I had Berry Gordy on and he told me all about how the first night he slept with Diana Ross his willie wouldn't work. It is unusual for someone to tell you that."

Today on the bed, however, she just seems hunted and haunted, traumatised, terrified but with a force that is fuelled by anger. I mean, you just don't ditch a saint and get away with it. Oh, no. You are punished by being the subject of a witch hunt. "It is so distorted and weird," she says. "They have chased the kids and shoved them around. When I left Bob, they followed me for four months, non-stop. Apparently they had six teams, so you never would have seen the same car, or anything. The night they broke the story of Michael and I in a country hotel, they apparently had all their photographic equipment in the fire extinguisher in the hall. It was just going off outside our bedroom. They were in the halls in sleeping bags. We had no idea. Now I always think I am being followed; it is like Jack the Ripper; it is paranoia-making. I stopped seeing my friends, I felt like I was contaminated, you feel so poisoned by all this sort of stuff. You have to keep it away from anyone you love."

Perhaps it is because Geldof and Yates have shared every itty bitty moment of their lives with the public in their remarkably candid respective autobiographies that the public now confuses them with daily soap opera. They have shared their glamorous lives like so many episodes of 'Melrose'. No tender moment unexpressed, no anecdote untold, no dirty linen unaired, even the bloodsplattered state of Bob's sheets when Paula met him have been written about for public perusal; they have invited the public in and now they won't go away. They want to know what happens in the next episode. Will Paula marry Michael? Will they have another baby? Or will he leave her for a lingerie model? Is the man she thought was her father really someone else? Did her mother really sleep with the game show host? Will Bob do more dirty tricks to get the children? Will Bob ever have another hit record? Tune in next week.

When Paula's autobiography was issued, things moved rapidly from bad to bloody terrible. Almost immediately, a former flatmate, whom Yates had described as a high-class callgirl but who these days is suddenly an 'unemployed actress', cashed in and sold her story to the *News of the World*, accusing Paula, at 16, of using heroin and one night bringing home two boys, both called, strangely, Nigel, for a sex tryst.

"I mean," she says indignantly, "I have never even had a drink in my life. I never smoked, drank or did drugs." But Paula, the career coquette, has always been accused by the tabloids of sleeping around. And Geldof of being a philanderer. 'Our relationship was completely shut,' she insisted in her book, though she later brought a warring Geldof into line, according to the good old tabloids, by threatening to name six women in a divorce settlement.

And her mother, a former B-movie starlet who now writes bodice-rippers, a role model Paula once described as a 'six-foot red-haired love goddess', had also sold her story to the *Sun*. "I have no idea why she would do this to us; it is so heartbreaking. She hasn't spoken to me since I left Bob," Paula says shakily, near tears.

"The only reason that book came out is because I left my marriage and I left my houses; I left everything. I have had to buy a house from scratch. Most women are not in that position after a divorce; it is entirely economic necessity. Everyone said, 'It was your house, why didn't you just stay put?' But it is the only way I would have got out and I wouldn't have left unless it was absolutely impossible for me to stay. Bob would have been too strong for me. I would never have been able to stand up to him like that, so I had to leave everything. And I am not going to live off some man."

This was, perhaps, regrettably stoic. Yates's girl assistant hovered briefly at the end of the bed. Yates asked her to do the more pressing bills and pay the carpenter for the renovations on what was certainly an original if work-in-progress house, shaping up to look like an Idaho bordello with leopardskin carpets, gaudily painted walls, bearskin rugs, a drawing room that looked like a Morrocan opium den, and pictures of children everywhere. "I did," said the assistant, looking slightly ill. "It, er, bounced." It was clearly one of those days in the life of a girl who was struggling to keep the show on the road.

Suddenly in a rallying moment of gallows humour Paula leapt up and started straightening the many scarves and the muslin which draped the sizzling love nest. The previous night, bawling her eyes out, she had phoned Hutchence in the south of France for a good wallow. Unfortunately, he had taken a sleeping pill. "He said," and she adopted a perfect quavering William McMahon Australian accent, "'rise above it. R-i-i-ise above it'."

This sadder, wiser, stronger, distractingly more curvaceous Paula, clearly in the thrall of passionate love—she talks about Hutchence all the time—is markedly different from the Paula I had met several years ago in Australia. Then, she was in the blissful hyperspace of breastfeeding a new baby, her then youngest daughter, Pixie, whose head was slowly covered in lipstick kisses as she talked. "I do hope Pixie will behave herself," she had said by way of introduction. "I live in fear of a baby deciding to be tempestuous when I'm supposed to be giving a thrusting interview. I'd dissolve mid-thrust if she started screaming." Paula then was very small, unprepossessing and pale; sweet, serene, funny and adoring of her husband. "He's so good at everything," she had gushed. "I struggle along with my writing and then he just goes and writes a best seller. I thought, shit, and found it very hard to be noble. But he's wonderful, he really is." Fifi, then nine, who had disconcertingly read my notes aloud over my shoulder and was now giving me a glamorous new hairstyle, chimed in. "Yes," she echoed, "he's wonderful." Yates had laughed. "He has a fan club at home. We just adore him. We all sit around gazing at him in adoration and wonderment." Well, no more Mr Wonderful. Hutchence gave a clue to this in an interview for *Australian Vogue*. "If people actually knew the truth about what happened . . . and why somebody has left somebody, they'd lower their head in shame," he said.

Such a perfect wife. This, depressingly, may be her secret. The little dresses, the underwear, the immaculately run houses, the adoring, the making his life perfect, the never arguing; she is the ultimate manpleaser. She is from the never-ring-a-man school, incidentally. Well, I guess that rules me out on all counts. I now know I will never have the allure, the wardrobe or the personality required for the snaring of the rock star.

"I did everything and became everything I thought he would like," she says now of why she suddenly made a break from her perfect life. "Then suddenly I was 35 years old and I was no longer willing to be told when I could chat on the phone or redecorate a bedroom. Bob is the most controlling person in the world. But, God, we lasted 18 years and we did so much; I was with him all my life, it has been incredibly difficult."

In her relationship with Hutchence, the endless comparisons with the lissom Helena Christensen have been rough, particularly since the tabloids have resorted to the old dastardly newspaper trick of publishing the most unflattering photographs possible to make their point. "It was just misogynistic, I thought. My confidence has been completely destroyed." She stretches out a freshly waxed leg on the bed and breathes a heartfelt sigh—an impressive sight as the new chest heaves mightily "I can't even remember what it felt like to feel pretty. I am lucky that Michael doesn't give a fuck about those sorts of things, how people look. I have put on two stone and gotten wobbly. I can't believe it. Here I am with Michael Hutchence and I have put on two stone." She said this last time I interviewed her; then, as now, she was wafer-thin. A pathology here, perhaps.

"My new bosom has been something I always wanted." She fondles it. "I always thought it would be fantastic and exciting. And it has been fantastic and exciting because I wanted them so much, but at the same time it has not really done anything for me because I feel like I have just been stripped away; I feel like I have nothing left."

Being destroyed by the tabloids has become something of a tradition in the Yates family. Perhaps she is attracted to the kind of showbiz men who draw tabloid attention, because her father was certainly one. Paula Yates has lived most of her photogenic life in the pages of the tabloids. At an early age she understood the potential power of blondeness. She was, she knew, a glamorous atomic blonde trapped inside a brunette scalp. By the time she was 17 the upper class schoolgirl had simply reinvented herself as a lingerie-clad sex-bomb. She met Bob Geldof back when he was merely a rock star. She had walked into the Boomtown Rats promoter's office in Dublin and sat on his lap. Said Geldof, "This weird girl walked in. She was about 17 and dressed in an outfit of ragged lace, which made her look like a cross between a hippie and a punk. She was small and waif-like, her hair was platinum blonde and she was gorgeous."

Like any self-respecting platinum blonde, she knew how to get her man. In the limousine going to the gig that night she leaned over and unzipped his fly because she thought that was what you did with rock stars. A shocked Geldof held on to his greying Y-fronts.

For the first year of their relationship she stayed in character and in bed. Geldof would come home to find a "dizzy peroxide blonde in shortie nighties, languishing between the sheets surrounded by magazines, detective novels, kittens and boxes of chocolates". She finally got up and got dressed when he informed her, in his inimitable way, that her talents were being wasted, confined as they were to the boudoir. "Why not be a journalist?" he said. "If you write the way you talk, you'll make a fortune." Together they scaled the dizzy heights. Tyne-Tees Television signed her in 1982 for the cult rock programme 'The Tube'; she was televisual heaven, an exquisite Barbie doll who was droll and sharp.

Paula and I are lying down now in the sizzling love nest, swearing and drinking tea, when I happen to glance out the heavily draped window. Sure enough they are out there, photographers, in the street, like flies buzzing around food. It is creepy here on the other side of what I loosely call my profession. Unnerving to be watched like this. Trapped. If only they knew how ordinary it is in here, just two girls lying a bed talking about children and boyfriends. "I have worked on those papers," she says, reaching up and toying with the canopy over the bed. "They are actually like a 1940s movie. They are all kind of going off to raid cut-rate wanking parlours. They are doing the seediest, most hideous things. They are all having affairs with each other, all taking enormous amounts of coke, all pissed as rats every night and all writing turgid moralising horse crap." Really, I think privately, maybe I should go and work for a tabloid, sounds like my scene. "I always giggle or gasp in the tabloids, I very rarely giggle or gasp. It's like I am an asthmatic," she adds indignantly.

Ian Hislop, the editor of *Private Eye*, later pontificated: "I wouldn't have an ounce of sympathy for her. She has courted them all her life, she has been entirely created by them and she will die by them. Without them she would be nothing. She appeared with Hutchence in every nightclub you could think of, she took her clothes off for the *Sunday Times*, she wrote a book about her sex life, what does she expect?"

Yates does not deny that her persona may have been a tad attention-seeking. "I can't wait until we have got enough money to get out of having to be in the public eye," she says. "It's not that important to me, it really isn't. Of course there are lots of perks, but it is not worth the pain."

You would think she might have learnt. According to her book, her father, Jess Yates, was an hilarious eccentric who dementedly played a mighty Wurlitzer late at night in his leaking, decaying mansion in Wales when the lithium he took for depression was wearing off; who kept his only child in an orange box at his feet next to the pedals in case something happened to her; and who made her wear a balaclava with a beret on top at all times in case she caught cold.

Later, her most irreligious father became famous as the sanctimonious 'The Bishop' on a religious television programme called 'Stars on Sunday'. 'One day,' she writes, 'they were shooting a huge, thousand-voice choir of nuns arranged on a large, tiered scaffold. As they began singing, my father was standing chatting to Grace Kelly about headscarves when one of the nuns fainted and plummeted off the top tier onto a large ornamental plant below. My father took a step to the side of the camera. "Keep singing, you fuckers," he shouted. "Keep singing."'

It was a showgirl that did 'The Bishop' in. Once the tabloids got hold of his relationship with a showgirl 31 years his junior he never worked again. He died in 1993. "I miss him so much," says Paula, misting up again. "He was so funny, so outrageous. He was terribly ugly, my father, but he went out with all these fabulous girls because he was so funny. It was good to have known a man like that."

Paula's parents divorced when she was young and it was her loneliness and unhappiness as a child, she has said, that has led her to keep her children close at all times. "I used to pine like a dog for my mother," she told me in our last interview. "When she finally came home I would lie prone outside the toilet in case she tried to escape through the window." Geldof too, had had a troubled, fractured childhood, losing his mother who died when her brain burst in her sleep when he was six. The day she died he developed asthma—a condition that would not lift until he left Ireland at the age of 20. He too, fretted for his mother, talking to her, as to a guardian angel. "I remember sitting on her knee before she died," he told me. "It makes me feel terribly, terribly sad. I look at old home movies and I see this young woman playing with me when I was three. I see her but I don't know her. And I would quite like to have known her."

And so the groupie found the rock star. No wonder they were drawn together, these two clever neglected children, to find shelter together, to make a family, to become famous together. Famous for all the right reasons: charisma, talent, brains, humour, altruism. Then when, as these things do, it spontaneously combusted and imploded, infamous.

Geldof agreed back then when I spoke to him in 1993, before it all fell apart, that their backgrounds had brought them together and kept them together. "It is probably that that shapes our feelings of the family as being inviolate and paramount. We discovered it anew. Paula had this Norman Rockwell view of the family. She is terribly disheartened when she sees our three daughters beating the crap out of each other on the sitting room floor, giving her lip, breaking her heart. I say that is actually it, you know."

It must have been a terrible shock for Bob, when she buggered off. When his fan club moved out.

Yates's book, it has to be said, does have its moments. During Band Aid, she wrote, David Bowie pressed his 'huge hard-on' against her bottom while she was attempting to do a live television interview with Bono. "I hated writing it. I wrote it in three weeks," she says of the book. "It went whoop, like the exorcist. I had never told anyone about my dad and the orange box."

Paula Yates is sitting on the floor nervily packing the lingerie to take to see Hutchence in the south of France. The underwear thing is, according to Marianne Faithfull, very important in getting your rock star. It took Paula quite a long time to capture Geldof because, as he wrote in his autobiography, 'the world and its legs had just opened up to me. I wanted to explore my options because it was the first time I had had any.'

Finally she resorted to the heavy artillery, the old ballgown-in-the-snow trick, turning up unannounced to a concert in Paris. Wrote Geldof: 'I came out of the gig that evening and there she was, standing in the snow, with the Eiffel Tower behind her, wearing a stunning pale blue ballgown, off the shoulder, sparkling with iridescent sequins. She was beautiful.'

Hutchence, too, is known for a long string of girlfriends. "Paula is a great woman," he says. "He is like Cary Grant," says she, "old-fashioned, very gentlemanly and very dry. When I was with Bob I was so frenzied, trying to make everything perfect. Michael is a different kind of person. Now that I am with him I don't feel the same need to flirt and I don't feel the same need to work. He has made me very laid-back. It has taken that whole drive out of me. It has been an incredible feat of will on his part to see it all through. It has been very much directed at me and so nasty. I have been very distressed, I haven't really coped that brilliantly and he has been incredibly strong and so kind. He has had to get used to having a totally instant family. They are incredibly noisy and Fifi is very adolescent, so Michael and I can never use the telephone and we have to live with the strains of Shampoo playing 24 hours a day. I think all of that is a bit of a shock."

As we go back down the three flights of stairs Paula Yates lightens up as we reach the children's rooms. "I overhead two of my daughters talking about it the other day. Pixie said, 'People ask mummy for her autograph.' And Peaches said, 'Yes they do, because she has written a book.' And Pixie said, 'Do you think they think she is pretty?' And Peaches said, 'Nooo, they think she is our mum.' I thought that was healthy."

I hug Paula as I leave. And I wait for the next instalment.

# Fuck Them if They Can't Take a Joke

There is a humour that underlies everything in English life. Irony. Dark, dark irony. Humour that turns in on itself when it starts getting dark in the afternoon and the cold comes up from the ground. The tabloids are mostly engaging, at the basest level they can possibly manage, in that great British sport of taking the piss. Well you do need to have an indoor sport in London, a hobby, the weather being what it is, like darts or snooker or, say, laughing at others' misfortune.

"It is entertainment," says Ian Hislop, possibly the most spiteful man in a deeply spiteful town. He is talking about the tabloids. And he should know. He is the editor of *Private Eye*. He takes the piss for a living.

It is that strange counter-balancing combination of the quality papers, the tabloids and *Private Eye* that make this civilisation what it is. Civilised. By and large. Amused. The ability to laugh, if not at themselves, then viciously at other people. The greater the height the funnier the fall. "The tabloids are not actually newspapers. They didn't replace people buying newspapers actually, they are very inventive, they are a new type of thing that the working classes now buy."

Is that a muffled snigger I hear as I struggle to escape the sofa? A relic of the dinosaur age, its jaws snapped shut when I sat down. Yes, that is definitely malevolent tittering on the wind as I discreetly try going out sideways. The sofa has no springs. None whatsoever. It looks normal, in a shabbily genteel English kind of way. It has arms, a back, a framework, but no insides. Like most of my former boyfriends, in fact. You sit in it when the receptionist says "Do sit down" with a flourish of her hand towards the sofa and an evil smile, and you sink straight to the floor. Then you are stuck. At first you try to remain poised, you try to keep your dignity and remain nonchalant as you writhe, hopelessly entrapped, against the decaying leather. "Ian will see you now," says the receptionist, her shoulders shaking. So you take another approach. You will beat the crap out of the fucking thing. You will wrestle it to death. Bastard. Engaged in this ugly fight with the furniture, teeth bared, face contorted, you are suddenly discharged. You shoot forward and plunge into the wall opposite with a dull thud. That was your head, that thud. Reeling round in a concussed circle you knock over a side table and a pot plant. You have been in the so-called reception area for about 10 minutes and you have trashed it and yourself. You have not even been drinking. Yet.

As I stagger up a dark and narrow flight of worn stairs I turn to survey the damage. The sofa seems to smirk.

When my eyes stop watering and begin to focus they are assaulted by a wide and pulsating flowery tie. Fluorescent flowers, they don't look like any garden I have ever seen. But then I have just sustained serious head injuries.

Ian Hislop jauntily leads me up another narrower, meaner flight of stairs. I start to feel like I have walked into a Dickens novel, illuminated by a strobing tie. He could have a disco party with that tie. The *Private Eye* offices appear to have remained untouched since *Oliver Twist*. Papers piled everywhere, yellowing, faded, encrusted with dust, the detritus and dubious trophies of many years of taking the piss. Notices and ageing cartoons peeling off the walls, backs missing off chairs, walls stained with damp, typewriters gathering dust, an old upright piano, an incongruous glimmer of frivolity. It wouldn't be at all surprising if the odd contributor hadn't fossilised here, covered in cobwebs under some of that paper. Haven't seen George for a while, old boy, he was sitting over there for a few weeks, didn't seem to be moving much, wonder what happened to him.

Ian Hislop sits down behind a desk which is so piled with paper it is unlikely that he would recognise its surface even if he were to see it. He clasps his hands in a priestly manner. "Paula Yates is a slag," he then says, with feeling. "She has always been a slag. That is her profession. Slag. Fuck her."

Well. Here I am at the pumping heart of a great English tradition. A national institution. *Private Eye*. Satire central. And its editor does not disappoint. Ridicule is his job. And he is just the man to do it. "I think anyone is game for a laugh if it's funny," he adds merrily as I warily eyeball the chair he has proffered. Uh, uh, not falling for that one again.

Every second Friday for over 35 years a quarter of a million copies of the slender, stapled together, sophomoric newsprint magazine has dripped venomously onto the news stands. To strike at the rampantly erring heart of the establishment, wielding garlic and a wooden cross. To mercilessly pillory the pillars of society, the posturing, the pompous; the lying, cheating bastards. Wit is the weapon. And no one uses it more cruelly, with more scalpel precision, than the English.

*Private Eye* is merely carrying on a tradition that goes back to the 18th century, to Swift and beyond. "I think what satire does," Hislop eagerly brays, "is tell the truth smilingly, it hopes to educate and inform"—he pauses while we both laugh at this blatant bullshit and I sit very carefully on red alert on the edge of the chair. "The point of the art," he gamely goes on, "is to do all those sort of basic democratic duties but in an amusing way. You just do straight comedy if you are not interested in how it works and what happens. There is a refusal to take political life at the value it takes itself. You don't have satirical magazines in Iraq. They aren't big on jokes in Beijing. We do jokes but they are jokes that are about things."

They certainly are. Local government, business, politics, the media, all up to no good and requiring constant surveillance. They are jokes about uncomfortable things that people do not want revealed, at any cost. Embarrassing things. Private vices. Little things like hypocrisy and corruption. The kickback, for instance, the snout in the trough, is a popular *Private Eye* theme. The things that the ruthlessly ambitious stoop to to get ahead, *really.* "People think no one is watching and then it appears in the *Eye* and a stink blows."

Nup, they are not exactly lining up to be mocked, for a stink to blow, out there. *Private Eye* has a long history of fearless investigative journalism, of breaking the major stories of the day, of sniffing out sleaze, long before any of the other papers. The Profumo and Thorpe affairs were illuminated early in the pages of *Private Eye*. "There are probably 50 or 60 stories in each issue that people probably don't want printed," Hislop continues. "They are not going to say, 'yes I did it' when you ring them up. So there is a certain risk. Often I don't get it right and I end up paying. The *Eye* does two things. We sort of laugh at people and then we run stories. I got into some trouble when I took over and said that I didn't particularly like leg-over stories. I mean I merely think someone's marriage breaking up is not particularly useful. I always try and justify a story. I mean what is the point of this story? What does the sex add? Someone has given you a job because he is fucking you, um, someone has told a lie about fucking someone else, someone is telling us how to live our lives but they are not doing it that way themselves. Any of those stories I will go with. Abuse of power, whatever. But it is better if it is funny."

Ian Hislop talks fast and laughs a lot. There is, after all, a great deal of fruitful misconduct to laugh at among the British orders. Even more hilarious when it occurs among the venerable, the patronising and the condescending. The powerful newspaper editor doing devious deals. The class-traitor Labour politician who has compromised his early principles, fingers jammed in the till. The kinky peer in the country house hotel, always good for a laugh. The standards slipping, dear boy. Crash. "It is a funny country, that is one of its great strengths. The class thing is always good for a laugh, it is part of what England is and it still provides endless amusement for people but I don't think it stops people from getting the sort of jobs they want any more, there was a report in a paper recently saying that social mobility in this country is exactly the same as any other and that the élite is actually more self-preserving in places like France," he gushes, a tad defensively. Well. Apart from the most ridiculous of all, those pantomime horses, those gifts to the satirist—the royal family. Really, really silly, as the *Eye* constantly and pitilessly points out. The Queen is always referred to as Brenda. Prince Charles as Brian.

But mostly Hislop laughs because he is a humorist. He is just a fun, fun guy. Yah. Ha, ha, ha. A humorist in a flowered tie, a waistcoat and an aqua jacket. He could be a sight gag too, but you fear, and sadly, that it is unintentional.

Like its office, the magazine has changed little since its inception in the satire boom of the early '60s. It retains its smelly sock, public schoolboyish appeal and the in-jokes that reside therein. Its genesis was at Shrewsbury School back in the early '50s, where Christopher Booker, Willie Rushton and Richard Ingrams all sat the scholarship exam together. In its early days it was simply smart-arsed public schoolboys having a laugh at other people's expense, xeroxing 500 copies and selling it to their mates in coffee shops around Knightsbridge. Momentum gathered with the Cambridge Footlights of the '60s. Richard Ingrams would go on to edit 'the organ' for some 23 years. Peter Cook remained its long-suffering majority shareholder, standing firm, well maybe listing a bit, through the court battles, the monumental feuds, the lurches in direction up until his death. "He was the ultimate proprietor," snorts Hislop, sadly now. "He didn't interfere at all, all the decisions were left to us, he was a good friend and also brilliant fun. He was the funniest man I knew, incredibly fast and incredibly entertaining. He would occasionally come in and just pace about. I would just write it all down, it just flowed out with Peter. He would take you out to lunch and get you pissed when you thought you were about to go down the Swanee over a libel action. We tried hard not to make him any money." Did he really drink himself to death, I ask, gingerly feeling a growing lump on my forehead that seems to be pulsating in time to Ian Hislop's tie, a distant Bee Gees number, I believe it is.

"Oh God yes," says Hislop, "he had a long period of not doing much. I liked him a lot but he was a difficult man to know, he was quite reserved really. He was great when he was performing but when he was himself he was not. At his funeral everybody said that. We were his friends but we really didn't know him very well. He invented a lot of it."

A small, balding man, Ian Hislop has a great deal of clamorous charm in a jolly rah rah public school way, in spite of his vigorous, bloodyminded invective. He speaks at the top of his voice and with the speed of the busy brain. The frequent impish grin often precedes the punchline like the placard to a studio audience. Warning: cruel joke approaching, laugh now. He works here every second week, doing editorial in the morning and jokes in the afternoon. The rest of the time he appears on BBC2's 'Have I Got News For You', writes essays for other publications and comedy scripts for television. What if you come in here and you just don't feel funny? If you are having a day where you just don't feel like cracking a sneering joke on demand? It's no joke, one would have thought, when the jokes dry up. "We write collaboratively," he says reassuringly. "We do it on a Monday morning. About four people come in and we try not to laugh at each other's jokes because we are very ungenerous. If one does come up and everyone laughs, then we go for that one."

It is in this way presumably that some of the more colourful and enduring euphemisms were coined by *Private Eye* and came into common parlance. Tired and emotional for drunk: "that was to do with a Labour politician". Ugandan relations became the phrase for sex, usually adulterous, somewhere back in the '60s. Will Carling, noted the *Eye* drily, met Princess Diana at the Ugandan Sports Training Centre and thus kamikazied his marriage. "That was to do with a man called James Fenton who was a poet and who was caught upstairs with a Ugandan princess at a party. When he came downstairs he had obviously been doing what we thought he was doing but he said he had been discussing Ugandan affairs. It was an immortal phrase, so from then on it was Ugandan relations or Ugandan affairs. We invented luvvies, of which we are very proud. I started a column called 'Luvvies' because of an actor friend of mine who I think is the ultimate luvvie. It's only a few years old that one, it is fun making up language."

Not everyone, of course, sees the joke. There have been some spectacular defamation actions. And these have been no laughing matter. James Goldsmith—'Goldenballs'—once relieved the magazine of a vast sum of money. Robert Maxwell—'Cap'n Bob'—probably would have won his case against the magazine for suggesting he was taking money from a pension fund, had he not gone overboard in the middle of it. Sonia Sutcliffe, wife of the serial killer Peter Sutcliffe, won £600,000 in defamation, to which Hislop responded memorably, "If this is justice, I'm a banana." At any one time he has around 25 writs outstanding. It costs at least £1 million a year to rock the foundations. It is expensive at the cutting edge. "It would be a terrific failing here if you hadn't had a writ. I mean if you worked here and hadn't had a writ I would probably sack you"—loud laughter. "I was in court two weeks ago. The Maxwell trial judge rang up and said something I had written was contempt. That was slightly worrying because I was in front of the appeal court once and they said if I am done for contempt again they are going to put me inside, so it was slightly nervy. I have an awful feeling they mean it, they have that look about them," he says cheerfully. "I lost four hundred thousand in November, through a libel writ, I had to cough up, it is tax free too. It is a terrific deal we get over here. You sort of cut your losses really. It gets to a certain point. We get a lot of writs, but writs disappear, people go away. A good settlement is fine. Our production costs are not high, this office is luxurious obviously but nothing actually costs much, so we do have money and we do blow it."

Not though, on the staff. They do it for the glory, darling, the glory. The deep satisfaction of subversion. Of kicking the shit out of someone better off than you. The faint sound of breaking crystal in the stately, the hound kicked in the magnificent country house, as the sordid details are dished up on cheap newsprint. *Really*, Philippa, how *could* you? He's the *huntmaster* for God's sake.

"I have a tiny staff here," chirrups Hislop. "Most of them are

30-something, like me, or 60 and still hanging around. I sort of pay them like shit really. Always works. Then they think they are doing it for the privilege and they enjoy each other's company"—ha, ha, ha—"and if you have got the best then everyone wants to be in it. I don't really fire people."

Most of the *Eye*'s stories come from leaks. Everybody leaks all over the place to the *Eye*. Who, after all, is going to pass up the opportunity to see their friends and colleagues look foolish in front of quarter of a million readers? "Most of our stuff is written by people from outside and given to us. A lot by other journalists and a lot by people in professions. One of our columns about hospitals is entirely written by doctors. They are not allowed to say anything about the places they work so they just tell us. We run it all. So do local councils. And journalists. There is too much vested interest in their own papers, advertising and so on, so they just send it to us. If you are a journalist in this country and work for the *Telegraph* you can't write about Conrad Black, who is really interesting, and you can't write about the *Telegraph* board, who own the rest of the businesses in this country. If you work on the *Times* you can't write about Rupert Murdoch, and he is the best story there is. So you end up dumping it on us."

Mostly though, and far more typically, they end up dumping on each other. Never, ever underestimate the spite or the bitterness of the rivalry in journalism. When your correspondent gets home to his/her lonely maisonette after a hard day of trawling the depths of humanity, what better light relief than sinking even lower, stabbing a colleague in the back where it really hurts. Cunts. The 'Street of Shame' column in the *Eye* is satire at its best. Not, of course, that I am salivating at the ritual disembowelment of my peers. Certainly not. Rarely a week goes by when two of its favourite targets, Brendon Parsons and Kate Thornton, are not flayed alive. Like this gem from September 1995, which came only two weeks after Thornton had been taken to task for reporting wrongly, in a 'World Exclusive' planted by rival hacks from the

*Sun,* that Paula Yates had two ribs removed to boost her new boobs:

> 'Hysterical laughter greeted news that the *Daily Mirror*'s deputy editor Brendon "Chucky" Parsons was trapped while holidaying on Antigua by Hurricane Luis.
>
> The bullying Parsons filed such drivel—mainly concerning the heroism of holidaymaker Brendon Parsons—the paper was unable to use a word of it. Upon discovering this the indignant hack yelled insanely: "Then give it to the *Independent!*"
>
> To universal dismay the *Mirror*'s travel editor was ordered to pull out all the stops to get the absurd hack on to a plane and back to safety.
>
> However, far greater danger faces him at Canary Wharf where ex-*News of the Screws* editor Piers Morgan is due to take over. As Hurricane Gormless he is expected to cut through the *Mirror*'s useless executives like a typhoon.
>
> Meanwhile Chucky's protégée, libel-prone showbiz corr and micro-skirted ex-secretary Kate Thornton, continues to dazzle. Her latest "scoop"—that Liz Hurley's contract with Estee Lauder stipulated that she had to have a lip implant to give the "bee stung" look—attracted immediate writs the following day from both Hurley and the lipstick company.
>
> Hence the new *Mirror* joke: "Knock, knock."
>
> "Who's there?"
>
> "Kate!"
>
> "Kate who?" Pause . . .
>
> "That's showbusiness!"'

That is about the delightful level of it. "Yeah, hacks always love stuff about other hacks," says Hislop. "I could probably run about ten pages of stuff about journalists but I keep it to a page because I think the public are *quite* interested in how journalists behave, just given how much power they have, but not *that* interested. It is staggering that editors in this country are much more important than ordinary MPs. They are much more important than cabinet ministers, they have all this power and no one ever criticises them. I think that is one of our bits of public service really, attacking other journalists." Evil chuckle. "Journalists write absolutely disgusting stuff about other people but they can't take criticism. About half the writs I get are from journalists, which is pathetic, utterly pathetic."

Hislop's secretary is hovering meaningfully at the door. "Richard," she says to Hislop, gesturing towards the telephone. Hislop picks up the phone, dials it and has a brief booming conversation, during which, unaccountably, 'Ha, ha, ha, ha, stayin' alive, stayin' alive' reverberates in my head. "I have lunch with Richard Ingrams once a year to celebrate taking over the mag, which I am doing today," he whispers, his hand over the mouthpiece, his tie dancing. "Of course, he has forgotten."

As if as a parting cruel joke, it was Richard Ingrams who nominated Hislop as his successor in 1986, unleashing this small, savage satirist on the nation and thereby causing an almighty stink to blow. Ian Hislop has not been immune; he, too, has been comprehensively pilloried, whipped, stretched on the rack. By experts. The very best in the business. Former *Private Eye* commandos like Auberon Waugh and Nigel Dempster. The tabloids were onto it like a rat up a drainpipe. Hislop was slagged all over town. Flailing for invective, since his behaviour appeared beyond reproach—just the one wife in Clapham, just the two children by the one wife— and therefore 'boring' and 'young fogeyish', his caring peers resorted to endlessly criticising his corrugated countenance. Even the *Sunday Times* lowered itself to such superficial spite as the old vegetable metaphor: 'He is certainly not God's gift to womankind. His lumpish features are reminiscent of those exotic vegetables left for months on the grocer's shelf because nobody knows how to cook them. His sultana-style eyes blink behind huge tinted spectacles and his Friar Tuck haircut looks as if it has landed accidentally on his head.'

Expecting an eggplant with hair, I can only report that he isn't *that* bad.

The élite Old Guard at the magazine were apoplectic that a 26-year-old upstart from a *minor* public school, my *dear*, had gotten the job they had all coveted for so long. Civilisation as they knew it had ended right there.

Nigel Dempster, thereafter known at the *Eye* as Nigel Pratt Dumpster, who left the magazine after falling out with Hislop over a story about Cecil Parkinson, described him nastily. 'I don't think people like midgets, especially pushy midgets. I think he is a deeply unpleasant little man. He is the one and only reason I left. He knows nothing about life, living or journalism.'

Auberon Waugh thundered that he was 'representative of the yob generation which is stupid and can't read.'

But what a tough little cookie Hislop turned out to be. "I'm quite shameless." Ingrams did not, after all, select him for his qualities of compassion. "I was very surprised when Ingrams said 'I'm off' and offered me the job. I did accept within a nanosecond, opportunity doesn't come your way that often. I did revue at Oxford and I did stand up things. I knew what was enjoyable, I just didn't know you could make a living out of it. It is amazing that you can."

Sometime in the '70s *Private Eye* lurched to the right. Richard Ingrams was mild-mannered, teetotal, conservative and deeply religious. "I think I lurched it back," Hislop assures, "that is one of the things I have done since taking it over. Rightly or wrongly the magazine was much more associated with the right and now it isn't. It's back in the middle." His enemies, however—and there are many—have accused him of middle-class conservatism. "I hope so," he gushes, "I hope so."

A Labour Party breaking all its election promises yields a different kind of joke than the Tories and their continuous sex scandals which so enlivened their long tenure. "Adultery is just a way of doing sex," Hislop sighs. "Most people in Britain aren't having sex at all, they're just reading about it."

Not me. I have got myself some Ugandan relations lined up this very night.

In the meantime, I am going out there into the streets of Soho to bang my head up and down on the road a few times. And then get tired and emotional.

# England's Treasure

"If you don't have a slightly gloomy view of things there is no impulse to write about it really." Alan Bennett is sitting in his own dark and gloomy front room in Camden. "You tend to write in your diary when you are down and not when you are happy." If bleakness in English life engenders a great capacity for being silly, Alan Bennett has been among the silliest. He was the fourth member of the legendary *Footlights* team which included Peter Cook, Dudley Moore and Jonathan Miller and which conquered first the West End and then Broadway in the early '60s. "If I was older I would have enjoyed it more, you were too young to really enjoy it. I wrote pieces subsequently that didn't make it to Broadway," he says in a high-pitched Yorkshire accent. "We all did have slightly different approaches. It was happy coincidence. It is like another life when you look back on it. I just stayed on at university by sheer accident and auditioned. If I hadn't done it I don't know what would have happened to me. It all seems miraculous in that way. I thought I was the least funny of us four; although we got on, we weren't naturally suited to each other. Peter and Dudley were glued together, I always felt the odd one out, but then Dudley felt the same way. It is kind of a drug really, making people laugh like that. Even when it is not quite as orgasmic, if you have made people laugh and then you are trying to write something more serious, if they are not laughing you feel it is a failure."

While the undergraduate humour of Ian Hislop is vituperative, gleeful and malicious, Bennett's comes from a more lugubrious place, the working-class North, the depressing industrial town. "There is a kind of attitude associated with the North, about not putting it on. It is being more down to earth. It is quite self-mocking and self-deprecating. Not being able to resist a joke even when it is bad taste."

For many years though, Alan Bennett's immediate gloomy view was of the imperious Miss Shepherd in her van in his garden. Miss

Shepherd was a madly eccentric old lady who lived in her van, which gradually moved from the street outside, to his driveway, and then into his garden where it and she stayed for 15 years until her death, in an uneasy fondly fractious alliance between what she described as 'two celibates'. From *Writing Home*: 'Miss S.'s daily emergence from the van was highly dramatic. Suddenly and without warning the rear door would be flung open to reveal the tattered draperies that masked the terrible interior. There was a pause, then through the veils would be hurled several bulging plastic sacks. Another pause, before slowly and with great caution one sturdy slippered leg came feeling for the door before the other followed and one had the first sight of the day's wardrobe. Hats were always a feature: a black railwayman's hat with a long neb worn slightly on the skew so that she looked like a drunken signalman or a French guardsman of the 1880s; there was her Charlie Brown pitcher's hat; and in June 1977 an octagonal straw table-mat tied on with a chiffon scarf and a bit of cardboard for the peak. She also went in for green eyeshades. Her skirts had a telescopic appearance, as they had often been lengthened many times over by the simple expedient of sewing a strip of extra cloth around the hem, though with no attempt at matching. When she fell foul of authority they put it down to her clothes. Once, late at night, the police rang me from Tunbridge Wells. They had picked her up on the station, thinking her dress was a nightie. She was indignant. "Does it look like a nightie? You see lots of people wearing dresses like this. I don't think this style can have got to Tunbridge Wells yet."'

The garden is resoundingly empty now that Miss Shepherd is dead and gone and her putrid van winched over the fence by a crane. But when she did die in his drive, Bennett knew almost nothing about who she was or where she had come from because she had refused to divulge it.

"I did used to think I had heard her, I got so used to her. When my work was going nowhere I could watch her and make notes." Not everybody gets to observe a genuine eccentric—an arch-Tory, committed Catholic who wrote political slogans on the footpath—going about their daily business right in front of their window I guess. Rather like performance art, or living theatre.

And theatre is, after all, Alan Bennett's business. He is one of Britain's most popular playwrights, described usually as 'The National Teddy Bear' or 'England's Treasure', warm and cuddly, like a sort of aunty. What an insult. He runs his hands through his hair and scrunches his face. "I'm not. I am quite sharp really. I don't have the self-possession or self-confidence to repel people and so people will come and say nice things. I am quite timid, that is why people think I am nice. Even now when I walk into a room full of upper-class people I go back to being a stammering 16-year-old."

He stretches out in his chair, jiggling change in his pocket. The room is full of clutter, paintings, books, beloved objects, pieces collected in the course of an interesting life. England's Treasure, too, has been mauled by the tabloids. Everyone thought he was gay until he revealed in an essay in the *New Yorker* that he had been living with his former charwoman for 15 years. An odd thing for a deeply private person to do, suddenly start mentioning the s-word. "One's personal life is almost of no interest to oneself," he laughs shrilly. "It is ludicrous. I think the public has always got far, far more sense than they are given credit for by the tabloids. Far more tolerance and decency. What you feel is that people feel so bad about Murdoch, it is a deliberate attempt to debase them, to pull them down."

As I leave, Alan Bennett walks down the road with his bike. He is right. He does look like a prat in a helmet.

Emerging from the legendary gloom of El Vino's—once the haunt of the Fleet Street hack and now the haunt of the haunted—one day after the completion of a difficult story and the meeting of an insane deadline, I stumbled, as one does, out into Fleet Street and strolled along past its medieval buildings. Like any self-respecting hack I was not a stranger to stumbling out of El Vino's; it is mandatory, one does not walk from El Vino's, one stumbles—the only possible exit given the quality of the food and wine there. Once, fresh off the plane from Australia, I was interviewed for a job in book publishing at El Vino's, a place that had to be strong-armed by irate '70s feminists into letting women in at all. I do not recall any actual food at the lunch but bottle after bottle of wine was brought to the table as the afternoon changed gear and then jammed. Somewhere around five o'clock in the morning, surrounded by lascivious Arabs in a nightclub down by the river, I was told that if I could get up and be in the office by ten the following morning I could have the job. I got the job but my boss, who doubtless continued this interestingly selective interviewing technique (if you survive you've got the job), later drank himself to an early death. He did not, sadly, turn out to have the stamina he expected from his colleagues, though a number of his hand-picked-in-the-pub protégées have gone on to greater glory. Which just goes to show.

I walked along Fleet Street where the legal system grinds inexorably from the old newspaper offices, and the dome of St Pauls Cathedral rises spectrally above it all, keeping a Godly eye on things, past the Wig and Pen Club, past the Supreme Court and all its antique ritual and the labyrinthine Inns of Court, past the ancient crumbling chapel that divides the road, and turned left into a champagne bar. It was a slow night on a fast street and I was personally welcomed by the proprietor. Frequented by barristers and esteemed members of the legal profession, those sons of rolling acres and hunting fields, it immediately became my local as I embraced the notion of pub life. Your local pub is like the lounge room for its regulars. Or a French farce with the characters entering and exiting stage right and left and the dramas, the sub-plots and the sub-sub-plots played out with characteristic English understatement and wit. The men in their pinstriped suits and cashmere coats always made me laugh, they seemed so pretentious and affected and condescending at first, but then I laughed because they were funny.

Rocking up and down the country on British Rail to interview wild eccentrics in sagging cottages and crumbling spoils of success, spending nights in narrow single beds in grey hotels where the food was defiantly bad, I would return here to regale them with the latest and they, in turn, would devastate with stories of failed career criminals called Keith and Crash and Tel and their bungled break-ins. Or the failed corporate criminal caught in the process of nicking off with the billion-pound pension fund. Not sporting at all, old chap. Then they would return to the wife in Surrey or retreat to their club.

And we picnicked on mid-summer nights on Hampstead Heath, the huge yellow sun sinking, London dirty in the distance. Under sighing ancient oaks, beside beaten paths and trees tangled with time. The smell of long summer grass, the sound of owls hooting, the moon shining on green ponds. Magical mid-summer nights dream.

A notice went up in Kensington Gardens. William was on the warpath and William takes no shit. 'Last week,' the note warned, 'William and Mary hatched six cygnets at their regular site on the Long Water. William will insist on walking his brood uphill to the Round Pond and back again to the Long Water. As in past years, for the next three months the family will be seen during the day foraging on the grasses between the Long Water and Round Pond. Last year, two cygnets were savaged by dogs and one died from the injuries it received. All dog walkers are warned to keep their animals under control and advised to keep a good distance from William, who can become extremely aggressive if he sees a dog nearby, even if it is on a lead.'

Hey, William and Mary rule okay? Better to be a swan around here than to be from a dusky subcontinent, as racial violence escalates. As long as you are in the right park.

# Staring Out to Sea

Sensible spinsters slump in deckchairs along the promenade. Seagulls shriek and swoop across a grey, sagging sea. A sea that whispers palely across sharp, shingled beach. The long evening light, hazy with heat from the day, catches the peaked roofs of the town, glances on white cliffs and dances down the ancient stone walls of Lyme Regis.

This is it, I hum, as I skitter down the steep cobbled street to the bay. This is IT, I silently sing as I skip through hurtling, screeching children and torpid tattooed parents grimly taking the air on the Marine Parade, and fly out onto the seaswept Cobb.

This is where she stood in the gathering storm, Sarah, her black cloak billowing, 'motionless and staring, staring out to sea'. This is where she slowly turned her unforgettable, tragic face and looked straight through Charles, poor doomed Charles. In that lancing moment, in that face from which pure sorrow flowed, he was undone. Shipwrecked by the mysterious French lieutenant's woman. By the shatteringly tragic look I once attempted to perfect on the headland at Bondi during a particularly anguished romance. No one, however, was undone. Except me.

The magnitude of this religious literary moment is somewhat undermined by the strong smell of septic tank seeping across the lamely swelling sea out there on the battered Cobb; still pushing back the ocean after seven centuries. And by the Mr and Mrs Manchesters, pallid and varicose, pulling loaded pushchairs, permed, peroxided and blaring; shovelling fish and chips, flocking into the sea and swarming the sea-wall. It is the summer holidays and the English, unfortunately, are at play.

On the hill above his beloved, maddening Lyme sits John Fowles, fulminating. From the Cobb the chimneys of his looming Georgian house glower through the arboreal anarchy of his garden.

"Grockles." John Fowles is pointing an invisible gun in the shrill direction of the beach below and firing it with flourish. "We call the tourists grockles. They ruin this town for two months every year. And a guilt I have to live with is that people go on a pilgrimage to the Cobb and try to relive the book, you know. A lot of them pose in silly sorts of ways, with cloaks and things, as if they were the French lieutenant's woman. You can only think of putting a bullet through their head."

Ah, yes. Er, I don't think that will be necessary, John.

Fowles lifts his imaginary gun to the busy, busy sky and lets off an extended round of ammo. A thundering helicopter has risen above the trees, menacing the sky and drowning all hope of conversation. "There are two big military air schools just up country," he says, shuddering. "Ark, ark," go unnaturally large and audacious seagulls, wheeling in its wake. "Ark, ark, ark." Fowles snorts. "Herring gulls. Most people in Lyme hate them. They are very big and dangerous if angry but I am very fond of them."

But then John Fowles is fond of lower invertebrates too. "When I was very small I used to love earthworms. Apparently I was often seen kissing them. It used to horrify my mother. But when I think of all those little boys pulling wings off flies, I think it was rather nice that I kissed earthworms."

They are nature, you see. His great, great love. His muse.

'Again and again,' he elucidates in *The Tree*, the elegant entreaty to leave nature alone that he regards as his most important book, 'I have told visiting academics that the key to my fiction, for what it is worth, lies in my relationship with nature. Again and again I have seen, under varying degrees of politeness, this assertion treated as some sort of irrelevant quirk or eccentricity.'

Indeed John Fowles, now 70, is a particularly English eccentric. What? There he sits under the tumbling wisteria, the great novelist, holding my hand, his disregard for his appearance absolute. His hair a stranger to the comb; in khaki shorts, decaying sandals wrapped around gnarled toes, a crumpled maroon shirt suddenly, spiffingly topped by an immaculate cravat. As if he might be about to pop into the jungle for a quick safari. Toodle pip.

And then there is the peculiarly English self-neglect. The

immersion in matters of the mind. The indifference to the temporal, material world. The dark brown rotting teeth, the bandaged
legs and rotting feet, as if he is slowly going bad at both ends.

"Gout," he says, painfully lifting one bound leg. "I wouldn't
wish it on my worst enemy. It has been very, very painful. Bad circulation and so on. Not having looked after myself and so on. It is
one of those illnesses where you realise that you only have yourself to blame. Of all the English kings the one I really disliked was
Henry VIII. And then one day I read that he suffered from it and
now suddenly I am very fond of poor old Henry VIII."

The civilised Englishman in his wild garden; bees buzzing, vines
clambering, flowers flinging themselves open. The Englishman
offers elderberry wine: "It is a good flower." We could be in *The
Ebony Tower*, a typically Fowlesian story of sublime, thwarted
sensuality. The young man, the writer, has come to interview the
great renegade artist in exile at his manor in France, now elderly,
irascible, almost impotent, full of bitter mischief and living in a
shaky *ménage à trois* with two young Englishwomen. 'What he
[the young writer] would finally remember about the old man was
his wildness, in the natural history sense. The surface wildness, in
language and behaviour, was ultimately misleading—like the
aggressive display of some animals, its deeper motive was really
peace and space, territory, not a gratuitous show of virility. The
grotesque faces the old fellow displayed were simply to allow his
real self to run free. He did not really live at the *manor*; but in the
forest outside.'

Like the old artist, like his ungovernable Sarah, like the wildness in his work, the real John Fowles—the spirit not bound by
illness or encroaching age—roams free here in his unchecked
garden, in the wild countryside beyond Lyme, in the tangled undergrowth of Ware Commons, where Charles stumbled upon Sarah
sleeping under a ledge; where ancient ashes and beeches soar and
high grass and rambling blackberries froth at beaten paths.

Sarah slept 'tender and yet sexual' on a carpet of grass and
marjoram in a dell at the foot of the chalk cliff, in the wood that

Fowles loves the best. From *The Tree*: 'I used this wood, and even this one particular dell, in *The French Lieutenant's Woman*, for scenes that it seemed to me, in a story of self-liberation, could have no other setting.'

Self-liberation is the theme of all his work; of the mystic *The Magus*, that flawed masterpiece of illusion and shifting perception, of point and counterpoint. A cerebral game of fantasy written, says the author, in a state of endless flux. "*The Magus* is probably my favourite novel. But it is like asking the mother of a large family which child they like the most. It is probably the one which is crippled. And so *The Magus* is probably my favourite novel because it has so many defects. The thing about writing, one of the things you discover in the course of it is yourself. That is why it is liberating. I am a great believer in freedom, the world must some-how achieve freedom. I am an atheist and I think that on the whole freedom is possible for all of us, but it is bloody difficult."

Published in 1965, *The Magus* captured the hearts and minds of a generation with its thesis of sexual and personal freedom; a cruelly magical story played out by a group of young intellectuals to show that absolute knowledge and absolute power do not exist.

Today, as a work of literature, with its breathtaking evocation of the Greek islands and its beguiling complexity, it still stands. Like his protagonist Nicholas, the young Oxford graduate John Fowles taught English at a school on the remote island of Spétsai; and his gift to us is that he was utterly haunted by one of 'the purest and most balanced landscapes on this planet'.

Repeated in *The Magus* is the theme of the *ménage à trois*. The selfish young Nicholas is enticed and denied by beautiful ethereal twins; clearly a tantalising Fowles fantasy. And in *Daniel Martin*, the most reflective and autobiographical of Fowles's books, the young Daniel shacks up with two sisters and the older Daniel shillyshallies between two women. "I am un-English in that the erotic rather interests me," he says with a sly sidelong glance. "It doesn't mean that I am constantly demanding it personally"—chuckle—"but I do like the flavour of it in all fiction. I am not afraid of the erotic or of sensuality. I never get embarrassed. God knows, I am not ashamed of myself."

Down there on the Cobb things are getting Pythonesque as the Lyme Regis Junior Brass Band marches along, crashing through 'When The Saints Go Marching In', jarringly out of tune; crash, crash, crash go the cymbals, scattering startled beachcombers. The local postman, however, waving his metal detector across the filthy beach, is impervious to the racket shattering his evening constitutional.

And there seems something achingly sad at the core of John Fowles, tactile, touching my arm, as his sentences trail, as he loses the thread and lurches to waffle, struggling to recover himself. The lingering aftermath of the stroke eight years ago that stole his imagination and robbed him of his ability to write fiction.

Something, too, of the melancholic deep loneliness and poignant sense of loss from which he has said all his work comes. "Loss is essential for the novelist, immensely fertile for his books, however painful to his private being," he says. "I think all you create does come from a deep sense of loss. To take that on a literal sense or on a profounder sense, it is a realisation of all the worlds there might be. There could be so many worlds, and some of them are quite enchanting."

Great loss came to Fowles when his wife and devoted companion of many years, Elizabeth, suddenly died in 1985. "I am just about getting over it now." He looks at the ground. "She died of a particularly brutal form of cancer. We knew she was ill, but nobody ever said a word about cancer. We took her to hospital and the doctor took me aside and said, 'Can I have a word with you? I think your wife has about one week left to live.' That was a nasty shock."

There have been others since, but they have not stayed. "I do have somebody now who comes to visit me, who has just been here . . ." he trails off and looks across the trees where the land plummets seaward, as if she is out there somewhere watching.

His friend Terence Stamp, who was so beautiful, so damaged and so tenderly evil as the abductor Clegg in the 1965 film of *The*

*Collector*, was greatly intrigued several years ago when Fowles fell conspicuously in love with a young doctoral student he met on a trip to North Carolina. But, says Fowles wistfully, "she came and went. One thing I have learned is never buy an 18th century house and never try to have an affair with a 23-year-old. It is doomed to disaster before you even start. Never buy a house this size. But I suppose it is the one luxury I have. I don't drive a car, I don't travel, I can't eat what I would like to eat. I don't think I am a spendthrift. Most of my money is spent on books."

Fame for the true artist is an equivocal by-product of success. Particularly if, like Fowles, your work comes from a natural reclusivity; the need to be alone with the mysterious hooded women of his imagination. "Fame is shit. Honestly. I mean it in quite the literal sense. It is the excrement from society, I think." His solitude is vital to him. 'I think you have to keep most people at arm's length, which I do. But don't imagine that authors ever get tired of talking about themselves. We don't. We are selfish, I'm afraid," he laughs mischievously, "but I couldn't stand it every day. I shan't see anyone else for a while now."

He has a flat in London, which he rarely visits. "I loathe cities. I don't get out in London or society at all." He rests his hands on his legs. Actually, come to think of it, he loathes England. "I hate everything about it, it is a dreadfully bound society, it is so tied up."

But, still. Some of the locals in Lyme Regis are so awful that they are strangely compelling to John Fowles. "They amuse me, there are a lot of small town toughs here. There was a famous slip here and a lot of things had to be rebuilt. I got a famous architect from London to design a marvellous plan for these new buildings. There were going to be gardens and all that shit. But the town council sent a notice that said nobody who has not lived in Lyme Regis for two generations has any right to an opinion about it." Raucous laughter. "Absolutely marvellous. That is typical of Lyme. It is a fiercely independent town. It has always been bloody-minded. If anyone is going to object it will always be Lyme Regis."

The fishing boats are coming in now, down in the dreamy

twilight across the bay as the English Channel washes below us, and the greedy, greedy gulls shout and children walk painfully across the pebble beach to greet the boats. A teenage love affair is going spectacularly wrong on the Cobb.

Fowles's vast house seems to shuffle behind us, uneasily guarding its secrets. Paintings lie stacked against the walls, books teeter in piles.

John Fowles believes that most writers are haunted by some primal experience. And at 15, at Bedford School, the fragile boy suffered a nervous breakdown. "They kept me away from school for it. But I don't think I knew what was happening to me then. But now when I look back I think it was becoming school captain and head boy. Head boy at school is an awful situation because you are responsible for the discipline of the other boys. So really every day I had to cane other boys and at the same time we were fighting the Nazis and the holocaust was going on. It was horrible. I hate sadistic cruelty."

His father was a cigar importer with a small chain of tobacconist shops who had literary aspirations but no talent. "I had good parents, for what parents were in those days. But my mother was a weak woman. I don't think she ever questioned my father. I think she was the first person my father met when he came out of spending three years in the trenches in the First World War. I gather he was very ill and she nursed him."

Many years later, on his deathbed and in a near coma, his father suddenly began speaking in strange staccato sentences, talking to an invisible third person about a friend who was killed beside him in a trench in Flanders. This unsettling incident and fragmented pieces of a stiff unpublished novel his father had written about the war would appear in *The Magus*.

Two years of national service in the Marines turned him into a devout anarchist, and then Oxford University changed everything for this brilliant, sensitive man. "It blew away all the past. It had never occurred to me that I had an artistic side, or that the arts weren't rather suspect. The existentialists helped. I was mad about them at the time. I am profoundly grateful that I could get to Oxford."

It was at Oxford that he wrote the pretty much unreadable *The Aristos*, his manifesto, oddly prescient, stating his lifelong and deeply held ideas about freedom and equality.

He was teaching English to foreign girls in a secretarial college and 37 years old when he wrote *The Collector*, the chilling account of a psychopathic clerk who becomes obsessed with a beautiful art student, kidnaps her and keeps her in his basement. This darkly male fantasy became an immediate bestseller. "I remember I could hardly breathe when the publisher said he would give me what seemed an enormous sum, two or three hundred pounds. I couldn't believe it. And then very soon somebody bought film rights, I now realise very cheaply."

Much of Fowles's work is an awed and fascinated study of the female. His men are often emotionally dead, leaden. At the end of *Daniel Martin*, Daniel the disillusioned screenwriter realises that 'It is not finally a matter of skill, of knowledge, of intellect; of good luck or bad, but choosing and learning to feel.' The women who awaken them take on the proportions of the goddess. They are women who can see through people. "I am a feminist really, because women have a much greater knowledge of feeling."

So, in *Mantissa*, Fowles explores startling and sometimes sado-masochistic variations on the theme of feminity, deconstructing the female, awed by her dominant sexuality. "As I told you, the erotic doesn't frighten me as much as most English writers and I did want to have a go at deconstruction. I wrote it not quite as a joke but as something light, the publishers paid far too much for it."

They are all shades of Elizabeth, these women, his lamented Elizabeth, whose death was so hard. "Most of what I have learned about women, which I realise is only a small part of what women are, came from Elizabeth."

He had met her during that magic time, on Spétsai in 1952; she left her husband and child for Fowles and their tragedy was that she was unable to conceive again. Bedridden at the end of her life, she poured out letters and poems full of hate and fury; resentment at the endless attention bestowed upon her famous husband, most particularly that of women.

And John Fowles—the admirer of Jung—dreamed once that there was a luminous woman standing on the Cobb. It was Sarah. That fallen woman searching for freedom and independence, trapped in servitude in provincial Victorian England, pining for the dastardly French lieutenant who has seduced her, abandoned her and condemned her never to conform. "I had the idea for *The French Lieutenant's Woman* in a dream. I think you can have very good ideas in your sleep. The girl I saw on the Cobb was a black girl. I have got Sarah dressed in black, but that is not good enough, I suppose . . ." he says, waffling sadly into the distance. "She is a pre-Raphaelite woman."

The novelist shifts his aching legs, his shining cheeks flaming pink in the sun. Bereft, now, perhaps, of that soaring imagination, the enchanting profusion of words and ideas that once sustained him, but not of an innate eccentric charm. "Sometimes the ideas would flood in so fast I wouldn't have time to write them down. Suddenly you are overwhelmed by the incredible richness of this world which, of course, you have created yourself. The most exciting moment is the moment of creation. Those mysterious moments, you wouldn't want anyone to see you. Nowadays I can go for weeks and not write anything at all. I am trying to write an essay and I am constantly behind with my correspondence."

John Fowles listens to music deeply, you can tell, it streams tremendously through his books. "Well, I always used to write with an accompaniment of music. I used to put records on." He is leaning forward, animated, explaining in his thick, blurred voice. "For *The Collector* it was Bartok concertos. When I was writing *The French Lieutenant's Woman* I was listening to Bach, I was mad about Bach. I was big on Gregorian chants and Greek music for *The Magus*."

And he suffered agonies of grief when each book was finished. So much so that he went back and reworked and republished *The*

*Magus.* "I am sure that part of it is that you do not want the novel to die. As soon as you put in the final full stop it is locked up, it is dead, in effect. And you can't bear the thought that these people aren't still alive." He has never quite recovered from killing off the unfortunate kidnapped Miranda in *The Collector.* "It does hurt you to kill people. You don't do it lightly. I felt such remorse at having to kill her."

I know now how richly imagined *The French Lieutenant's Woman* was, as I walk back along the esplanade of the town that Fowles says had its heyday in the Middle Ages; from the bleak Cobb where Sarah stood, past the somnolent senior citizens in their floral frocks sipping warm beer in the White Lion, the pub where Charles and Sam, his uppity butler, lodged in *The French Lieutenant's Woman.* With his wild, winter tossing sea, his dark cascade of trees and undergrowth on a Ware Commons studded gold with primroses, Fowles in his book created an idyllic world where there is none. The charm of all his books is the tremendous sense of place; he takes you all the way into the long grass. But it is this beloved southern English landscape that he evokes with the rarest poignant power and passion.

Tonight, Ware Commons smells of freshly mown hay. But tonight there is a weird Bible class happening on the beach. Tonight, fat white legs are crossed as hyperactive children and their parents sit with bad posture and a man explains the Bible with great fervour using a whiteboard. The callow youth of the town lurch down the esplanade red-eyed and clutching bottles of liquor. And back at my hotel with its mean and narrow bed (dinner inclusive, dogs £4 extra a night), the dining room doors have slammed shut sharply at eight. And all that is left is a lone old lady who snores in a chair in the corner of the lounge.

# Blowjobs on the A3

The dirty old river is changing from brown to black as it rolls into the malingering dusk. Fat seagulls cling to its swelling surface like crumbs on a wet tablecloth. The egg-shell dome of St Paul's Cathedral, rainwashed and pious, hovers celestial pink, bathed in the toxic Waterloo sunset. Red buses rumble and lurch across Waterloo Bridge.

Down the dirty river the ornate serrated roofs and turrets of Westminster and Whitehall gather their guilty secrets and slowly disappear as the sky fades from exhausted blue to London night. 'As long as I gaze up at Waterloo Sunset I am in paradise. Sha la la.'

As a teenager Ray Davies stood here and watched the high tide nearly flood the banks of the Thames. 'The water was a bright brown; almost red. This was probably caused by pollution but it gave the impression that the water was like blood flowing through a giant vein that led to the pumping heart of the Empire,' the composer and singer of the Kinks wrote in his autobiography *X-Ray*. 'I felt that there was a bigger tide coming that would completely flood the banks and submerge the Houses of Parliament. This was a tide of reality and change that was soon to turn England on its head.' This is where Terry met Julie at Waterloo station every Friday night and walked across the river as darkness fell. 'Terry and Julie cross over the river, where they feel safe and sound' go the lyrics to one of the great '60s songs, 'Waterloo Sunset', on my Walkman, as joggers and walkers and cyclists sniff the warm summer wind on the bridge, and I palely loiter in the laneway, having A Moment. 'Waterloo sunset's fine.' Cue in the chorus of female back-up singers here.

But Ray Davies has just snapped his swizzle stick. Clean in half. Snap.

"*Blowjobs?*"

A smile smears slowly over his face. "Blowjobs." The smile

slithers. It is somewhere round the ear region when it broadens into a wide grin. A famous grin. That famous gap between the teeth now bared in my direction. "Er, yes." I clear my throat. I am blushing. I can feel the heat rising. Shit. How uncool. "I gather from your book that it is true what they say about rock stars and, ah, you know, well, blowjobs."

The smile gets dreamy. He is having A Moment. He is somewhere in the mid-'60s. It is London. He is a famous pop star. He has had seven hits in a row. He is 22 years old. He is coming off the stage. A girl with lacquered hair is waiting. 'I considered it to be part of the job,' he wrote of the ritual of the groupie and the rock star. 'Perhaps if I hadn't I would have been branded a queer.'

Davies reluctantly zeroes back to the present. The rather less tantalising present, a beer garden in Guildford. He sips his beer. "I think it started at the Filmore gigs. But not all rock stars like blowjobs. For the most part a rock star on tour just wants to have a drink and go to sleep. I think the supporting people were more into the blowjobs and the toot. The roadies who will say to girls 'no blowjob, no backstage pass'. They work very hard for a start. The person who is the focal point is usually shaking hands with people and socialising afterwards. I remember a famous groupie in the States in 1980. It was almost like getting an appointment with the Queen. She wanted to meet me in a bar. She had been with everybody, Jimi Hendrix, Cream, everybody. I was the one conquest she hadn't had. I had to go and meet this wretched woman. But I passed because I didn't want to be another notch." Davies notices half a swizzle stick in each hand. This has clearly been on his mind for years. He looks doubtful. "I *think* I did the right thing. There were women who would walk up to the dressing room and say 'where's the cock?'."

"Um, were they interesting women?" I ask, attempting to recover the situation. "For the most part they were quite interesting. I found them fascinating." Dirty laugh.

Suburban Guildford, Surrey, is not Waterloo Bridge. It is not a landmark. It is not romantic. It got bombed in the war. It is a boring town. Davies, now 50, leans across the plastic outdoor table at the faux-tudor Guildford Travel Inn, to make himself heard above the traffic screaming past on the A3 and a pneumatic drill which is creating a vertebrae-dislocating stereo effect on the other side. The earth is moving, yes, but for all the wrong reasons. Running shoes, jeans, bomber jacket; bulging tendons in the long neck; a neck still scarred from a childhood accident. Big, beak nose; strong face, exaggerated features. The sort of beak you could imagine on an eagle cleaving the horizon looking for fresh road kill. Long, fluffy, hair, receding hairline. The old rocker special, that hairstyle.

In his book, Ray Davies used a shifting literary device and two personas to tell his story. He was just 19 when 'You Really Got Me' went to number one and made him famous. In skintight hipster trousers, the Kinks rapidly became the pre-eminent band in the first wave of British music, eclipsing, for a time, both the Rolling Stones and the Beatles. They caused teenage riots, auditoriums got trashed. Songs like 'Sunny Afternoon', which satirised the upper classes, symbolised '60s London and the sudden celebration of the working class. 'The taxman's taken all my dough / and left me in my stately home / lazing on a sunny afternoon.'

In his book a 19-year-old is interviewing Ray Davies as an old man, brooding, bitter, difficult, at the end of his life. "I took myself out of the book, in a sense, to put myself in it." He portrayed himself as shattering easily, subject to fits of paranoia, insomnia, rattling insecurity ('the most insecure of the insecure') and anxiety, which has caused him to act real peculiar, to take to his bed, and on one impressive occasion to throw the television in a gas oven when he saw himself singing 'Dedicated Follower of Fashion' on 'Top of the Pops'. 'The cord was still attached to the wall and through the glass in the oven I was still performing.' 'Oh, yes he is / oh yes he is . . .'

"I write on my nerves and on my emotions," he says now, "and I think it is inevitable that at some point they should feel the strain a bit. And then I suppose the brain gets confused, I don't know what is happening, I feel disjointed, nothing connects up."

When he was a child, the seventh of eight in a big, chaotic working-class North London family, he was a difficult child, a loner who simply stopped talking when his elder sister died. "I withdrew from the world, it didn't exist for me." Somehow his mother understood his distress and tried to help him, even with all those other children. "She was typically hard, she was quite hard. She didn't scream at us too much, she had no need. She was quite a good aim with a broom. She would throw the broom. When she had me she was 42. She was quite a good aim with kitchen utensils too. By that time she couldn't get around too fast, so we used to dodge in and out. If she used to corner us at some point then we would get it, yeah."

There were times at the height of stardom when he would refuse to come out of his hotel room. "I wouldn't open doors, I seem to recall, I just locked myself in." This is a man who knew how to throw a tantie.

"So you were an arsehole? A pain in the arse?" I sensitively ask the man who wrote 'Lola'. Going really well here, Susan. "There's no 'were' about it, I am an arsehole." Joke. "I was afraid to open doors, especially hotel doors." Today, just quietly, he is doing an excellent impersonation of being good-natured and amused, sardonic, gentle. Normal. In spite of his own admissions of quivering neurosis and bad behaviour.

And rather endearingly human in admitting to going on benders when his relationships break up: "I would rather go on a bender and get over it than live through it." We nod tacitly. I am not exactly a stranger to the old heartbroken bender myself. Playing records over and over. Well, you do get over it quicker. You feel like shit, you gnash your teeth, you lose weight, you howl at the night sky, and then you get over yourself.

That would make quite a few benders for Ray Davies. When Chrissie Hynde of The Pretenders dumped him for Jim Kerr of Simple Minds, in Australia, he first heard about it from the newspapers. He was devastated. He never spoke to her again. But that wasn't as bad as when his first wife left him, taking his two daughters. Bit of a drama queen over that one. During that particular bender there were two suicide attempts, narrowly averted by having his stomach pumped. At a gig in a stadium, he told 17,000 people he was retiring from music because it had ruined his life. And then, theatrically, he collapsed.

"She had left me. I blamed it on the music industry. It was funny," he says of that Christmas spent going round and round on the underground drinking beer. "It was even funny at the time. But there were a couple of years build-up to it, the butterflies in my stomach, the anxiety whenever you are around each other. Horrible. I had been in the music industry straight from college. People could tell me how to go on tour, how to do photo sessions, or how to be on TV, but I didn't know how to handle personal relationships." He shudders and laughs. Kind of. He is now married to a ballet dancer.

"Love is very important to me"—hollow laugh—"obviously. The trouble is when you fall head over heels with someone and you just lose all control. Your ideals go out the window. When you get overpossessive about it and you get overanxious about it, you are just killing it. If you fall in love with someone and they are not what you imagine them to be, then you are only going to be disappointed down the line. If you go into that relationship saying, 'I am just going to have this fling, I am going to imagine that he or she is the greatest person and I am going to forget these negatives', if you imagine it like that, and that it is going to last for a month, you won't get too hurt down the line."

In fact, much of the time he was a rock star, he was a suburban husband. What a *drag*. And his songs about 'leaking kitchen sinks' and 'roast beef on Sundays' reflect the ordinariness of life in the suburbs of London, no rich symbolism here. "They were simple songs, but they said a lot. We made impressionistic records. People picked up little subtexts and bits of information through the harmonies. But they weren't very deep. Suburbia was and always would be a major influence in my writing. I do have a great feeling for London." He is yelling now as peak hour hits the A3.

Ray Davies and his brother Dave began performing at drunken family parties in the front room. Everybody had a party piece. His often-unemployed father would do 'Minnie the Moocher'. "Eventually it would be Dad's turn, and he would stagger over to the piano and belt out his song. He was often so drunk that he would not so much sing the words as assume the attitude of the lyrics so that an impression of what they meant came across. Then he would trip over the carpet during his hoochie-coochie dance routine, thus bringing the performance to a premature end."

With Dave on guitar, 'You Really Got Me' was written on the old piano in the front room, "because all the important things happened here. All the family parties and singsongs had contributed in some mysterious way."

Soon he and Dave had formed the Kinks and were surrounded by suave spivs, strutting wide-boys and gobbling groupies, travelling up and down Britain, arguing, in the back of a van. Dave was particularly feral, fighting, fucking, drinking. The fights on stage were notorious. Beer bottles were more likely to be hurled from the stage rather than the other way round. During one famous fight in Cardiff, Dave demolished the drummer Mick Avory's drum kit. Avory retaliated by emerging from the wreckage wielding a cymbal stand and knocking him unconscious, nearly garotting him. The venomous kinship of Ray and Dave Davies is a long-running show-business soap opera. Ray once offered his younger brother to a gay retired major, David Watts, in return for his fancy house. That inspired the song '(I Wish I Could Be Like) David Watts'. Dave has called his brother 'cruel and creatively draining' and 'miserly'. When I tell him Dave's loutish behaviour could only be expected from an oversexed adolescent who suddenly had money and could have any woman he wanted, he gives me a questioning sidelong glance. "You can only keep that excuse up for so long, can't you?" Then softens: "I think he was driven to it. Like all these things, there is a cumulative effect. If you do things when you are young it can only escalate from then on."

But they celebrated their time, their youth. "Our songs captured a moment." And there was innocence too. They were so young. "I was very confused when it first happened. I went through a few years of real concern because I liked it but I didn't understand it. I am very introverted and I wouldn't turn up for interviews." Later would come massive law suits and recriminations. "Everybody made money and did the best deal possible because they thought it would be over in a year. They didn't think about long-term careers in those days. A lot of musicians got stiffed. Our back catalogue is still selling amazingly well. We don't get very much money from that. Nobody thought the band would last, they just thought the industry was having a good flush season. Managers would say 'just give us another hit', that went on and on and on. Until I reached a point where I just couldn't keep aiming towards something I didn't believe and I just couldn't see my way out of it." And the fall from grace. Or, in the perverse Kinks' case, the kamikaze from grace. Davies spent time writing grandiose musicals, getting self-indulgent and alienating practically everybody. In his book he expressed his image of happiness. "Loneliness without desperation. Work without frustration. Love without the fear of it being lost."

"I was never a sex symbol," he smiles seductively now. "It wasn't my sole purpose in life to be fancied. That really worked for me in the long run. I didn't come across that dreadful time when I confronted myself in the mirror and saw that I was washed up. How awful."

They were dead impressed in my local, all those lawyers and lawyerettes, when I arrived with my friend Steven Berkoff. He was rehearsing *Salome* round the corner in the Aldwych and had come out to play. Suddenly, everybody wanted to know me. Pretty girls in suits kneeling down beside my chair, trying frantically to remember the name of the close friend they just happened to be chatting to, furtive eyes flicked at Steven. That always happens with Steven.

I remember a literary party in Sydney. A book publisher smarmed up like I was his best friend. "Susan, lovely to see you, how are you?" he said, holding his hand out to Steven. A man who, the last time I saw him, had made a withering remark about an article I had written. There was no love lost between this man and myself. Next thing, he was all over Steven like a cheap suit, handing him his card, quoting his plays, "You simply must publish your next book with me." It was pathetic. Next time I saw him, sans Steven, I was back to being invisible. It was business as per usual. The man looking over my shoulder for someone more important in the room. Celebrity. It brings out the worst in people.

But it is not just celebrity with Steven. It is his physical presence. He is a gleaming and arresting presence in any room he enters.

"No one wants my stuff," he told me that night over dinner in Covent Garden, vulnerable, hurt. London brings him down but he needs it. It fuels him and his work. And in his turn, he kicks the shit out of London. In Sydney, he lightens up. A bit.

# ■ A Scream of Pain

Steven Berkoff is at the wheel of a white sports car. Flying along. Nostrils flaring in the breeze. Top down, wide open, here we go now. Up the winding road to the sea. It is tempting to say that the warm wind is in his hair as he rides through Sydney in a sports car. Well, his shorn, lamented hair. But no, alas. He is wearing a cap pulled low. Face in shadow. That extraordinary face. The light that comes off the skin. Planes and curves and angles.

Steven Berkoff is slouching forward in the seat. Savouring the potency of this day. Eating up the open air, thick with promise, the sea, the sky, the unfolding frangipani. As if he seeks to absorb the fragrant essence, the sensuality of this city, somehow, through the skin. "I like to get a city inside me," he says. "I like sniffing in all the corners."

Complacent, congenial, content. Like a large dangerous lion lolling in the sun after a kill, claws sheathed, momentarily benign.

Because there has always been that quality about Steven Berkoff. Dangerous, menacing, the scent of towering rage. Of festering fury. It informs all of his work. That unnerving possibility of imminent apocalyptic explosion. No survivors. Eyes flickering, facial muscles flinching, black electricity. Scary on the stage. "It is passion," he says of his power.

You glimpse it in his daily interaction. The continual struggle to push back the immense frustration of living in a world that is slower, duller, less inclined towards magnificence. Moody, complex, turbulent. Ever vigilant lest those unseen enemies—banality and apathy—creep up on little cat feet to ambush him.

But as forest gives way to open sea there is one crucial difference. The lion's paw never does lash out. The fat cat prefers, instead, to purr. It has become something of a ritual, this drive to Palm Beach. The instinctive dash of a disoriented man to the sea; a man who has passed through several time zones to be here with us today.

## ■ STEVEN BERKOFF

Riding sidekick to him is like being permanently in the front row of a Berkoff play. A less exaggerated version perhaps, but outsize anyway; the mind constantly roaming, the performance shifting, the accent always altering to illustrate the vignettes of his life, the voice silky and deep then suddenly something else. A fascinating work-in-progress. An everlasting one man show. Acting all the time. Testing, pushing, furtively flicking watery blue eyes to gauge the audience. Even an audience of one.

"You've mellowed," I tell him as we sit on the sand eating fish and chips. No, he counters, gazing out at the bucking sea, he is angrier than ever. Still angry as hell at 'moral turpitude'. But there is an uncertainty about him, on this day, that I have never seen before. As if he has been somehow humbled.

He was drinking in the sea and the sky the first time I saw him, in fact. That and rum punch. That tremendous appreciation of place, the ability to be fully in the place that he is in. On location in Fiji for a film about Errol Flynn that was never released. Sitting beside a coral lagoon, as was his custom, for cocktails at a gold and scarlet sunset, he was suddenly overcome with emotion. Three burly Fijian resort employees who were strumming ukeleles and singing in harmony became his accompaniment and chorus as he opened his arms as if to embrace the universe. "Being in this place, I can see how simply wondrous life is," he shouted as he got on a roll. "I think how marvellous the cycle and the mechanics of the universe are. I see this and I think what a shame it is that people are not a little more civilised and do not look outside their greedy, mendacious and stupid, hypocritical lives." Subsiding into a plastic chair. "I think I am going through menopause," he confided theatrically. Well, he is a famous and consummate dramatist, after all.

Steven Berkoff has always been a man of classical proportions. But he seemed more dangerous then, back in 1990, marooned on a South Sea Island in an unmistakable turkey. Maniacal. Fulminating. As if he might soon split his own seams. Listening to him on the subject of England was like standing helplessly on the slopes of an erupting volcano. The veins stood out on his neck as the venom poured from his mouth. "I would have loved to have lived in a bigger country with a bigger heart and soul and spirit and got involved in the big themes. People in England aren't involved with the big themes, they are all so kind of bitter, twisted and esoteric. England is twitty; inexorable boredom and small minded pettiness. It reminds me of a can of worms that fishermen have and they're all moving around feverishly getting nowhere. They are weighed down by their traditions, crushed by them." Words that seemed to resonate and hang in the heavy heat of the tropical afternoon.

This is Berkoff in interview mode. For reasons best known to himself he finds it necessary to turn into a complete wanker when a microphone is put in front of him. To fill his lungs and roll his r's in a loud declamatory rant; to become BERKOFF, the *thespian*. To speak in thundering arias as if he were addressing a sceptical first night audience at the National Theatre. Revving it up, winding himself into a monologue so over the top as to be in orbit. Like the Elizabethans, he admitted in his autobiography *Free Association*, he likes a long speech. With female journalists he can be like a cat with a mouse. This persona has, it needs hardly be said, led the British press to mercilessly take the piss. 'When you interview Berkoff,' noted Lynne Barber in the *Daily Telegraph*, 'you are never at any point required to speak. All that he requires is that you sit still and admire.' I thought it rather a shame, really, that first tirade, that such grandiloquence should fall only on the ears of one journalist and a startled mongrel dog snuffling across the lawn.

Seemingly unware that he offers himself up for ridicule, he kicks back, hurt. Aggression that has reached the point of trench warfare. "Anything that is indulgent is frowned upon. Anything that has sensual input or some effect that is generous and heartfelt is abhorrent, sneered at," he says cheerfully and without conviction one morning over coffee and Turkish toast in Kings Cross. In 1995 he successfully sued *The Times* and Julie Burchill for calling him ugly, not once, but, gasp, *twice*. He even took on the almighty Frank Rich of the *New York Times*, a man capable of closing a show overnight. And he famously threatened to kill the theatre critic from the *Guardian*—for saying his beloved *Hamlet* was 'fatally miscast'—so convincingly that the police were called. "They just thought we were a couple of pansies from the theatre," he snorted in an interview with me on Bondi Beach in 1992, still unrepentant. "Critics are a kind of toilet roll. They become like sadists and worn-out old tarts. You wouldn't write that vindictive, nasty criticism where I come from or you'd get a punch in the face."

Perhaps it is testosterone, all that Attitude. Certainly it is a bravura performance. Because if you were to peel away the layers, strip back the masks, cast off the posturing and braggadocio you would probably find a small, shy, Jewish boy, bullied in the playground, berated by his father, unhappy as hell. 'I was desperately lonely at school,' he confessed, tellingly, in *Free Association*. 'That sort of need for friendship and affection makes schoolboys turn from you.'

At his most pretentious and stentorian, playing the role of actor, he is almost a parody of the worst aspects of the ruling classes he so affects to despise. Hard to tell, though, how much of that stuff is tongue in cheek. This is, after all, a monster of his own creation. Once he became an actor, by his own admission, he systematically eradicated all traces of his background and invented somebody else. Someone rich and famous. East End meets chutzpah and mutates into something else altogether. In unguarded moments when the veneer wears thin he seems only a heartbeat away from the heavily Brylcreemed, unsure adolescent amid the casual territorial violence of the East End, who would strut his stuff in a sharp suit, skirmishing, scabrous and profane, and beyond that to the outcast Jewish boy so desperately excluded in the playground.

"I did it," he said in mild amazement one night as we sat in the smoke haze of a Sydney pool hall after he had dispatched the balls with ruthless efficiency, a killer on the baize, legacy of that frittered youth. "Here I was, an uneducated slob, tossed out of school at

14, interpreting the great works of the century, designing it, acting it, at the National Theatre." He was gleaming that night, I remember, in the dim dirty light, the face filled with shadows, fluorescence playing tricks on the trees outside.

But then, but then again, the private Steven Berkoff bears almost no resemblance to any of those poses he strikes in public. Then, he is a kind man. A civilised man. A man who can summon sumptuous charm; generous, tender, playful, funny, hypersensitive, often depressed, always negotiating his angst. Mature angst, tortured genius angst. Weighed down by the capacity to feel the tallest love, the highest hate, the most profound pain, but condemned to live in a world that finds honest, unleashed emotion embarrassing. "I get attacked for the things I write," he told me, as the waves bowed and broke in long, clean lines on Bondi Beach, "but the best things I write are written out of huge vehemence, an extraordinary belief. If I censor myself I find that I don't exist anymore. A good 90 per cent of my work has been stimulated by pain." The agony on that occasion, as I recall, when he brought *Salome* to Sydney, was woman trouble. Agony which even in the alcoholic anguish of my own latest romantic catastrophe would have me weeping with laughter as he acted out all the roles of his trouble to his audience of one lying helplessly on the sofa in his hotel room. Because way down past all the pain, all the unhappiness, and underlying everything he does, is robust satirical humour. Survival in the East End depended, above all, on being entertaining.

Only once have I glimpsed one of his famous tantrums. And I was very glad he was in Los Angeles and I was in Sydney when it happened, I'll tell you that for free. When he screamed toxic abuse down the phone it was awesome. Pure malevolence that seemed to snake down the phone, wrap its fingers around my throat and press hard against the windpipe. Windows rattle, dogs cower, babies cry. I heard several interesting new ways of describing female genitalia that day. Then just as suddenly as it erupted the tirade was gone, over, forgotten. "Right," he said into the shaken silence as if it had never happened, "got that off my chest. What do you want to talk about?"

His father too, it might be noted, was subject to 'enormous screaming rages'. Berkoff projects a warrior stance, one suspects, learned in a swaggering adolescent apprenticeship in the East End, in order to shield his vulnerability. Which, as it turns out, is considerable. Fear of exposure of weakness. Egotism concealing diffidence. Said Joseph Pap, who first invited him to direct *Coriolanus* in New York, "As an artist he is very vulnerable. He gets himself hurt. There is always tension on the stage when he is on it."

In private he can be defencelessly open about the peculiar daily obsessions that torment him and the dull ongoing anxiety of his existence; those kvetchs that lurk like poisonous snakes in the long grass, eager and waiting to bring him down. 'It is the demon that wishes to taste your blood and sucks at your confidence,' he wrote in the author's note to his midlife play *Kvetch*. 'You may want them to go away and shout at them, confess them to shrinks or drown them at birth in drugs, but they will always return in some form or other.'

However grim and painful his background might have been, it became the imprint for his life's work, exploited, now, to the max. It all came pouring out in his first play, *East*: The monumentally wasted adolescence, the terrible theatricality of the street, the pugilistic push against poverty. 'Why don't we chat up classy snatch? Why is it that we pull slags?' 'We pull what we think we are, Mike . . . '

'A scream or a shout of pain,' he wrote about this play for *The Collected Plays, Volume I*. 'It is revolt. There is no holding back or reserve in the East End of youth as I remember . . . you lived for the moment and vitally held it . . . you said what you thought and did what you felt. If something bothered you, you let it out as strongly as you could.' It is there in Sylv's fighting Speech of Resolution as she dreams of getting out: 'We will not end our days / In grey born blight, and stomp / Our hours away in fag-end waste.'

Winning a scholarship to the hardly illustrious Webber Douglas Academy of Dramatic Art undoubtedly saved Steven Berkoff from god knows what. Or perhaps, more accurately, society from Steven Berkoff. By then he had had a hundred soulless jobs in six years and had already been before the juvenile courts for stealing. He once joked that he would avoid jail if he could possibly manage it because he wouldn't be able to stand 'the wardrobe'. The idea of a rampaging Berkoff pursuing a full-blown life of crime is, frankly, terrifying. As is evidenced in his chilling negative-charisma and powerful physical presence, now fortunately discharged in a lucrative, late blooming earner playing villains in movies like *Octopussy, Rambo II, Beverly Hills Cop, The Krays* and even an astonishingly convincing Hitler in *War and Remembrance.* "I thought I could be an actor because I had chutzpah, I thought because of my background I maybe had energy. All I wanted to be was a movie star. I thought that would be nice. I am not a bad looking fellow. I had never been to a play in my life when I went to drama school," he said as the sun sparkled on the water and he rolled a neat cigarette.

*East* and its successor *West* were, like all his plays, almost pure autobiography, though raised, naturally, to Berkovian pitch and altitude. Fighting and fucking appeared to be the primary leisure activities in the East End of his youth. Oh, and dancing. One night after a dinner in Covent Garden, Berkoff stopped and stood reverently in front of the massive edifice that was once the 'great' Lyceum Dance Hall, lingering at its Corinthian-columned portico, awash with nostalgia, transported back to tender, twirling, tumescent times.

*West* was based on a revenge fight resoundingly won by Berkoff's cousin Sid. Walloped the fucker: 'Like stepping round the back was what was expected of you / like a clobbering now and then / was mixed up with pulling birds round there for stand-up charvers . . .'

"What a play should do," he thundered across the empty lawn

that day in Fiji, "is push people away from laissez-faire attitudes, and show them something else. It should be driving an audience away from stereotyped attitudes. I think the theatre has the ability and the duty to shock and disturb and excite." Indeed, he did not so much challenge the boundaries as blow them up. A typical Berkoff play features great arias, descriptions of swollen, dripping genitalia; vivid, colliding images, sharp edges, imagery that rears up and slams you in the solar plexus; and a resounding social message which basically amounts to a strenuous Fuck You. And the language. Let us not forget the language. If the combat against mediocrity is mortal, then language is the weapon of choice. And Berkoff uses the lacerating and highly evocative Cockney slang as poetry in toxic motion. Stream-of-consciousness language, language to be shouted and savoured; sexual and violent. 'Shakespearean prose meets skinhead spleen', as journalist Helen O'Neill pointed out in the *Australian* newspaper, adding that meeting him made her feel like Jodie Foster in *Silence of the Lambs*.

"*East* was a kind of joy and exuberance," he says. "*East* was the euphoric joy of suddenly becoming aware of this sensuality of my person. It was dealing with a young man's awakening desire, a charge of language. I felt that was missing in the theatre. The playwrights of England were all kind of wanked-out wrecks who were detailing their neuroses. I wanted to be loud and screaming with joy."

Indeed, the great Shakespearean speeches reel incessantly though his head. On the treadmill at the gym, bathed in sweat, on his rollerblades sailing round the park in the misty early morning. The habit of a lifetime. Formed as a young actor fine-tuned, fit as an Olympian athlete, ready and roaring for the great roles that never came. 'If I had an audition I would stay home for a week and work and work on the speeches, hour after hour like some demented maniac from an Edgar Allen Poe story, until they no longer yielded meaning,' he wrote in *Free Association*. 'And I thought I was marvellous, bloody sodding marvellous . . . but then a few days later the inevitable reply, "Thank you but no thank you." How could this be?'

He might bore it up the establishment. But they started it. They rejected him first. He was working class, bred to work. Even now he likes to leave the stage drenched in the sweat of exertion and toil. Like his father before him, he was working from the age of 14. His father was embittered for life at his lot as a tailor. "My father imbued me with the guilt of unemployment; if you are not working you are a bum. He abused me all his life with verbal harassment and never praised me. Rejection caused me grief and cold fury, and that too may have had its roots in the barking end-less criticism from old Dad," he said without rancour as we sat by the saltwater pool at Palm Beach, blinded by late afternoon light dying on the water, turning then to trill in an Irish accent to an Irish mother happily bossing her many, many children.

It was after a particularly excruciating audition, cut short by the underlings of his hero Laurence Olivier who was setting up the National Theatre, that he began to suspect that he might have to depart your traditional career trajectory, the mainstream alto-gether, perhaps civilisation as he knew it, and fend for himself in future. He, for one, was never in doubt of his own genius, even if it was not immediately obvious to anyone else, and he was a man in a hurry. For him acting is a religion, spiritual. And so, already outcast, he became a radical. The hard man of theatre. His satiri-cal piece *Actor*, performed to screaming laughter in his one man show when he brought it to Sydney in 1994, is a litany of the frus-tration of the out-of-work actor whose destiny is not turning out to be as dazzling as he had envisaged and whose life, consequently, is coming apart. 'Hallo Peter how are you / I'm doing well too / working / you are / that's good / bastard he couldn't act his way out of a paper bag / the slag.'

Steven Berkoff was sitting in the Sydney pool hall, having a beer, muscular arms folded. The tape recorder was running and he had drawn himself up and gone into Interview Mode; the vowels becoming rounded, the voice both caressing and molesting before speeding along the runway and taking flight. "To me unemployment in a fully grown man was humiliation. I was low and weak and unfit to partake in human society. I tried to feel I wasn't unemployed. I filled those days going to the gym, learning movement, taking dance classes. But I had this guilt that made me feel I had to do things. So I got a group of like-minded people together to perform. Learning movement was like learning a lot of magic tricks. I took a class for a friend of mine and found I could teach. So I went to my old drama school and volunteered to take some classes. I didn't have a clue how to direct but after a couple of months I ran out of ideas so I started to invent. That process led me to thinking about doing my own work. So I ransacked the novels. This was a source of tremendous ideas. My desire to write was a pragmatic functional role. I was an out-of-work actor and I wanted to give myself great socking parts to play. It was a product of necessity but as I got more and more involved, I got more inventive and bizarre."

More drawn, too, to the pure, wordless world of Jacques Lecoq, with whom he studied mime in Paris. "It was another way of escaping from the claustrophobic atmosphere of middle-class theatre," he told his drama school buddy Terence Stamp. He had been appalled that two East Enders were rehearsing *The Reluctant Debutante*. "They are castrating us here," he told Stamp.

For him theatre is magic. "I come from a Jewish background and the world of mysticism, surrealism, expressionism, music, literalism really belonged on the surface. From a very early time I was interested in mysticism. I would read science fiction or occult, Aldous Huxley or Kafka. Therefore plays from modern English writers had no interest for me because they were an immediate reflection of society which was picayune, trivial, emasculated and dead. People wanted to see themselves in the mirror and make sure they were OK. These plays said nothing to me because I was living in an imaginary world."

Mime and music, then, would become the final, distinctive ingredients in the physical, stylised, polemic Berkovian theatre. His choruses are fluid lines of actors like dancers or athletes bringing the subtext to living, breathing life. His chorus in *Coriolanus*, for example, moves seamlessly in enacting class warfare. From stormtrooper soldiers to East End wide boys to gibbering Arcadian hilarity as they vividly illustrate the mood of the body politic. "What comes into play is another language, which I think is a visual language which is to do with the language of bodies telling you a story. I try to create a visual language which tells yet another story. It tells somehow the underlying motives and dreams. I want to squeeze as much energy out of the ensemble as I can. Normally if an actor only has two or three lines he is just sitting there. Very often you see actors just standing there limply while another actor speaks. But in my plays he is a vital, integral piece of the ensemble, this adds to the heightened drama, it can take theatre to another level. The language of gesture is very, very powerful. I bring the actors together like a football team or a basketball team. I started with the greatest short story ever written, the most powerful, demonic, exhausting Kafka story, *Metamorphosis,* about a man who changes into an insect, and made the leap into metaphysical theatre. From there I went on and on and on. I did *The Fall of the House of Usher*, I had the idea that the usher was the house itself, I would enact a house. What I did with *The Trial* was turn everybody into the furniture in Joseph K's house."

Steven Berkoff has a gallant, old-fashioned way of taking a woman's arm as we walk down a street dense with determined shoppers. We are doing some retail therapy in Oxford Street, Sydney, another favoured Berkoff recreation. He adores checking out the shops but it can be a fresh form of torture. Even after all these years of working bloody hard for his money he has never overcome the ingrained guilt of spending money on himself. Especially when it comes to the deeply satisfying but imagined frivolity of shoes. Should I? Shouldn't I? Yes. No. Maybe. In ecstasies of doubt over a pair of boots in one shoe shop, he twirls across the floor doing a samba with the middle-aged shop assistant. Real sexy, da, *da,* da, *da,* oh yeah, he's got the moves, all right. "As a child I didn't get a lot of the things I wanted. So therefore I had to adjust my goals, like children do. Then when you get older and you can have more you give yourself guilt for giving yourself more because the child in you is going beyond the parameters of what you are permitted." And somehow, no matter how many clothes he buys, he always seems to look more or less the same. Black, bulky and baggy. Apart from one memorable trip to Sydney which featured a pair of white patent leather shoes, a fashion crime that lingered in more than one mind long after.

Heads jerk round as we roll on down the street, sensing a charismatic presence, stopped by that powerful, omnivorous face. People approach him, even when they don't know who he is, sort of helplessly awed. He moves through crowds, through rooms, through flattery flung from all directions with the utmost grace and charm, a smooth performance in humility. The lion loves the attention. He sat with his Akubra hat on his knee backstage after seeing Marianne Faithfull perform, as they oozed mutual admiration. "He is dangerous," she whispered later.

I asked him one evening, when he was relaxed and in repose after his second 'marg' (he is a connoisseur of the margarita) where he thought charisma came from. "Testosterone," he shot back. "It has a chemical basis, the balls. Women can have it equally. Once you have triggered that kind of charisma the mask is made and when it is gone you still exude it."

Women flock to Steven Berkoff. Drawn by the danger, by the seductive fat cat smile, the animal sexuality. Who among us, after all, will easily forget the infamous 'cunt' speech in *East*: '. . . juice-ridden knicker, hot knicker, wet knicker, swelling vulva knicker, witty cunt, teeth smiling the eyes biting cunt, cultured cunt, culture vulture cunt, finger biting cunt, cunt that pours, cunt that spreads itself over your soft lips, that attacks, cunt that imagines . . .' And a story in his spurting book of short stories about sex and loneliness *Gross Intrusion* begins: '"Of course I like the feeling of a full cunt," she thought.'

Yes. What can I say. "I wrote that more than 20 years ago," he protests now. But still. This is a man who loves women, in all their infinite variety. "I don't think I could go on the stage if I didn't feel I was loved or had somebody who I loved, or whose life mattered absolutely and beyond and paramount to anything else on earth," he told me in an interview in 1994. "That is my justification for living."

That he is no stranger to sexual thrall and/or obsessive love is fairly clear in his play *Greek*. Get a load of this:

'I love her / I just love and love and lover her / and even that one / I could have loved her / I love everything they possess / I love all their parts / I love every part that moves / I love their hair and their necks / I love the way they walk across the kitchen or put the kettle on in that lazy familiar way / I love their baby soft skin / I love their voices / I love their smaller hands than mine / I love lying on them and them on me / I love their soft breasts . . . and their desperate passions and their liquids and their breath against yours in the night / and their legs across mine and their feet in the morning and I love their bellies and thighs and the way each part fits into mine . . . and love and love and love . . .'

And women do love men who love them.

Even so there is an aura of loneliness about Berkoff, the outsider. He is, as Kenneth Tynan said of Laurence Olivier, 'an uneasy guest on earth'. Steven Berkoff, in all his brilliance, in all his allure, with all his acolytes, is condemned somehow to loneliness. He spends much of his life in hotel rooms, far from home, untethered, unquiet, a bit lost; lonely, lonely, lonely. Solitary, writing in his journal, ruminating, wishing you were here. Says Les in *East*: 'Just lonesome, basically I think, like is one born that way, I always felt lonely as if it was something like a habit, or the colour of your hair.'

But with reluctant maturity comes some sagacity. Sitting by a swelling Sydney Harbour one day in 1994 he admitted that, contrary to his enlarged reputation, the blistering passions of the past, "Sex is not remotely important to me. I don't have a huge libido, I discharge a lot of that stuff in my work. I used to think life wasn't justified unless one was thrilling oneself. But that is a negative because it should be a playful thing and an enjoyable thing. I learned many, many times that to think otherwise is a one way ticket to pulukerville. That leads to neurosis, loneliness and low self-esteem. Your life is ruled by the density of your protuberance. Love to me is the most important part."

On the stage he is on fire, both controlled and over-the-top, playing the audience with consummate skill and daring. His Herod in *Salome* was manic obsessive, quivering malevolent sensuality, the last chilling line, 'Kill that woman', delivered in a different way each night. One night murderous, another comedic. His *One Man* a walloping, virtuoso three-part programme of Edgar Allen Poe's story of an obsessed murderer *The Tell-Tale Heart*, *Actor* and *Dog*, a working class yob and his violent pit-bull terrior Roy, which the *Sydney Morning Herald* critic Angela Bennie described as 'onanism'.

Walking along the white sweep of Bondi Beach one day he said drily, "A more uncharitable critic would accuse me of chewing up the scenery. You try to reach that state of putting yourself into another level of consciousness. You open a Pandora's box and all these creatures are in there kind of thrashing around. You change the chemicals in your brain when you do it. I try not to lie. When I am on the stage I try to live every moment. I don't know who I am. I am possessed."

Although he was embraced by the establishment in 1991 when he won the *Evening Standard* award for *Kvetch*, which he described as 'the unburdening of my middle-aged self', he has never compromised. The abrasive angry young man, the terrifying *enfant terrible* who had to direct and produce his own plays because no one else would, may have spread into his sixth decade, may have become a middle-class gent who likes to live well, but he has never lost that vitality, never stopped writing about the working class, never departed from his original tenets. "The tenants are very pleasant people as far as I am concerned," he quipped with a huge and sleazy smile, when I put this to him. Said Terence Stamp, "For us, Berkoff's work vibrated like a railway track before you caught sight of the train." And so they came: *Decadence*, his play about excess which he made into a film with Joan Collins; *Lunch*, where a man picks up a woman and goes through all the stages of romance, the man a space salesman, a job the young Berkoff once held for a day; *Greek,* a love letter to a difficult relationship and an Oedipal allegory of London life; *Harry's Christmas*, a lonely man suicides at Christmas; *Sink the Belgrano!*, an anti-war play about the Falklands War; *Brighton Beach Scumbags,* about two couples at Brighton Beach.

His plays, as he said in *Free Association*, 'are the living embodiments of my life', and he takes an evil pleasure in young actors auditioning using his work for theatres that would once never deign to stage it. And that actors who are the same age as he was when he wrote these socking great parts for himself breathe life and youthful exuberance into his words all the time, all over the world; his gift to them. Before he wrote them, "for years I had to be happy with crap" in rep, going home each night to damp hotel rooms, in depressed small towns of Britain. And grateful, too, to be working at all. "The charge of getting on the stage was so intense it didn't matter if I was doing a play called *The Amorous Prawn*."

Steven Berkoff is taking a childlike delight in the brilliantly coloured parrots that swoop into the café, hop across the table and peck the cake from his hand. His face lights up as they jump onto his shoulder and clamber across his chest, round blue eyes shining. Waitresses always flirt with Berkoff, innocent, irresistible and dewy as they are here at Palm Beach. Suddenly he puts his face in his hands. He is remembering a recent film shoot in France. He had arrived on location only to realise that it was little more than a skin flick. "I don't read the script, I just read my lines. I would probably have an epileptic fit if I read the whole film." His eyes narrow. "Not reading it is just being kind to my brain. I nearly packed up and left right then. Then I thought I would hide. So I went to wardrobe and organised a disguise. I wore a wig and a little moustache."

He could have done so much more in film, had he not been so utterly contemptuous of the medium. A classicist, a dramatist, he seems not to care what he does, self-destructively selling himself short in a medium that is writ so large. "I just look at what they send me," he shrugs. He does it for one reason and one reason only. Money. Money to subsidise his theatre runs. "Very few films have engaged me to the point where I think, 'I really want to do this film'," he said as he sat in dappled sunlight on the set of *Flynn*, in Fiji. "In fact, I can't think of any."

In each film he plays more or less the same villain, with minor variations, based on the hard men of the East End of his youth. Not so much evil incarnate as sardonic and amused. "I try to squeeze an element of humour from them. Villains are interesting because they are obsessive people and this obsession requires a certain kind of drive. It is the pursuit of power." It is the face, you see: it does good cruelty. Like his personality, it can compel and repel simultaneously.

His mother adored him. He opens his autobiography with his weekly visit to 'Ma', for breakfast. 'The work would receive the most curses as if there was some kind of conspiracy working against her angel son, simply because he was so angelic and wonderful and talented . . . and so both of them fumed, inveighed and seethed against the drab world which had no time for Mum's angelic son, who in the meantime was scoffing down bagels with cream cheese and salmon, washed down with abundant cups of tea.'

I once saw him burst into tears during a film about Scott of the Antarctic. It was the voiceover of Scott's final stoic letter to his mother that did it.

But the world does have time for Ma's son now. Or some parts of it anyway. He has made it take notice by sheer force of will. But what does an *enfant terrible* do when he is no longer young and rocketing through space? This is the question he asks himself now.

Berkoff is well aware of his own mortality. Ever since I have known him he has seemed to be searching for some kind of happiness for the "few years I have left". Peace of mind remains elusive. Beside the coral lagoon in Fiji he leaned back in his plastic chair. "I walk down the street feeling that I'm 22. Then I look in a shop window and I'm a bit shocked," he said. And then, as if on cue, a young actress sidled nervously to his side. "Where I come from you are God," she blurted. From *Free Association*: 'I don't want to be acting past sixty or fighting for a place or getting angry when I should be calm and serene, nor feel sick when I take too much notice of reviews.'

Still, he enlarges the moment, feels it, shouts about it with the highest drama he can possibly summon. And still, the world would be a far less interesting place without him in it.

# Famous Seamus

They call him Famous Seamus. He won the Nobel Prize. He surveys the room with a certain wary scepticism.

The journalists seated untidily in rows before him clear throats, rustle papers, click equipment, murmur among themselves and regard the Great Poet as if he were a rare and precious endangered species on display. A live Great Poet in captivity. The scarce cable-sweatered naturalistic Irish Great Poet, hunted down and brought in from the wild. Indeed with his flying white hair, his rough fleshy face, his uncomfortable gaze, Seamus Heaney has the look of a cornered animal. He lowers his hooded eyes to the floor and keeps them there.

He is an imposing presence nevertheless, his unsmiling sheer size, his stern black eyebrows, the weight of his eminence. Of classical proportions; he looks exactly like a Great Poet should.

He wrote a poem about journalists in Northern Ireland once: 'Where media-men and stringers sniff and point / Where zoom lenses, recorders and coiled leads / Litter the hotels. The times are out of joint / But I incline as much to rosary beads' and of: 'Northern reticence, the tight gag of place / And times: yes, yes. Of the "wee-six" I sing / Where to be saved you only must save face / And whatever you say, you say nothing.'

And we wait to hear him speak. You can't say nothing when you win the Nobel Prize. Not after all those years of being fruitlessly nominated. Great Poets are usually dead, extinct. Unavailable for interview, at this time. "I let it all wash over me," says Seamus Heaney in his deep muddy Irish voice, all the more pronounced against his publisher's precise pristine preamble. "In Ireland everybody is famous from birth."

Emboldened now, the press want more. Details, details. How did you feel? what did you say? what will you do? where? what? tell me, tell me, clamour, clamour. "I was bewildered," he looks modestly bewildered, "I didn't know about this until I phoned my son from a small town in Greece where I was holidaying. I had planned to read a book, have my lunch. My son Christopher said, 'I'm so proud.' He thought I knew. I said, 'What are you talking about?' It is a bit daunting but a happy accident that the activity is being celebrated and a carnival is being made of it, it is wonderful for a value to be promoted by festive means. I never usually made statements about poetry and prizes," he stumbles.

Seamus Heaney is the shaggy product of generations of humble farmers, the eldest of nine. Like Les Murray, whose widowed father was an illiterate farm labourer, like so many brilliant men and women, there is nothing in his antecedence to explain his academic brilliance or his poetic gift. Even in a country of innate everyday poetry, he is a dazzling aberration. A beloved poet who writes about the psychic tragedy and painful beauty of his country. Or as Clive James once described, Seamus Heaney ("bogs, eels") and Ted Hughes ("crows, violence") when the two appeared on television together. Their staggering combined charisma made James worry for the future of poetry (not to mention jealous) because, he felt, poetry is meant to sustain itself, not to be put over by a charismatic author.

'When the lamp glowed / A yolk of light / In their back window, / The child in the outhouse / Put his eye to a chink.' (*The Henhouse*.)

"That," says Seamus, "was based on a news report about a boy who was secluded in a henhouse. The mother was so stricken by blame and by the shame at the time of this child born out of wedlock that she kept him away from the house. I do believe that this boy is still alive." But when they found him he couldn't speak.

'With a remote mime / Of something beyond patience, / Your gaping wordless proof / Of lunar distances / Travelled beyond love.'

"If he is a poet he must be struggling," muses a pretentious man in a tweed suit aloud, as though all poets are scrounging money for cheap red wine. "How long have you been making a living, as it were, from verse?" the man asks, rocking back on his feet. Love those 'as it were's' slyly slipped in because this is an interview with a Great Poet. I too, once practised saying this in the mirror when I had to go on a previous television book programme as *a literary critic*.

"I taught for a living. I came from a home and a culture generally that presumed and expected that you would work for your living. I taught at a college in Belfast for a few years, I taught at Queen's University. At the age of 33 I resigned from the job in order to connect myself to writing and rites of passages but at that stage we had three children so I consider I have had some training in frugality. I accepted when I was offered a position at Harvard University which allowed me to teach eight months of the year. I still teach four months a year. It has become a habit. Like all teachers I dread the thought of it but I enjoy the action of it, the fulfilment and pleasure, the contact, the tedium and verity of that kind of relationship. I like to think I teach by example." Seamus gets defensive. "Poets are supposed to be poor but several were sprung in the past from large middle classes purses."

A bearded man from the Voice of America is burning up. He is *dying* to know. "What are you going to do with the Nobel Prize money?" As if the Great Poet is suddenly going to confess to a life-long ambition to build a large and vulgar house with leatherette furniture; buy a red Cadillac and do a bit of recreational kerb crawling, take up nude water skiing, hire a phalanx of high-class hookers and hit Vegas. Seamus Heaney's eyes lift briefly from the floor. Mind your own fucking business they say. But what comes politely out of his mouth is the prescribed script. "I don't know. Money is not an art of mine. I don't think about it. It is the thunderbolt aspect that is the real thing." He keeps talking when he sees the bearded man leap up again, to be on the safe side, just in case he is going to ask another question and not dance the first act of the *Nutcracker Suite*, as he appears to be attempting. This is how media savvy is born. Keep talking, anything but questions. Instead Famous Seamus obligingly gives us the soundbite story of the poet in training. "Being born and brought up where I was, being the kind of creature, the kind of temperament I have, the kind of teachers in my country. I have had good luck in terms of publishing. From the first moment I sent poems out in Belfast to local newspapers they were accepted by editors. I had no names, I had no connections, I just sent the poems to the editors and they accepted them. That was the first magical thing to have happen. They turned aspiration into text. People outside my own community read my poems. Faber wrote to me. That was another bolt from the blue. My experience has been unusual, it has been immediate acceptance and benediction. And so I gained a trust in process."

A blonde bob pops up with another stunning question. "What is your favourite poem?" Seamus pauses and pretends to take it seriously. "I am not sure that consistency is all that important a virtue. I really couldn't say what my favourite poem is."

A man from *The Times* wants to know if he is a poet of the Troubles. "I thought we got rid of that in 1972 myself," retorts Seamus witheringly. "There has been a lot of crap about it, a lot of journalists go on about it. We had irony and resistance from the start," mumble, mumble, "exhausted subject."

"Why don't you live there?" asks the impertinent man from *The Times*.

"I don't think one is ever absent. When is history? History is every moment. I was in Spain in 1969 when the first violence started in Derry and it changed from protest to violence, so there was a sense of massacre. History was changing. The aim of the artist is to keep history turning."

A complete prat from a quality newspaper seizes the moment, clears his pale throat and asks, "What's it like being famous?"

Seamus laughs. "I have an Irish wife and family who have a very combative sense of the world and a sense of protecting the house and its occupants."

The Voice of America does a *jeté*, a pirouette and the splits mid-air. "What relevance does poetry have in today's world?" he enquires as he lands.

Seamus pronounces it "potree". He is ready for this one.

"Potree always has relevance in any world because of the relevance within the individual spirit. Relevance doesn't really apply to potree, it is a deeper spiritual thing. It is part of the cultivation of our lives."

What is the value of the Nobel Prize, *The Times* would like to know. Apart, presumably, from fame, money, prestige, adulation, babes, the best tables in restaurants. Apart from that. "I think the value of the prize itself is that it is a multiplication system not for the individual but for the art form. If you hear of the Nobel Prize for literature it is one of the few magic words in the world. It is credible for people who don't believe in much. It promotes good activity, it blesses the art of potree, the art of literature, the sciences. It is not quite a personal thing, it is a statement of value."

Asked to read one of his poems to what is giving a very good impersonation of being an uncomprehending audience, Famous Seamus has a trick up his woolly sleeve. "This is called 'Bernard and Jamie McCabe'," he says with a sly smile. "'The riverbed, dried-up, half full of leaves / Us, listening to a river in the trees.'"

They are sitting back, the shabby press, affecting suitably incipient expressions of transportation, when they hear footsteps. The Great Poet is leaving the building, ladies and gents; that poem is only two lines long.

"Poets," he admonishes from the door, "are never dead." They can be quick though, damn quick. He is on the other side of Queens Square before they realise that the beast has given them the slip and returned to the wild.

# The Damned

He lopes into the room, this man who needs no introduction. Lopes with a stoop as if the burden of all his troubles, all the troubles of the world, have been carried on these sighing shoulders too long and too heavy. The stooped back is silent heroic eloquence. It has been six years since Salman Rushdie was sentenced to death by the Ayatollah Khomeini for defaming 'Islam, the Prophet and the Koran'. Six invisible years since he vanished into front pages all over the world. Six years since he precipitously assumed his drastic place in history.

And here he is still, ladies and gentlemen, coming down the corridor in billowing white shirt and trousers; manifestly alive, unrepentant—"they were worth upsetting"—and utterly ordinary. But not free. Never, ever free again.

He couldn't have put it better himself, really, when he began *Midnight's Children* with these words: 'I had been mysteriously handcuffed to history.'

And so it would come to pass. As so much of that first fabulist novel would come to pass. He realised even then that his words had a strange supernatural power. He should have ducked for cover then. Taken up quilting as a creative outlet. "It was spooky the way that novel prefigured what happened." But by then it was already too late.

*The Satanic Verses* was, of course, even more terribly prophetic. "It is all in there. It is terrifying, even for its author, to find out how much that book knew. It is one thing to sit in a room and dream up what religious fanaticism might be like. It is quite another to discover just how accurate the book was."

It angers him, this 'thing' that keeps happening. He is sick, sick, sick of it. Martyrdom sucks. Even though he has turned out to have a flair for it.

"I think if I were to examine it I would be very, very pissed off. I am bored with it. I would like to leave it alone for another 10

**SALMAN RUSHDIE**

years. It is characteristic of such an event that a kind of false self gets invented by other people and projected onto a very big screen. You think, 'Who is that guy? That is not me. Who is that guy with my name?'."

The guy who subsides cross-legged into a wing-chair in his publisher's office is a small, rotund, balding intellectual with a greying beard and rosy cheeks. But the scourge of Islam looks, alarmingly, as if he might be about to drop off to sleep. So heavy-lidded is he, behind the professorial rimless glasses, that he gives the impression of sleepwalking. It is hard to imagine anyone less dangerous to East or West, less satanic, than Salman; than this apparently mild, talkative man holding a paper cup in lily-white hands.

"If you had asked me six and a half years ago, if you had described to me what was going to happen and asked me how I was going to stand up to it, I would not have expected to be here in one piece. I haven't been calm or wonderfully strong all along. I have had very bad passages. I have made mistakes. The early period was by far the worst. We had no idea what was happening. There was no way to judge what was coming at you. I was quite off-balance for a while. It has been very hard." He says this so mildly, however, this man whose bounty is $3 million, and with such understatement, that he might be asking you the time.

These are merely the facts of his distorted life. Death squads, armoured vans, policemen carrying 9 mm carbines, surreal, high-security, covert operations; days in the life of a moving target. Get used to it. It is hard to vanish when you are as recognisable as he. Plastered over the papers like a giant arrow pointed at his head.

Out of the question, still, are the small kindnesses given and received, the daily cruelties, the ordinary nuances of everyday human interaction that layer our lives. "You miss the small freedoms a lot when they are taken away. I found it so humiliating to have to ask friends to buy clothes for me." Like a recalcitrant child, he has rebelled against his guardians. "I think what I did from the first moment was try to get my freedom back. That has been an invisible fight that nobody knows about, what I have had to do to get that stuff back. The ability to come here and talk to you, for instance; three or four years ago we wouldn't have been able to do this"—his hand flails.

Indeed, today, the posse of policemen who elaborately orchestrate his every outing, much to the mirth of London literary society, is disappointingly stationed out of sight. I was rather hoping to be frisked. Recently he told *The Times* of London that groups of assassins had been routinely dispatched to kill him and that he had changed residence some 30 times since 1989. But in this interview he smiles mysteriously.

"There is an awful lot of exaggeration, and mistakes about how it is done, fortunately. I am quite happy for people not to know how I am protected. Almost everything that has ever been said about it is wrong." He contributes large sums of money to his protection, which, when he goes to America, is "what Arafat gets".

There are flashes of the underlying, percolating, festering anger, the monumental outrage at the injustices of his life, that simmer within Salman Rushdie. There are bursts of the petulance that has hardened public opinion, a glimmer of the guts, the refusal to roll over and play the victim that has been interpreted as super-egotism, but which may have saved him.

"I don't want to talk about it," he says, abruptly snapping off the charm, when asked about his announced conversion to Islam in 1990 as a plea for clemency at a time when there were still British hostages in Iran. "It was a mistake. It was done at my lowest point, I shouldn't have done it. Full stop."

Says a literary insider: "He is a difficult man; he has a huge ego; he has made this something that other people wouldn't have made it into."

But most of the time during our long conversation there is the calm, the knowing acceptance of the survivor, the resigned at-least-I-am-alive stoicism of the trauma victim who has walked through the shadow of the valley of death and who, profoundly changed, is beyond fear. "I am not afraid," he says of the real possibility of eradication.

We will never know, most of us, what we are truly made of. Salman does. Salman has been persecuted. Salman knows now that he is a fighter. To the death. "I guess I have learned that I am quite stubborn and not easily shut out. A lot of people have committed crimes against me and against people I care about and that makes me want to fight. But this is a fight one has to win because the consequences of losing it are not conceivable. At least it is the right fight; it is a fight about the art of the novel and free speech and the right of the ordinary person to say what they like and not have your word defined for you by fanatical purists. I guess what I thought was that, insofar as these guys ever read 500-page literary novels, they wouldn't like it. No doubt several of them would say so. One or two might fulminate and I would fulminate back and that would be it. It was basically a comic spectacle with an irreverent voice. On the whole I thought *The Satanic Verses* was a story about somebody who does not weaken in the face of persecution and is merciful at the moment of victory"—dramatic pause to make sure the interviewer understands the parallels—"I don't wish I hadn't done it. I don't propose to be told when to shut up by a priest. I am right and they are wrong. There is strength in that. I don't want to lose."

The attacks on Rushdie's translators in Italy, Turkey and Norway, and the murder of his Japanese translator, were, he says, "completely obscene. The Japanese man was a completely innocent bystander, the last person in the world who had any right to feel endangered. It made me a thousand per cent more determined to fight even harder. I felt it was about things that were bigger than me, my work or my book."

He has spent six years as an ambassador for his own life, travelling across the Western world, speaking to world leaders to demand stronger sanctions against Iran. "The degree of inertia from the world's politicians was quite stunning. I still think that if there had been any genuine political energy to solve this case it would have been solved years ago."

As a left-leaning Indian in Tory years, he was not exactly fashionable. And his case has not been high enough on the British political agenda, in his view, to warrant economic sanctions against Iran, a situation Martin Amis has called a "concentrated disgrace".

But, says Rushdie, "I used to find it difficult to get an appointment with the British government, but I am quite close to them now. The Clinton administration has been very helpful. I think that the very strong line they have adopted towards the Iranians is the only way to do it. These guys don't get appeased; they respond to strength and weakness."

And if by the seemingly awesome consequences of his own words, with which he had the impudence to challenge the sacred texts, he has become the *cause célèbre* of the century, despite other dissidents and other *fatwahs* in other places, then Rushdie, by that same power, may have delivered a triumph of the human spirit with his book *The Moor's Last Sigh*. A series of stories, *East, West*, was published in 1995 and a defiant children's parable, *Haroun and the Sea of Stories*, was written for his son in 1991. "Not being able to see him is one of my greatest regrets."

He has not been silenced.

He has turned the nightmare into the dreamlike quality of his writing. Anxiety, as any writer knows, is not the place from which great writing springs. Nor is anger. Or hate. Rushdie has transcended the ugliness, found love where there was hate, strength where there was suffering, beauty where there was none, light where there was dark. And that is his victory.

"If people are hurling hatred at you, write about love. If people try to silence you, speak and do it with force."

He has not been defeated.

"There were times when I thought I wouldn't write again. I was sucked into a campaign where I lost a couple of years talking to politicians. Then I began to feel that if this thing stops me from writing then that is a victory I am not going to permit them to have. I felt that the best way to fight was to be the writer that I am and not turn into this kind of cowering politician. At least writing a novel is a thing you can do in a room by yourself. I do have a great deal of anger about what has happened but I did not want to write out of that, I wanted to write out of its opposite, which is love."

*The Moor's Last Sigh,* set in the southern India of his childhood, is a series of dazzling images. An exhilarating flight of an imagination at the height of its power, comic, profound, satirical, full of eccentric, preposterous characters, colour and sound, allegorical, fantastical; the story of a chaotic fabulist family in terrible decline, set in the polyglot of Southern India. Furiously paced, there is an urgency, a breathless quality, as if everything that has happened, all the struggle, has been to lead him to this spirited profusion of language, this colour and sound. "I do think this is the book that has taken me all the other books to write. *Midnight's Children* was about the beginning of the century; this novel is about the sense of it ending. It is the culmination of everything I have ever done. There was a lot of emotion flowing through me in the writing of it."

In it we find the familiar Rushdie themes, those which he somehow brought upon himself—exile, ostracism, bewilderment and banishment. From a middle-class Bombay family, he was sent to Rugby, a public school in central England, where he was subjected to constant racial abuse—ostracism from which, perhaps, his anger grew.

Rushdie's fictional women are fabulous, strong, treacherous, powerful and dangerous. Deadly. "I am the only son of an only son of an only son. There was a boy shortage in my family. But there is a vast army of sisters and aunties and nieces. I think one of the reasons why this is a book with so many loudmouth females is that all of my life I have been surrounded by noisy women."

He has, presumably, in the last few years, had plenty of time to contemplate the idea of romantic love. Since his wife, Marianne Wiggins, left him he has had small affairs and now has a girlfriend.

"I have always been rather keen on the idea. I am a falling-in-love person. I have been the recipient of all sorts of love through this time and so I have become very interested. Actually, as one goes on as a writer you intensely discover that it is the only subject worth writing about. Like India, it is an inexhaustible subject. Even love that is invested in the wrong place is better than any possible alternative."

Rushdie has always been troublesome, always had a lot of nerve, been a provocateur, has always deliberately antagonised. President Zia, the late Pakistani leader, banned his book *Shame*, an angry examination of women's lot in that country. In India, Mrs Gandhi sued him for libel for *Midnight's Children*. The press in Britain remains polarised on the Rushdie Affair. His critics see his consorting with rock stars on stages, his appearances at literary parties, as posturing, un-martyr-like behaviour, his self-interest and statesmanlike status irritating. That he lacks the humility and nobility that are somehow expected. Humility, he readily admits, is not a feature of his personality. Others, like Prince Charles, who told Martin Amis he had no sympathy for someone who "sets out to offend people's deepest convictions", feel he is the author, literally, of his own fate.

The mullahs, with internal political divisions of their own, continue to toy with him. "It is characteristic that there are mixed signals. One moment they are making statements that they are calling off the dogs, but on the other hand, when they are asked to formally put that in writing, they don't do so. So we will see."

Day by day, bit by bit, he is winning his Biblical fight. "What seems to be happening is that other things in the world are moving in such a way that it has become convenient for people to deal with this issue." Rushdie is getting tired and a tad pissed off.

But if words are his weapons, he will have the best revenge. The last word. "Everybody will be dead and my book will still be there." So there.

It is getting colder now, lurching along on the number 23 bus down the Strand on a grey afternoon. Water splashing cold in Trafalgar Square. The rain whines and whinges and cries down the windows. The sky gets turbulent and starts lowering into autumn and you begin to feel like you are in an underwater playground. Gardens are wet with rain. That grey gets into everything, it gets into the tissues of your brain. A weekend by the filthy grey seaside made Fawlty Towers seem like social realism. "Nup, no decent restaurants around here," said the man at the reception of our hotel with a triumphant smile. In an act of absurd British macho my male companion actually went swimming in the freezing, grey, greasy sea. When he came out he was blue and wrinkled like a newborn baby. Along the seashore at Great Yarmouth the rain dripped off the arcades, theme parks and Ferris wheels as they flashed their neon lights in hopeless gaiety. Such watery intensity and melancholy in the colours of the country-side as it recedes into rain.

# ■ Slave To Love

"People say, 'oh, you are such a cool guy'," says Bryan Ferry, placing one immaculate black suede cowboy boot on the windowsill and running a long, sensitive hand through the famously artful sweep of hair. "And I say, 'oh, fuck off'. I am very emotional. I feel things very deeply. I am cool on the exterior but I'm actually very Latin."

Bryan Ferry, suave dude, cool crooner of the '70s—who could forget 'Slave To Love?'—languid aristocratic-style queen of the '80s and '90s, suddenly stops as if surprised by his outbreak of, well, emotion. He squirms in his chair in a tall, carefully rumpled, large dog sort of way, looking soulfully out from under the spaniel hair, appealing, appalled.

The studied romantic rock star gloss, it is rapidly becoming apparent, is calculatedly surface. Image, darling, as I seem to say ad nauseam, is everything. But the slick suit of celebrity, it seems, is a mask. Ferry appears a man not comfortable in his own skin. Wearing his beauty like a crumpled suit that he might, at any moment, shrug off to release the darker demons seething away in there that drive him.

Those ugly, dark, scary places of self-doubt and introspection that we are all too familiar with in this book. Like all great obsessives, he seems doomed to an unquiet centre. "I can be pretty bad," he says of the torture of obsession. "I can be an absolute nightmare, you ask the people around me, I can be absolutely weird. Until the next thing comes along and takes over. You are longing for the next thing to step in. I can see it in one of my sons already, it makes me laugh."

It made me laugh too when I took his advice and actually asked one of those people. He had, only the day before, locked himself into his hotel room and refused to come out until a woman working on his tour wrote him a letter apologising for, get this, calling him a prima donna. He is an artiste, darling, he has an artiste's temperament. But he is nice man really. In spite of himself. Shy. Easily hurt. Fastidiously dreamy. "I've always run over dead-lines and screwed up release dates rather than say 'OK, that'll do'."

Ferry approaches an interview as if he is taking a final exam. He is not your talker, Bryan. More your rambler. When he goes off at a tangent it can be a bit hard to get him back. Oi, Bry, over here. "I am not a great talker, I don't talk much, you know." Actually he would rather be singing. On the stage he is charismatic, it's the way he moves, controlled but sensual, knees slightly bent forward, what *Arena* magazine described as the Ferry Effect. "I have never been very confident about speaking. I have always been more com-fortable on stage singing than, like, talking." His struggle, for a man who is by nature shy and introverted, to lay himself open gives him a pained vulnerability. "I have still got a long way to go before I can really enjoy my own company," he admits. "Maybe that will never happen." He turns on the dazzling smile. Girls, I have to tell you that when he does that you pretty much want to faint. He is very neurotic and very beautiful. And those long, long legs, man oh man. Who needs a personality anyway.

Ferry's album 'Mamouna' was the end result of a fairly major obsession. For six years he strove for perfection, sculpted and chipped at layers and layers of sound for a masterpiece, his magnum opus, his passion. "You do go on a journey, it can be good or bad, it's the luck of the draw really." He spent all his money making it. Unfortunately the journey was bad. It failed, dis-mally. He took it badly. Rejection is hard for a slave to love.

In the lyrics we find the bleaker vistas of love, nervy love songs. In the complex, experimental, strange notes, in the hypnotic arrangements, there is a sense of aching loneliness, of being lost, not knowing which way to turn. It is an atmospheric mood piece. "I make it so hard for myself. I did get more abstract. I like that myself but it's not a very commercial way of doing it, that's for sure. People find it a bit strange or a bit remote, a bit hidden, a bit inaccessible or something. I had a lot of turbulence in my life, I had two children in that time, but it wouldn't be worth anything if it was easy. It is sad because you always want your work to be commercial, inasmuch as you don't make any artistic sacrifices. I know my music is soulful. I put a lot of myself into it."

And Bryan Ferry does like a good yearn. He is a yearner from way back. "For me the yearning of music is what drew me to it in the first place, it wasn't, like, image or clothes, it was a pure emotional thing." The strange notes were always there, but this new mournful layered music is a long way from the blasting exuberance of Roxy Music. From the songs like 'Let's Stick Together', 'The Price of Love', 'Love is the Drug' and 'This is Tomorrow', hit after hit, emblematic, a perennial party soundtrack of their time. "I don't let that bog me down."

And like many a writer he has discovered the unnerving power of words to make things happen. "People say, 'That song is about that girl, isn't it?' and I say, 'No, it's from my imagination'. But sometimes you write a song and something happens a few years later so that life imitates art. I don't know why I fuss about the lyrics so much really. All those people who listen to opera don't know what they are singing about. They could be singing 'open the door' or 'turn the heating up'. Most music is rubbish, most music is terrible. About 10 per cent is worth listening to and about two per cent is beautiful. I often think how great it would be to have one great idea and live off it for the rest of your life, like inventing Guinness or Tabasco or something. With an album you are expected to come up with 10 winners."

The technical remove was always there but there was great good humour and irreverence too. "I hope it will come back but maybe it won't." Now, Bryan, put that razor blade down. Ferry looks out the window of the 21st floor of his hotel, across the city, as if help might arrive from out there.

The work became more detailed, lush, rich and beautiful, with songs like 'Slave to Love' and 'Avalon', but in the late '80s he seemed to have got lost, becoming a millionaire recluse, disappearing into aesthetic living; exquisite houses, a society marriage to a woman who is photographed at fashion shows, and his art collection. A man of wealth and taste. "'Avalon' was quite a hard album to recover from, I was pretty burned out and then I made the album 'Boys and Girls', and that was pretty hard work as well."

It is surprising, for a man whose photograph appears in the society pages, how much of his working class, outside bathroom, northern upbringing he has retained, how much of the Geordie he remains. His father, whom he adored, was a miner who looked after the pit ponies and who once knocked the teeth out of a man for hitting a pony. It is there in the language, in the work ethic, the approachability, the raw honesty. "My parents would have done anything for me. I am not spoilt because I remember what it was like living in that tiny house. One interviewer in 10 will make some crack about 'How can a Geordie lad like you live in such style?'. As if to imply that I have betrayed my roots. It drives me crazy. I sit there looking at them and thinking 'How can you be so stupid?'. All I have done is grown from something which I am totally proud of. I wouldn't be me without my background and I certainly wouldn't have the drive that I have."

He is the father of four young boys. "I'm very relieved that they are boys, I don't think I could handle girls. It is quite funny with boys, it is all these egos asserting themselves, it is all me, me, me; it is quite humbling because you see yourself in them. I suppose it would be nice to have girls fussing around me when I am old. But maybe my boys will find girls who will."

He spoke to me of his wife Lucy's fashionable rehabilitation from alcohol and drugs. "My wife's generation was a very bad generation for drugs, they all ended up in the programme." In recent years, for Ferry, there have been troubles, pain. He has a tentative optimism, a febrile, hesitant happiness.

"I feel better approaching fifty than I did approaching forty. I went through so many horrible things in the past 10 years that I feel I can cope with anything now. Both my parents died, it was just one thing after another. I feel more comfortable, I dunno, happier."

Squirm, squirm.

The leaves in Kensington Park drifted from the trees like orange snow and crunched sharp underfoot. Turning back towards Kensington Palace the park was awash in autumn, filigrees of yellow, brown, orange, vast splashes of crimson like the last dance at the ball, the last blazing blast of exquisite colour, of violins and party lights, of rustling taffeta and lingering caresses, before it all falls to the ground and is gone. The afternoon mist floats down through the trees like gauze. Stamping feet and white plumed breath. And suddenly, thundering through the mist is an apparition. A white charger, its neck arched, its delicate nostrils flaring red, its black eye rolled white, canters across the emerald grass. On its back is a medieval knight, his green and orange tunic overlaid with heraldry, his face red with chill and purpose. He is carrying a scroll, unfurling down the horse's haunches. He jerks the scalloped reins, the horse turns heavily and, enveloped again by the mist, they ride towards the palace. Surreal, ghostly, like the centuries never passed.

# Bend Me, Shake Me

The smoothly sadistic landlord strips to his black underpants and drags the thin, pale girl by her hair to the tatty bedroom. There he systematically rapes her from the rear. The characteristic defeated passivity in her gaunt face is replaced by the surprise of fear and, much later, a kind of resigned anger. She had expected love but what she got was pain. As usual.

This sequence from the film *Naked* is played with such cruelty and cold violence that it has haunted Mike Leigh ever after. The brutal sexual and emotional humiliation of women, the nihilistic landscape of post-Thatcher England, the violent alienation of the young and damaged, lost and drifting, thwarted anger, pissed-off, divided audiences and turned his film into a polemical blast into the public arena for its director.

While he is regarded as a cinematic visionary whose view of *fin-de-siècle* Britain is powerfully bleak, Leigh's detractors vociferously found his searing images offensive and misogynistic.

Mike Leigh was still recovering from being comprehensively misunderstood. He threw himself into a chair in his office. "The famous thing about *Naked* is the preposterous accusation of my being a misogynist," he said, "whereas it is perfectly obvious, apart from anything else, that you couldn't possibly make a film like *Naked,* you couldn't do those female characters with actresses who were anything other than feminists. Only the toughest, most intellectually astute women would do those parts, and they wouldn't do it if there was anything remotely dodgy about it."

Mike Leigh thoughtfully poured from the bottle of wine he had just uncorked and assumed the position of crumpled heap in his chair. "But that rape scene," I venture. He instinctively raised an arm across his face as if warding off a blow. "It is an awful scene, I know, but Katrin Cartlidge, who played the character, is an extremely sophisticated, very intelligent, very centred woman.

■ **M I K E   L E I G H**

Therefore she is able to go into character and work within character and to be completely detached about it in every sense. In the end you just get on with it. To say that I am sadistic and get enjoyment from other people's misfortune is a load of crap. What I do is motivated by compassion and by the human condition, by a sense of how we are. We are less than perfect. The fact is that in society there are erotically disoriented, lonely and frustrated people kicking around. I do make things that are rooted specifically and unapologetically in the culture."

A small, round, hunched, bearded man, Leigh has a kind of shambling untidiness about him. He has been compared to a rabbinical hamster and a bearded polytechnic lecturer. You would not think by looking at this small *auteur* that he is a great British success story, as some proclaim him to be. A resolute outsider, he was nevertheless awarded an OBE in 1993 for his services to the British film industry. An endearingly idiosyncratic English intellectual in the corduroys he always wears; who walks everywhere or uses public transport and is indifferent to anything other than the life of the mind and weighty matters of an aesthetic nature. There were hints, though, of the irascible fighter who has thrived on adversity.

Conversing animatedly in his broad North Country accent, brown eyes gleaming mischievously, he waved his little arms around, tearing off into tangents. There was no evidence on this London winter evening of the allegedly depressed personality whose allegorical films form the cutting edge of the recent British tradition of black, disturbing, political kitchen sink and social realism.

"I have been reported widely as being a glum and humourless person, or indeed a taciturn person who doesn't say very much. But everybody who knows me knows this is simply ludicrous. I have a great deal to say and I am always a barrel of laughs," he asserted defiantly, suddenly pausing mid-sentence and pointing towards the persistent and rhythmic thud coming from the ceiling of his Soho office. "Sorry about that," he smiled. "There is a brothel upstairs."

With the black clouds rushing past the window it seemed as if, for one weird minute, he had scripted an ironic Mike Leigh Moment and delivered it on cue.

Leigh was then, as he settled to talk, in post-production for *Secrets and Lies*. Perhaps this was the reason for his outbreak of optimism. "This is the good part actually, it is very much an actor's film and it was a very good atmosphere, comparatively." The word was that Leigh had lightened up and returned to his pre-*Naked* form of *High Hopes* and *Life Is Sweet* with humorous observation and satire about families. "One thing I will say is that *Naked* is a hard act to follow. It is. The more you live the more pressure you put on yourself not to repeat what you have previously. I think we have done it. This is very much an actor's film and it has had a very good atmosphere. But more than that I cannot say." And so it proved to be.

He could not say, because he did not know, even then, towards the end, what he had done.

As a filmmaker, Leigh is the consummate artist with a technique that is complex and profound, and for whom the process of creating is the thing. And as the artist uses brushes and paint, so too does Leigh use the actors to build and build the picture. He does not script. Instead he takes the actors through a gruelling rehearsal process where he strips them away, layer by layer, in improvisation, beginning by asking them to describe 100 people they have met. It is a constant state of exploration where everything is up for discussion to find the film, to find the alchemy. To find the caricatures for his devastating comments on the hidden aspects of English working- and middle-class life, the aggressive resignation where these two intersect. Bad times in bad housing, cups of tea, cheap furniture, the pub, the stoicism on the faces through the cigarette smoke. Leigh gets in the cracks and fossicks around, finds the frailties and quirks, the inadequacies and redeeming decentness. "It is just ordinary pain in the lives of ordinary people." He is at the kitchen bench now talking over his shoulder. Knowing of the artistic struggle in making his films makes the tension all the more palpable in the viewing. These actors are laying themselves bare in a giant experiment.

We can leave it to Clive James, really, who reviewed *Home Sweet Home* and countered the argument that Leigh's work has nothing in it. "It had everything in it. Every tortured inarticulacy took its place in a fearfully symmetrical confection. There were arias on loneliness and struggling pretension, in which daydreaming wives haltingly poured out their anguish. There were passionless duets in which hang-dog husbands were brought even further to hell. 'Stop treading on the *rug*! You're *squashing* it!' There were long, Mozartian, end-of-the-act ensembles in which everybody said nothing. His communities of zombies speak clichés when they speak at all, but their emotions are real. Even if they feign passion there is genuine deprivation underneath."

For the actors, working with Leigh is a life-changing experience. "Certainly," he agrees, as the brothel bangs away above him, "there is a kind of fraternity of people who have been through it and done it. Certainly you couldn't do it with an actor who was emotionally locked up. You couldn't do it with a thick actor, either. I work with them in private, one-to-one. It finally does sort out a source for the characters and connects it with things in my head. It helps to get a relationship going. I do think that is terribly important, to have a private communication right through to the last day of the shoot, a rapport; it is just, sort of, you care, to me it is a personal and very involving business. In the end what turns me on is just people and their individual way. I am responsible for a number of marriages and a number of children."

When he feels that everyone is ready he starts shooting. "It has to gradually cogitate and percolate. My problem is that I am locked into the well-known syndrome of total procrastination. But when you have a gang of actors on the payroll and a deadline to meet to start shooting, you can't procrastinate any more. All art comes of improvisation. I see my job as being to create a working environment in which other people can be creative in their own terms, while not necessarily expressing the views that they expected to express, so that what we get is something that is organic."

I tell Leigh that an actor once told me that there is a moment on every film where the actor looks into the director's eyes and sees that the director has lost it. In Leigh's case, it would seem that he never has it to lose.

"The answer to that demands a certain degree of modesty to answer honestly. On the one hand, you always see serious panic in my eyes in the sense that I can never say, 'oh well, bugger it, let's just learn the lines and wait for it to come out' because there is no film. I went to dinner at an actor's house shortly before we started filming and he said, 'how is the film?' and I said, 'ah, it is fine except for the fact that there is no film', you know, I said, 'I am mad'. But on the other hand because we rehearse for months on end and everybody really is so *there*, there isn't a kind of paranoia on the go. It really is to do with OK, what is the film, what is it? The actual foundation of the film, the organic base for it, if it works at all, if it seems to be quite solid is because it *is*. It is rooted in something that is real and tangible. I do have a vision, a conception; when things finally start to click depends on various things. It is so knackering you don't get time to be nervewracked really, but it is great, it is just great."

Leigh's perspective in charting the social mores and nuances of Britain's working classes comes from his childhood in the depressed North Country, where smoke poured from chimney stacks, horses shat in the cobblestone streets and men wore cloth caps. "I did grow up in the monumentally ordinary world of the provinces of the 1940s and '50s. But my dad was a doctor. I was a middle-class kid in a working-class area. But that world, the perception of that world, is the perception that shaped my life, absolutely."

As I leave Mike Leigh there is an extremely loud crash from upstairs. We look at each other in tacit agreement that another Mike Leigh Moment has occurred. All by itself.

Mike Leigh and Steven Berkoff have often been lumped

together as great maverick artists working out of the working-class experience, succeeding in spite of the system and establishment and not thanks to it. But it does not necessarily follow that there is admiration among mavericks. I took Berkoff to see *Secrets and Lies*, well, OK, dragged him, he had wanted to see something else. Well. He went berserk. He talked loudly about its banality for 20 minutes—"People don't talk like that. It has started with a funeral, what a downer"—and then to everyone's relief walked out. But, like everything about Berkoff, his tantrum was, I suspect, about something else, something he had recognised in the film.

# All the Way Home

The dirty old river shrinks from its bank as the tide ebbs to the sea. Now and always the lethargic Liffey slides like a black ribbon through the city of Dublin. A city that seems smothered in stale cigarette smoke on this lambent late afternoon. Under the vaulted spires of dusty St Johns the pious and recently sinned kneel contrite over polished mahogany. And over at the Shelbourne Hotel, under crystal chandeliers, the bar is bursting with badinage.

In she comes, Marianne, moving fast. Thin legs in black leggings across the lobby, negotiating deep upholstery, gathering speed at the corner and, oh my God, darlings, thrilled to find old friends ensconced in conspiracy at the bar. Friends, wicked and vivid and wildly eccentric. Friends who would soon, very soon, be responsible for my disappearance.

Marianne, Marianne, oh Marianne; fallen woman, scandalous blonde, one of the truly great bad girls; risen now from the wreckage of her life. Bitten-down nails sail through the air trailing veils of cigarette smoke.

Damaged and raw and still getting straight, Marianne Faithfull came here to Ireland seeking sanctuary and healing as she emerged from deep shadows. "I don't feel I have to watch myself all the time in Ireland. I don't know whether it's the church or the drinking, but they are very forgiving"—filmy chuckle from the bottom of the throat. "I guess all I mean is that they like me. In Ireland my friends have sustained me through a very fragile period of my life."

And here they are at the infamous Shelbourne bar, her hilarious, generous friends. Garech, mad Irish nobility on day-leave from his magical house in the country, resplendent in pinstriped Savile Row and grey ponytail; Roderic, Machiavellian and mischievous, hatching yet another nefarious scheme; John, famous actor, vigorously drowning interestingly complicated marital problems in whiskey.

**MARIANNE FAITHFULL**

Marianne coils untidily into an armchair. Legs splayed, arms waving. "It was good for me to come and see you," she grins, "otherwise I would have lounged around in bed all day." And a girl does require a doona day, we agree with alacrity, every now and then. Well, quite a lot actually. Hair twisted up, long white shirt, black waistcoat, bluebird in flight tattooed across her hand; she is freckled and pale with smudges of black under clear blue eyes.

Marianne Faithfull is still here. Oh yes, manifestly, raucously, emphatically still here. Still here and practically vibrating with gusto. Marianne Faithfull has never held back. Even after everything. Even after her own continuing efforts to extinguish herself. To self-destruct; to simply disappear. "That completely crazy despair where you don't give a shit," she grimly recalls of one of her longer and more interesting dark nights of the soul.

Marianne the cracked goddess of the sex and drugs and rock and roll ethos. Who took it all the way down and made it all the way back, but came back profoundly changed. Came back with defiance and anger and hard-earned street cred; the pain and edgy power that would be folded into every crevice of the unforgiving 'Broken English', the album that broadsided her back from oblivion in 1979 after ten lost years of being broke with bad men, living in squats, scrounging money, beating herself up, pretty much unconscious, sick, sick, sick.

Fighting songs, shockingly explicit anthems about lost youth and the agony of sexual betrayal, sung in the bruised, broken, bitter voice of experience, toughened and deepened by the extraordinary past it describes.

"It was a surprise to a lot of people, that album," she says, tinkering with a fancy teacup, "but not to me. You must remember I know who I am and have done for a long time. Part of that pain was being me and not having anyone else recognise that." She speaks now in that gravelly, grand, cigarette-stained voice; the smashed-up aristocrat with the huge, genuine smile and the low laugh that rumbles across the room.

"Marianne," her pianist Paul Truelove will later tell me, "is her own work of art."

"Obviously I had a very, very serious case of low self-esteem," she says drily, a woman who once spent two years sitting on a wall in London's Soho blitzed on heroin, skeletal, looked out for by other derelicts, trying to become invisible.

Still wearing her fraying finery, she literally hit the wall when she walked out on Mick Jagger and the relentless glare of flash-bulbs as the '60s faded to black. Suddenly the photogenic pop angel with the seemingly enchanted life disappeared from tabloid pages all over the world, mortally wounded by the negative pub-licity after the Redlands drug raid in which the police discovered her on acid, wrapped only in a rug. And a conversation overheard where Ahmet Ertegun, head of Atlanta Records, advised Mick to get rid of her because there was a great deal of money at stake and her drug-taking was a liability. "People can help me by forgetting about me," she said at the time. And so they did. Sort of.

Vanished into a prolonged breakdown pickled in narcotics; a spectacular fall from a dizzying height. Abdicating from myth-ologised rock royalty, she crashed to street junkie with a vengeance; no telephone, no address. Something she still seems to be coming to terms with. Confusion, still, over how such a massive slide could have happened, how she could have ended up on the streets.

"Everyone would say to me 'How could you walk out on all this money, all this fame and most of all, all that security?' Being with Mick Jagger and him protecting me. You can't believe what I walked out on. I felt there must be something wrong with me when I walked out, but I didn't yet know about 'Broken English'. On certain levels I could have what I wanted. But what I wanted he couldn't give me. So I had to go. I didn't leave him because I didn't love him. I say in my book that I left him because I wanted to do drugs. But I think the drugs were a lot to do with it because although I knew I loved him I couldn't stay, I had to go. I couldn't have done what I have done if I had stayed with Mick and I couldn't have got where I have got. I didn't know what was coming, so it was like walking into outer space. It took me a long time to get over the Mick thing; it was a very important relationship for me. There is this sense of failure about it that I have to deal with constantly. I did get over it. But by then I had another problem. I was addicted to heroin." Hopelessly, for years and years. It is as a result of this perhaps that her conversation jumps all over the place, as she waves her arms about. She seems slightly, harmlessly mad; contradictory.

But she speaks with the candour of the survivor who is beyond embarrassment, who has fallen down drunk too many times to care what people think. My colleague Richard Guilliatt remembers seeing her in New York on a panel of politically correct musicians at the height of her various addictions. "She was smoking a cigarette and in full flow of telling them what a bunch of wankers they were when she slid off her chair and disappeared under the table."

She once destroyed a friend's house when she nodded off in a heroin stupor in the bath with the tap running. Water cascaded down two flights of stairs, out the front door and into the street. When she came to, the ceiling on the landing had collapsed and bedroom walls were caving in. "We didn't laugh about that for many, many years. None of her children have got into drugs because they remember what I was like." Well, control was never Marianne's forté. Her acting career pretty much stalled when she made a habit of shooting up before auditions and passing out when she got there.

On the day Mick married Bianca, Marianne spent the night in Paddington police station, having had her own celebration in an Indian restaurant and ending up face-first in a curry. When she received a cheque for £90,000 from her record company for the album after 'Broken English', she rapidly blew the lot on narcotics and clothes with not a great deal of music to show for it. It was shortly after this that Island Records boss Chris Blackwell recognised how dope-sick she was and put her in for six months hard-core detox at Hazelton Clinic.

"There are many stories about my terrible behaviour. I hate them, but I do know they are funny. You lose real control. I couldn't do anything when I was high. You fall and fall and fall and fall. It just keeps getting worse, until you are in the lowest circle of hell and you know you are still going down and there are other circles underneath that. But eventually you fall through the lowest circle and then you fall into the light."

Her autobiography, *Faithfull*, is hilarious and harrowing in its honesty. She has never sought to deceive, she has flaunted her frailties and faults. It has, on her account, been one hell of a life. "It was awful doing the book. I had to keep going back in time." In New York "I just wanted to die. I got very, very frightened. I ended up with someone I didn't even like, didn't even want to speak to, just because I was sort of hopeless. And so it has become a really big deal for me to look after myself, to make my own food, to do my own laundry, wash up my own dishes and not depend on people. It is very difficult. I am an only child and I was very spoiled. I can easily let myself relax into a spoilt life if I want, so I have to definitely turn away from that. I have had a lot of accidents but actually I am very steady and very sure-handed and sure-footed. I don't cut myself when I am chopping onions. I do a lot of forgetting the keys to the house. That's one of the reasons I don't drive, this isn't to do with drugs and alcohol, there just is a part of me that isn't very functional, never has been. I think I would be dead by now if I drove."

Marianne and Mick were young, staggeringly rich, oh so very beautiful, and famous. Privileged, spoilt, on display and on the move, experimenting, with fabulous houses and doing fabulous drugs, they epitomised the last word in '60s chic. But Marianne, just quietly, was never cool. "I am not the slightest bit cool. I say too much, I always have."

Fragile and insecure, she would weep, convinced of her unworthiness, her saturnine unsuitability for adoration and envy. Swallowing 150 Tuinals in Sydney in 1969, when Mick was shooting Ned Kelly, and remaining in a coma for six days, was clearly an indication of the clinical depression, anguish, dangerous games and darkness underlying the glamour. "They were working nearly all the time, that's why the whole thing with Brian Jones was so sad; if you couldn't keep up you couldn't be there. I was a fragile person. Now I feel very connected to the music when I go to see the Stones and they play all the songs and a lot of them are about me. I know that. I get very sort of touched by it. I helped on a lot of those songs, you can see my mind at work quite clearly. I would never claim any of that work though."

As her drug-taking escalated, and after she passed out in the soup at a grand dinner at the Earl of Warwick's castle, Jagger gave up trying to take her anywhere. "Clearly I was not the right person for the job. Being with someone like Mick, it is part of your job as consort to be turned out perfectly, looking wonderful, in very good form, in good humour, always charming. I am not like that. I was never going to be an ego massager for a great star. It is not one of those things where you can really be friends. One of the reasons I can't go to parties now is that I am too embarrassed by not remembering people's names. I feel ashamed. So I don't really go anywhere where I will meet too many people I don't know. I get easily overwhelmed, especially by men. I can't bear it. I have to take it in small increments. I think it is a long time in a dark place."

Marianne knows how easily things come to the beautiful. But only she knew that the person lurking darkly inside bore no resemblance to the outward perfection of her ethereal beauty. "I was so beautiful that I would meet somebody and they would just fall in love," she says without vanity, waving the cigarette, spilling ash. Her compulsion was to tarnish and destroy. "I am very complex indeed." She shrugs.

During the wipe-out years she wilfully ravaged her greatest asset, the great, great beauty that had captured Jagger's heart and compelled the Rolling Stones manager Andrew Oldham to pluck the convent-educated daughter of an Austrian baroness and an eccentric former spy and academic socialist, who had long since divorced, from a bookish adolescence. "I saw an angel with big tits and signed her," he would later say of the innocent who became an overnight sensation with the hit 'As Tears Go By' and an affair with, ahem, Gene Pitney.

In a cocaine psychosis Marianne once took a razor blade to her face. "I developed a violent hatred of my appearance, of my face. Beauty was a curse. It stood between me and who I was." It was as if she had to systematically obliterate that person and live a different life to become another person, to inhabit the history she needed to find her true identity as an artist. She talks about being an artist a lot, it is what sustains her. Makes her more than just Mick Jagger's ex-girlfriend, famous for being famous. "What is very important to my work is that the same blocked emotions turn people into terrorists, I think it is very significant. I have always known that. If I hadn't been an artist, a creative person, I could have been a killer. It has been a channel for me, for my fury. I don't really know why, I am not even that interested, I have done therapy and it has helped tremendously. But why I am the way I am is not really that interesting to me. I had to learn to function in the world without drugs. But it is not easy and I am not necessarily an easy person to be with. But"—throaty laugh—"my friends like me."

A person immensely likeable on stage. Angie Bowie described Marianne back in the dark days as "riveting, magnificent on stage. That was one slow lady—until she had to hit her mark and perform, at which point she emerged from her cloud and flat-out nailed it. Then she would simply pass out until it was time to perform again or go home." Agrees her friend Martin Sharp, "She is a great chanteuse. It seems as if a purity has come through. She is very tough, an archetypal figure on a grand scale. She is a great warrior woman."

Looking at her now is to see that the twin evils of cigarettes and substance abuse do not guarantee premature decrepitude. Though nearly fifty, she is, in spite of herself, still gamely beautiful. (Although next time I see her, in Sydney, she has gained weight and the skin has somehow coarsened, like sandpaper.) "I sort of scrub up well, so I can see now that I was built to last," she allows. And now that her beauty has been sharpened and marked by time and by living hard—a scar runs down her jawline, the legacy of a fall while overdosing on heroin, and her smile is changed by having had two front teeth knocked out by a male nurse in a failed attempt to detox—she has grown into it.

"I am beginning to understand a lot more than I did and I have a lot more confidence." The arms wave as if to embrace everything and everybody. To talk to her is to understand how she survived her own assault. Open, friendly and vulnerable, she is literally full of life. A life force that could not be dimmed, an aristocracy of the soul, a dignity reclaimed.

The arm waving she uses to illustrate every utterance frequently gives the impression she is about to take flight. And maybe she is.

"It is a fabulous relief to live without drugs. I am not in the kind of pain I was. If I was in that kind of pain I would have to take drugs, I am sure. But I am not. I have got my music and I have got a really wonderful life now. My shrink says the reason I came through was because my mother loved me so much, I had the actual experience of real love, somebody who really loved me. He deals with a lot of addicts and he says the thing that is really heart-breaking is that it is impossible with many people because they really have no idea of the difference between love and hate. And I do. I think my mother was the love of my life. Nobody could be like that again. I miss her very much. I survive and always have on the love and goodwill of my friends who really do love me."

But, alas, her friends appear to have fallen in with some bad company, judging by the racket coming from under the hunting prints over there in the corner.

When Van Morrison asked her to sing 'Madame George' as soundtrack for the film *Moondance*, in which she plays a seeress character, they did it in two takes. "We don't fuck about, I don't know what it was about our generation that made us so quick, so talented and so fast, but you just go in and you just do it. My writing skills have come very slowly and very hard, I wasn't really a born songwriter, but I have really learned my craft, it didn't happen overnight."

You have to be so careful. We are doing girl stuff about guys. If the relationship with Mick Jagger damned her to hell for 10 years, her second husband, bad bass guitarist Ben Brierly, and his affairs caused the grief that pervaded 'Broken English'. "I loved him, he really hurt me."

Marianne has been married and divorced three times. She knows how dangerous love can be for the vulnerable and damaged, that the fragile self can be lost and fragmented in careless hands. "I am very, very careful with my sex life and my love relationships because that is the one area that is mysterious to me and I just can't take that risk. It is very sad really. I often meet people I could fall in love with but I hold back. I love men but they are terrified of me. I am afraid that if I let myself go and it didn't work out it would lead to the downward spiral. I fucked around long enough."

Marianne lost custody of her son Nicholas, now thirty and a writer, from her first marriage when she was blitzed on the wall. When he was seventeen he was horrified when he came to visit her in New York and she arrived at the airport in a limo offering him lines of coke. Now, astonishingly, she is a grandmother. "It is really lovely. Particularly because I was such a failure as a mother. It is so wonderful to have this little one who has come to us clean, without all the pain that Nicholas and I have had. We love each other so much but we will always have a lot of sorrow between us because I didn't really think about Nicholas. I will always feel very bad about it. He didn't like my book, nor would any son. But he is a very good friend."

As if all of it has been to lead to this late flowering.

Eventually she will return to Shell Cottage, with its shell-encrusted five-walled living room built for Queen Victoria, to have a cup of tea, near Dublin where she lives—the demons apparently vanquished—in self-imposed isolation. A house she first encountered on an acid trip in the mid '60s and tried to persuade Jagger to buy. But first there are extremely interesting matters to attend to at the bar. "Come and have a drink and meet my friends," she generously offered.

And this, dear reader, is where the trouble started.

Drink, naturally, followed drink at the bar of the Shelbourne Hotel. Every time we got up to leave someone would arrive well met and another round of drinks would have to be bought, another long and winding conversation would have to be started and never finished. More than once we made it all the way out to the front lobby, only to turn back to the bar. They were all there that night, the scroungers and chancers, the poets, the princes among men, the lawyers, the eccentrics, the artists, the actors and writers arguing, bantering, scheming, laughing, shouting, digressing, bullshitting, telling stories.

"There is the love of language that happens," a young actor told me. "It is all on the basis of irony. You are never quite sure if what somebody says is what they mean. There are all these kind of codes and signals that people get through and yet there is all this talk. If you are doing OK here it is a great place, but if people are down on their luck it gets dangerous, there is begrudgery."

Roderic and Garech were conducting boisterous business with barristers at the bar, fighting business that Roderic cheerfully assured me had already left people "not talking for several generations. It is a filthy fight."

They all drank and fought here, once, Behan, Joyce, Beckett, revelling in the musicality of their own language. I turned at one point to the darkly handsome man sitting next to me and realised with a jolt that it was the actor Gabriel Byrne. Sitting and smiling and sipping a Guinness, in Ireland everyone is famous. When I looked back he had vanished into the smoke, as rare things will.

The next day I staggered out of my aggressively narrow Catholic bed and went down to lunch in my rather less ornate hotel, across the depressed and sluggish River Liffey. Outside it was seeping grey to the ground and raining, dripping sadness. A Gaelic football game was playing on the television in the corner, its cheerleaders dancing in the rain, traditionally, arms chastely at sides lest an errant hand invite hanky panky. The three-piece band in the restaurant played desultorily, the singer smoking a cigarette and watching the television as she sang. And then the phone rang. It was Roderic, inviting me over to the Shelbourne. For drinks. Well that was it. After that I was pretty much AWOL in Ireland. I had fallen in with some excellent bad company, all right, and it would be some time before I would find my way clear.

The rain eased up as we drove through the formal Georgian squares of the city, their brass trimmings gleaming, past the literary pubs where political movements were plotted, great works shaped and promising careers drunk away, out past all the houses with their primly secretive lace curtains blurring like so many rows of frothing underwear hanging on a line. Out through Dublin and up, up into the misty hills where lustrous green valleys fall away into graceful sculpted curves and green fades to yellow and back to green, but a different wet and silky green, past stone cottages worn by wind and rain still streaming smoke from cracked chimneys, history seeped into the black haunted earth, where music and stories from times past are whispered on the wind, and across the purple plain where the twilight plays spectrally, and into the pub. The Roundwood Inn, County Wicklow, full of misfits and movie stars, with its fire blazing and its people roaring, and over there is Jim Sheridan grinning and across the table is John Hurt smoking, Neil Jordan is at the bar and I am discovering myself to be Celtic through and through after an absence of five generations. The madness, the wildness, the music, the garrulous warmth, the soft landscape, tapping on my shoulder and unleashing some kind of genetic memory. To my utter surprise I feel like I have arrived home after a long and turbulent epic voyage. Nah. Must be the drink affecting the cortex, getting fanciful. Until Garech puts his hand on my shoulder and says, "You belong, you are one of us." Something he will repeat in the surreal days to come.

The light wakes me up as the curtains are softly drawn and a man is standing by my bed with a tray. Excuse me. A what? Jaysus, I must have been drunk. But it's only Nicholas the butler with tea. I remember him now, he was ironing Garech's nightshirt in the kitchen when we stumbled in shrieking last night. And there are deer grazing on the smooth emerald grass out the window, ambling under great ancient trees and across the antediluvian landscape. And I am in the most beautiful place I have ever seen.

"No fucking," Garech had called last night as he leapt out of the window of his eighteenth century castle and weaved down the park towards the lake. "No fucking," he cried merrily as he poured his guests endless drinks and played haunting traditional Irish laments which required that we all join hands and bow our heads. Well, all except John Hurt, who snored softly in an armchair beside the large and dramatic Francis Bacon fireplace.

Garech Browne is an eccentric Guinness heir, an Anglo-Irish aristocrat, whose noblesse oblige and generosity are bred into the bone. He is the owner of Claddagh Records which has for many years recorded poetry and traditional Irish music and is a lyrical archive of this poetic race; it was he who put the Chieftains together and first recorded them. Luggala, his enchanted white house, built by the Huguenots, with its winding staircases and many rooms, its arches and crenellations, its cobblestoned courtyard, its treasures, is set in a hidden valley down a steep road and surrounded by moss-covered rock cliffs that rear up and bow like chiselled horses and fold reflected into a still, shining lake. On the edge of the lake is an elegant mausoleum for his brother Tara Browne, killed in a car accident in the late '60s, whose 21st birthday here at Luggala was attended by the Rolling Stones, among others of the beau monde.

Marianne Faithfull sat here by the fire barely articulate as she recovered, John Houston and his family stayed when he was filming Ireland. The house has always been full of music, it is that kind of house, open and shared with artists great and small. One night from the windows we saw a girl in a flimsy white cotton dress and wild hair come shrieking from the courtyard like an ethereal banshee. Richard Harris, big, craggy and handsome, his white hair falling across his face, strode across the grass and picked her up as if she were a rag doll and held her tight as she cried and shivered in his arms and the film crew stood around stamping in the cold.

I fell in love with it, all of it—they were so funny—and was drawn back again and again.

"You got Luggala'd," John Hurt would tell me later in London. We were sitting in Garech's club in Soho at the time, watching Garech, resplendent in a three-piece, loudly pinstriped ensemble recently stitched by his tailor, look for a phone number, during which piles of papers and envelopes, legal letters, the lot—an entire filing cabinet in fact—was fished from his many pockets. Then he swept his cloak across his shoulders and we went out into the night.

One morning Garech woke up at Luggala to find John Hurt standing at the end of his bed. "I dreamed of Kenya last night," said John, collapsing onto the bed with a theatrical flourish, "so now I must go there."

"No, no," said Garech, "don't go!" John, in terrible emotional pain, had sought refuge at Luggala following the collapse of his third marriage. He was not, Garech felt, in any shape to be going anywhere, let alone Kenya. Especially not Kenya. Because in Kenya was wife number two. Boo, hiss, sign of the cross. It was widely felt that he should move forward, not backwards. This was the whim of a heart-broken man who must be stopped from making a terrible mistake.

It was a crisis situation. Delay tactics must be urgently put into place. What followed was one of the funniest days of my life. The first and most obvious tactic involved getting John drunk. Which of course necessitated the rest of us getting drunk with him. I was enlisted to interview him to keep him occupied, but what with all the shenanigans and everything, well.

In the Roundwood Inn, Roderic sought to remind John of life with wife number two in a long discursive story about a swish party in London. John and wife number two had had a terrible fight at this party during which John had dramatically stormed out. Only he had stormed into the broom closet. Nevertheless, he stormed and bur-rowed in the dark for ages, determined to complete his departure. His friends stood around waiting outside the closet which heaved and crashed until finally, defeated, John emerged with a feather duster caught in his collar. "Well," said Roderic, raising his glass and completing his story with a flourish, "here's to new brooms."

The Machiavellian machinations went on around John as we drank. Hushed urgent phone calls were made—the manager of Garech's estate was instructed to drive a tractor across the road, the driver instructed to drive at no more than 10 miles an hour all the way to Dublin—until it was all arranged. John would miss his flight. Tomorrow he would feel better.

But there is a kind of determination that overcomes the drinking. Every obstacle secretly put in his path only served to make John more resolved. He got away on us, in the end, got his flight with minutes to spare. "Well," said Roderic when the news came through from the airport, "the operation was a success but we lost the patient."

# The Rocky Road to Dublin

It may have been a mistake to do the interview at the bar of the Roundwood Inn, as the mist drifted down from the purple hills and across the still, cold lakes. It may, admittedly, have been a mistake to accept that first champagne cocktail *quite* so early in the day. But here I was in what appeared to be a hoe-down situation. Dogs were barking and fiddlers were, well, fiddling.

Fortunately, and unlike my new friends or indeed myself, Paddy Moloney was not drinking heavily. But this was, of course, before the Barstool Incident occurred. Nevertheless, during what we will loosely call an interview arranged by Garech from his bed this morning there will be digressions and digressions from digressions as the crack goes down, cousins and friends join in, and the stories are told; the stories of heartache, illegal whiskey, drunken regret, grief, conspiracy and celebration that characterise the music of his band, the Chieftains. With a bit of a jig and a reel thrown in and Garech lurking dangerously in the background. Talk about laugh. Like the time Van Morrison somehow locked himself in the shower upstairs and they had to ram the door down. "Van came to see me about making an album. We installed him upstairs here, in a magnificent room. I came back the next morning at 8.30 to bring him up to my house. He was in the shower trying to get the hot water working. We heard this strange noise, we went up the stairs and said, 'What's wrong?' He said, 'I'm locked in the bathroom, I can't get out'. So I tried to open the door, I tried everything. There was no key and we couldn't get a locksmith. So we had to ram the door, a beautiful door. Only to discover that the boyo had only put the latch on it and it would have opened anyway. Out he comes with his hair all snazzed up and his suit on and we were standing there looking at this beautiful door. Actually I think I am responsible for bringing him back onto the drink."

Behind the bar the phone keeps ringing for Paddy, the tiny man in the jacket with the major nose, and we lose the thread all over again. And then Paddy and Garech are dancing and swinging along the bar.

The Chieftains are the result of centuries of the musicality that is seeped into the Irish skin; the ancient songs of loss and grief, love and war, that can be melancholy or happy or lonesome or wild or fighting insurrection, depending on the state of the musician at the time, stirring songs that capture the old landscape and make you cry or dance, depending on how drunk you are. Songs that wring the sentimental Celtic heart. Yearning. They like a good yearn, the Irish. "Music is the one source of entertainment that the Irish people had," says your man Moloney. "When I was growing up, there was no source of electricity in the country, only a tilly lamp, and a dry battery radio that my grandfather would only turn on on Saturday for the football. So you never heard anything except the people coming in and singing and dancing. We are a very proud nation. We never talk about the famine because we are totally ashamed. But we always went to each other's houses and told stories, and danced, played cards, sang songs, played music and composed some great music. The old sofa beds did wonders. Everybody would sing; most of the tunes are picked up by ear."

When they perform, the Chieftains are having a musical conversation. "What has happened over the years is that we have gotten to know each other so well that the whole thing blends, everybody knows how everybody else is feeling. We introduce automatic, unrehearsed, unorganised songs, we play musical jokes, we want to get close to the audience. Most of us grew up in traditional Irish families and most of the tunes were picked up by ear. All that music is stored away over a lifetime, it comes out in the middle of a session. If I have a party up at the house and some of the musicians come along, things just happen."

Indeed in Dublin with Garech one night at a traditional music commemoration I saw all the spontaneity and all the pain and all the passion that an oppressed people can pour into their music. The musicians sitting around in circles coming in and out of the tunes as the mood took them. The men all spruced up in terrible jackets and ties, grinning toothlessly as they squeezed accordions, hair slicked firmly down as they tickled their flutes and whistles, shy, cheeks shining, suddenly articulate when they played and keened.

Garech at times is overcome, the music touches him to the core. "It is the beauty of it," he tells me on the way to the Roundwood Inn, driving along past the lake, and the gatehouse perched on the rock, and up the steep valley road where the hills fold away as far as the eye can see and ruined stone walls tumble. "It is not the sadness that overcomes us, it is the beauty. Every time a tune is played it is played differently, that is why no musician is greater than another. When musicians gather together to celebrate something they join in and cut out. They don't know what all the others are going to do and they don't necessarily know all the same tunes. The real joy within the individual is playing something in a completely different way from anyone else, so when you turn on the radio you know the piper immediately. A fiddle player from Galway would be different from a fiddle player from Clare. The music is played in the house, in the pubs, in the street."

Small, perky, happy Moloney, now in his late 50s, looks rather like a dapper jockey. He has led the Chieftains for some 32 years and 31 albums—"We are a democracy but I usually get my way in the end"—during which their delicately shimmering traditional folk music has crossed over into the mainstream in a big way without ever losing its purity. "With the Chieftains we bring out the colour of the tune, you can't bastardise it for the sake of commercialism, the things we turn down are enormous. But the repertoire of traditional Irish music is vast," says Moloney, sitting down after an impromptu jig with an old friend. "It captures all the old landscapes, but you can pick a tune, happy or sad, for even the most lonesome jig, the slowest air or lament, is meant to be danced to if you listen for it. You can get whatever you want from it. You have first of all the ancient Irish music, which is lovely in itself, then you have songs which can turn into airs played on an instrument, you have different kinds of dance music, you have so much dance music it is incredible. You have music for the harp, you have music to do with events, summertime, winter into spring, birds and bees, fading away into autumn. We were the first band from the West to play in China, they probably didn't understand a word of the music but we had a standing ovation because the language doesn't matter when the music is true."

From the beginning, in the '60s, the Chieftains were intrinsically hip, taken up by the Rolling Stones and the Beatles. "We were always classified as musicians' musicians," says Moloney. "The music is true. I was doing some backing tracks for Paul McCartney the day John Lennon was shot. He came into the studio in Oxford Circus and met up with all his mates. It was a very sad day."

On their album 'Long Black Veil', which has sold several million copies, they have called on old friends to sing old songs, while they shade every note with mad fiddle and flute and demented tin whistle and keening pipes. Marianne Faithfull's is a cracked lament, Mick Jagger is in rebellion, Sinead O'Connor sings the Easter Rising lament 'The Foggy Dew' with absolute purity, Sting sings sad harmony and Tom Jones belts out 'Tennessee Waltz' from somewhere around the bowel region, a song that was playing on every jukebox in every bar in Manhattan. "They really come out of the woodwork"—Paddy has to keep stopping to greet people coming in—"they couldn't believe he would be on this album."

And in the middle of 'Rocky Road to Dublin' there is a weird moment when it turns into 'Satisfaction'. That day the Rolling Stones just happened to be rehearsing down the road at Ronnie Woods's house. "We sent a bus for them," says Moloney. "Heh, heh, and we provided the Guinness. A bit of a party started, people started dancing and at midnight we hadn't a note on tape. I managed to persuade them to suspend the party for a minute so we could record. I thought I had everything under control but it just went on and on. People were going mad in the studio. Once they were going they were going. At three in the morning we all retired to a pub and there were thirty or forty young people there banging out Irish songs and we guzzled pints of Guinness until six in the morning."

Those kinds of things happen around here; let me tell you, people were going mad in the Roundwood Inn. Or was it just me?

The twilight flickers across the hills, melancholy grey, and the mist touches the ground as night comes down. The secretive landscape from which the music comes is, says Moloney, "a very important part of your whole being. It is your language, your taste-buds. There is inspiration there. I believe in reincarnation of some kind. The ponds and little streams where we played as children. I remember at Easter it would be wet and miserable; I would be up a tree. A little story happens in your head. I can see the tunes in my head. I see the whole structure of how that fits into whatever I am writing for. The music is within you if you are Irish. When I was at school we sang a lot of the three-part Irish harmonies. We had these house dances where everybody in the room would sing a song. The dancing would stop and the tea would be served and everybody would sing. You were forced into it, it was coaxed out of you."

Inside the Roundwood Inn the fire roars, or is it the people who are roaring? Hard to tell. Oh. It's me. The inn was full, they were shouting and singing. The famous Anglo-Irish actor on my right was crying into his Guinness, I do remember that.

On my tape, there is the portentous wail of the tin whistle in the distance, followed by an extremely loud crash. It was at this juncture, it seems, that your correspondent became just a trifle unprofessional. I didn't think I was *that* drunk. But they said it was spectacular. They said it was a swan dive off a barstool. And then they suggested I might like to leave fairly soon. Coming from an Irish publican, this, I thought, was a bit rich, possibly a lifetime achievement.

■ ■ ■

I tried to escape after that, I tried to walk back to Dublin down the middle of the road, I am told. The rocky road to Dublin. But there was always someone arriving, another round to be bought, another story to be told. I tried to escape from a pub up in the Wicklow Mountains one night. Roderic said we would never get out because there was a semi-trailer jack-knifed in the road so we might as well have another drink. His friend Peter backed Roderic up, embellishing the full horror of the accident. Some time later Peter reappeared wild-eyed. "There *is* a truck jack-knifed in the road," he wailed, amazed to have been telling the truth.

# Shagging Joyce

There is a shagging lot of vomiting in Joseph O'Connor's shagging books. He is after all—throbbingly and achingly—a Young Irish Male. And that is what Young Irish Males do. Full of strange mischief, they get drunk, laugh, talk a lot, fight, try to have sex, fail to have sex, vomit, and then they shagging well pass out. Usually in the gutter in Dublin's O'Connell Street. In this respect the Young Irish Male closely resembles the Old Irish Male.

In *True Believers*, for example, the indefatigable narrator is trying to pick up a girl at a bus stop: 'Yes. She remembered me now. I was pretty flattered, actually, until she pointed out the reason she remembered me. I was the one who had puked over the aspidistra in the hall.'

They are howling down O'Connell Street on this moist Saturday night, that's for sure, as the elusive whiff of the promising encounter drifts across the old black river, up the dirty old streets and into the radiant pubs.

Large, and dressed in black, Joseph O'Connor strolls across the cobbles of Grafton Street, music pouring from buskers, and into Bewley's coffee shop. Fortunately there are no aspidistras here. And the novelist has disturbingly healthy pink cheeks. He extends a huge and fleshy hand. He stares shyly at the linoleum floor, blinking through rimless spectacles. He lights a cigarette.

In his book *The Secret World of the Irish Male*, he portrays himself as overweight, unhealthy, cocky and constantly rejected. "I am not actually as self-deprecating as I make out," he says wryly now. He is in fact, in person, kindly, gentle and humorous; a soft man, with a purring lyrical loquacity. And of course, being Irish, argumentative and opinionated. "I am a Virgo," he smiles, "and Virgos are great watchers. I like people who behave strangely." Well, he's in the right country for *that*.

And in exploring the wild frustrations and elations, not to mention the erections, of the Young Irish Male, O'Connor is clearly not bound by the constraints of the family newspaper. This is not always family journalism. 'Scratch and smell', he calls it. But the Irish do understand the playfully loud and profane. The great, satisfying beauty of bad language. "The Irish like to talk to each other, it is just a culture that expresses its longing in that way," explains O'Connor.

But, at 32, O'Connor is getting over his drinking and bonking phase now, his juvenilia. He is moving on to bigger themes. "To be honest, I think it is a very puerile affectation that a lot of young male novelists suffer from. Particularly when they come from repressive societies like this one. There you are writing your first novel and you know that your granny is going to read it and you are going to say to your granny: 'I have sex, I have drunk too much, I have taken drugs.' It takes you one book to get all that out of your system. I try to be more sparing on the bodily functions now."

Still, his novels do deal with the grittiness and the abrasions of urban life. As the Irish novel has moved from pastoral to urban, so, too, have its writers, writing in the scatological voice of their generation, against a tremendous and formidable literary tradition. "When I was a kid in the suburbs in the '60s, there weren't any novels about the world I felt I lived in. It just made no sense. But it is great to have the tradition because it is a very useful thing to write against. It is always good for writers to have that windmill to tilt at. It is one of the reasons why the English novel is in a lot of trouble, because the English own the novel. They have had the novel for 200 years and they have run out. Whereas I think we did nothing for a long time and this century we have had these giants, the greatest poet of the century and the greatest novels and the greatest playwright, so there is always this thing there in the background going 'you will never be good enough, why bother, why bother getting out of bed in the morning to write when Joyce was still alive only fifty years ago?'. It is a challenge, it puts it up to you, you know, it is a macho thing. It almost frustrates you into doing it. In some way, although we possess the English language now, we are also possessed by it. There is a playfulness about the English language here. It is just a culture that expresses its longing. Everyone knows it is made up but it doesn't really matter. One of the good things about being a writer is that you are young until you are over forty. If I was a footballer my career would be over now."

His novel *Desperados* is a big, ambitious, sprawling book set in Ireland, London and Nicaragua and is about a family whose son has gone missing in South America. "I had a dream about it and that is the truth. It really popped out in my sleep." His own family, which includes his younger sister Sinead O'Connor, is big, messy and obviously talented. There are eight children from three marriages.

"It sounds like a big, happy Irish Catholic family, when in fact it isn't. My stepmother is a Proddie from Northern Ireland, sort of unionist, and my dad is a working-class Catholic. So there are some very interesting political discussions over the Sunday dinner. There are a lot of Irish novels and plays about awful fathers, there are very few nice fathers in Irish literature. I started thinking about what that must mean, an entire generation, generation upon generation of Irish writers who hate their fathers, who were not dutiful. I think it is probably no secret that my parents didn't have the happiest marriage ever, they didn't get on very well. They didn't have much formal education themselves so I think they were always interested in the doors to those kinds of worlds being open to us. They would never have been pushy about it but I think it was important to them that we were interested in books and painting and music. I think they thought that to have respect for the creative process and the imagination was important, and the sacredness of that has passed itself onto us."

Well, his little sister has certainly carried the family tradition of debating the Irish problem into the public arena. "It took 800 years to create this problem, and what I detest is this short-term slogan-chanting that some people, including my sister, go on with. I think it is terribly unhealthy. This is a terribly fucking complex problem. In fact for people of my age who weren't born in the north, it made no difference and that is the truth. The north was a strange foreign place, with nothing at all to do with us. You saw it on the news, growing up in Dublin, and you saw it on TV, and I never thought of it as anything to do with me. Then, the way history was taught in schools at the time, there was a copy of the 1916 proclamation in every classroom, the call to arms. We were never once told in school that the situation was anything to do with us. On some levels, the sort of separation and national amnesia that went on throughout the north was one of the reasons it was able to get as out of hand as it did. And the truth is that people in the south just didn't give a shit about it. It is only very recently that they have, only in the past three or four years. We still regard the north and its inhabitants as having a completely different mindset to us. It is seen as a conflict between the British and the Sinn Fein. The key to the problem is the republic. We have to decide whether we actually want them or not and if we are prepared to remove the Catholic church from our laws to the extent that we would make the idea of the republic attractive to unionists. We have been left out of that completely, yet it is totally to do with us."

O'Connor is stirring his cappuccino thoughtfully. His books are written in flinty, seedy detail; you know about every wet spot, every painfully embarrassing failure. It is bloody hard work, that kind of detail. The personal hygiene starts to go. "I was living with someone when I wrote *Cowboys and Indians* and I just drove this poor woman nuts. She would come home at 6 pm from doing a real job and I would go, 'Look darling, look at what I did today. I wrote this paragraph.' And she would read it and go, 'I think that's really good.' All writers are paranoid and I would go, 'You don't think it's really good, you're only saying that.' And then, if I finally got her to say, 'Well I do think it could be better', I would go, 'See, you hate me.' I wouldn't recommend writing to anybody because it is hard to do and it is extremely frustrating. It is a terrible life. Most writers suffer from self-doubt and the secret feeling that they are crap and the constant feeling that you are going to be discovered. A lot of writing is incredibly unglamorous and just dull hard work. But from when I was a kid I wanted to write. I was trying to write at night and on the weekends, when I had a job. I just thought well, I am going to chuck my job and give it all up. If it doesn't work I will go out and get a job but either way I won't be the sad old bastard who sits there at the age of 50 going, 'I could have written a novel but I never got around to it'."

They are staggering down Grafton Street. The Saturday Night Special. Drunks everywhere, falling down in the street, sleeping in the gutter, kissing in the doorways. All the boyos. All the pretty girls, dressed up for a big night out. "I love Dublin," says O'Connor. "I think what is interesting about this generation of writers is to write about it in a contemporary way, an honest way. You don't have to be James shagging Joyce any more. You can write about what this city is really like rather than literary notions of what it is like. One of the things about the later Joyce is this idea that these books are so marvellously impenetrable that it is up to you the reader to do all the work. Well I just reject that, it is an amoral view. I think the writer is there to serve society, is there to change the world. And the way you change the world is that you change it in a small way. I think my job as storyteller is to reach out of the pages of that book and grab the reader by the lapels and put it on the plate in front of them in all of its garish fucking glory."

# A Savage Medium

A beam of celestial light suddenly breaks through the high leaden sky. It plays beatifically across the deep mist-shrouded valley as if guided by an unseen hand. Jim Sheridan smiles at the shining, strobing light as if he has arranged the scenery himself. You know, had a word. Cue in a hundred violins. While the actors posture histrionically in the ancient street, the Irish countryside is quietly putting on an electric light show of its own. Completely upstaging the actors, and throwing up a brilliant rainbow, it practically insists on being in the film. And it obviously knows a thing or two about lighting and timing.

Today is a particularly harrowing day in the shooting of *Some Mother's Son*, the story of Bobby Sands, the IRA hunger striker who starved himself to death in prison in 1981 after being elected an MP. Bobby by this late stage is pretty much on the extremely slim side.

The tall, formidable stone houses in the seaside village look on disapprovingly as if the vulgarity of a film crew is an affront. Lace curtains primly conceal their secrets.

It has not been easy finding the great Irish writer/director, Jim Sheridan, partly because he has that leprechaun habit of flitting off, partly because he is making two films back-to-back, partly because he gave me the wrong instructions and I have been chasing him across the countryside ever since, and mostly because of that playful Irish hobby of giving foreigners the wrong directions on purpose. The circles I walked in to bring you this interview, I tell you.

But Sheridan is grinning wildly as he ushers me to his ageing Mercedes. Short, stocky and with a shock of white hair, he saunters genially through the chaos of a film set on slightly bandy legs, greeting people as if they are guests at his party and me like an old friend. I have seen him in the past few days in that chancy pub, the

Roundwood Inn, hunched over his laptop writing his next film, about the early life of Brendan Behan, while they argue and yell and crash around him. That is where I cornered him, finally, to get this interview. "You can run, Jim, but you can't hide," I said, bailing him up in the corner. He cracked quite quickly really. It may, of course, have been the insanity that was in my eyes by now that did it.

He was thinking up, no doubt, hunched over his computer, more ways for actors to turn themselves inside out. It is not easy being an actor in a Sheridan film. All the more difficult, perhaps, because his films are about the real suffering of his people. These things happened, he did not make this stuff up. The Irish stories written in blood. The unrelenting sadness and pain.

John Lynch playing Bobby Sands had to convincingly starve to death—"he has had to lose a lot of weight"; Sean Penn would have had to drink himself to death as Brendan Behan if he hadn't pulled out at the last minute—"the pictures of Brendan as a kid are Sean Penn, you know"; Daniel Day-Lewis had to be completely crippled with cerebral palsy as Christy Brown in *My Left Foot*, then lose 30 pounds and spend 15 years in jail for a bombing he did not commit in *In the Name of the Father*—"he is very focused, Daniel, very pure, determined, a good worker"; and Richard Harris in the extraordinary *The Field* had to go mad with grief and wade into the freezing North Sea with no immediate plans to return. John Hurt, unrecognisable as a mischievous cackling miscreant. "Never trust a woman," says Richard Harris, "who has no contact with the earth. Our fathers' fathers' fathers dug that soil with their bare hands, I have learned the lesson of the land."

"Yeah, well, people like a challenge," says Sheridan serenely as the village rapidly recedes into the distance and elaborate churches, castles and flat fields flash past. "I think it makes it more real, more worthwhile, otherwise you are just looping around the place, you know, pretending you are someone else. That is debilitating. I don't believe Marlon Brando when he says acting is not important.

I think he said that after he had done his best work. I do think it is important. Film is a savage medium."

Sheridan's powerful, raw films use Irish stories to throw the injustices, the grief, the repression in your face. Writ large. A message of angry integrity tempered by the fact that he is a fine and unsentimental filmmaker.

"I think the truth of anyone who has been traumatised as a person, never mind a State, is that history is always there," says yer man, yawning. "Sometimes I get fed up with people who have problems, no names no pack drills, like famous people who have problems and are projecting them all the time. I think the same is true of a country. It is like, sure, there's problems in the past and there's traumas, you know, but there's not much point in reliving it unless you have an alternative vision to get you out of it, you know. Otherwise you go back over and over it. But we *can* get over it, eventually we can get over it. You know, the films I am making are to help get over it. I am not trying to drag everyone into the past. I am trying to make a future that is optimistic. But sometimes you have to confront the people who traumatised you, you know. I think that is what we did with *In the Name of the Father* and it is what we are doing with this film. The pain is in not expressing things. You know, pain is in keeping it in. It lightens me up when I do them, it is weird, it has the effect of getting rid of excess emotion."

A man of great good humour, Sheridan is the most mischievous and unpretentious of men, speaking in the working-class lilt of the rough Dublin dock area from which he comes, the eldest of eight. "A lot of people say it is a very working-class, tough area. It has gone druggy now because a lot of people have moved out, it is a kind of dumping ground. You know I was an altar boy and a mummy's boy, I was spoiled through the gills and I would recommend it. My mother's mother died when she was born. I was the eldest so I think she was very relieved when neither her nor me died when I was born. So I think I was even kind of more loved than normal which is not a bad thing. I suppose there is a price for any woman who tries to have a relationship with me," he is laughing now.

Everything changed with *My Left Foot*, nominated for five Oscars, winning two, the unromantic and unbeautiful film about a mother's love for her severely crippled child which led the current, inspired Irish film renaissance. Until then Sheridan had worked in fringe theatre in Dublin and run the Irish Arts Centre in New York for seven years, living in Hells Kitchen, always broke, writing tough social realism plays that never saw the spotlight. "I had a long apprenticeship"—hollow laugh—"I didn't get my teeth done for seven years. When my daughter Tess was born premature and had to go into the incubator, I didn't have the money to pay the $1500 a day." His only experience with movie making had been a six-week film course.

"I did the sound on a film about growing tomatoes," he chuckles. "*My Left Foot* was a kind of breakthrough"—he is hunched down and leaning on the steering wheel and yawning again—"because it was about an emotional cripple breaking out and, erm, in many ways it was kind of like the state of here, you know. The breakthrough to expression in a visual rather than a verbal way. I don't think it was any accident that Christy couldn't speak very well. Because every Irish hero up until then had unlimited gift of the gab like Oscar Wilde and O'Casey. It is a fact of Irish life that we like to talk, and when you've been deprived of power, words are your only possession. Our English is Joycean: hyperbole, all over the place, big story worlds and crazy storytelling. I mean the one condition in Ireland is unlimited ability to communicate verbally, whereas Christy hasn't got that and that dynamic is what the film is about. The film moves in a funny way from a verbal theatrical to a film culture. It is smashing through some walls. Success is a big instrument for change because it creates role models. When the moment occurred where we were shooting the scene where Daniel attacks the girl at the dinner party, well, I knew, God, this performance is amazing. And no matter what, I am going to be happy with this myself. And when you are happy with something yourself that is the best feat."

Suddenly he was famous and fêted. "I always say there is an ego thing inside that says 'I am right, I am right, they are wrong, they're wrong. I think I am right.' And then you are going up the hill all the time and suddenly you get to a level when you are on a plateau and you are saying, 'I knew I was right, I *knew* they were wrong.' As you head downhill you sort of think, 'I am always right, they are always wrong.' Before fame you know. But I have been up and down two or three times now. I wasn't bowled by fame. And I was actually surprised that other people were, you know. And that it affected them in a bad way."

Criticism flew in an appalled Britain reeling in the rubble from a spate of devastating bombings when *In the Name of the Father* was released. It was an unapologetic look at the ruined lives of those wrongly accused of the Guildford bombings in 1974, the acting seamless, the grainy greys and browns an incredibly sad evocation of stunning injustice and awful reality. An unrepentant Sheridan was denounced for maligning British justice, romanticising terrorism, boosting support for the IRA and playing fast and loose with the facts. "We were just describing the reality, you know," he says. "And the nonsense that sometimes the authorities come out with in England that we are either pro-IRA or anti-IRA is all just nonsense. Anything that is true hurts. And when it hurt them they had to react and, um, you know, the problem with England is that it was always so powerful. Everybody keeps saying to me, did you compromise on this and this. It never enters my head, you know, compromise. If somebody tried to make me compromise I would go the opposite way. I would become an anarchist or something. I think I give off a vibe, 'don't try to make me compromise'—not in a bad way, I think I am easy to work with."

As he says this Jim Sheridan throws the traffic into chaos because he has cruised majestically round a roundabout the wrong bloody way. "There are stories here, millions of them."

Indeed there are, you can hardly move across the countryside without falling over a film crew. Cameras rolling lovingly across the obligingly moody landscape with its changing, playful light have been known to find another film crew hoving into view. One day I stood and watched Stephen Rea and Richard Harris in an apple orchard in a film. It was a wedding scene at a big stone farmhouse covered in ivy, fairy lights in the trees, a bridal table covered with flowers and a bride frozen in her wedding waltz. There were some great Irish faces among the extras. I had passed two other film crews along the way. The film industry, revived by an ingenious combination of funding, training, generous tax-breaks and government support, is part of the new Ireland that is bringing big names to live and work here, that is telling the jagged Irish stories, that has the country engaged in a creative explosion. An explosion begun in the 1960s and '70s with the decision to provide free secondary education for all children, educated now beyond what the country can provide for them. There is unfulfilled potential, heartbreak and alcoholism in that. And there is emigration. The more I tried to understand Ireland the more confused I became. By the contradictions. By the secular and the clerical locked in some kind of deathly tango dance. By the illogical behaviour that contradicts the rules but does not quite break them, by the fabulous oxymorons. "The Irish can see round corners," Roderic told me. "It is all a conspiracy."

The past is there, unyielding and seemingly intractable in a country in the pincer movement of change. And across the top of all the intelligence, all the magical profusion of words, all the hope for the future, sits the old, conservative, Catholic Ireland, like a crust, a cracking carapace over a simmering cauldron. Thin-lipped, sanctimonious disapproval. The issues of divorce and abortion still hotly debated, issues that were resolved decades ago in the progressive countries in which I have lived. The old agitation over sex still evident everywhere: incest is widespread but birth control is frowned upon, even now in this time of sexual liberation. And the church losing its grip. It is there in infanticide—the killing of newborns has been practised in this country for centuries. The bodies of newborn babies are still discovered in fields and rivers around the country, poor country girls still unable to face the shame of an illegitimate child. No matter that she may have been raped or have been the victim of incest. I spoke about this to Alexis Guilbride, who published her Master's thesis on infanticide in Ireland In the *Irish Times*. 'The unwed pregnant woman in post-independence Ireland,' Guilbride wrote, 'could, accordingly, expect if her "crime" was discovered to be disowned by the family and thrown out of her home; to be expelled from her community; to lose any position of employment that she might have held and, with no social welfare to fall back on, to be reduced to prostitution or begging on the streets. Alternatively, she might spend the rest of her days, malnourished and ill-treated, working in a Magdalen laundry. The circumstances in which a woman was impregnated did not excuse her crime in the Gaelic Christian society in which she lived. Eoin O'Duffy, Garda Commissioner, told the Committee for the Report on the Criminal Law (Amendments) Bill in 1931 that there had been an alarming increase in sexual crime in Ireland, a feature of which was the large number of cases of criminal interference with girls and children of 16 years and under, including many cases of children under 10 years. A great many of these, he informed the committee, were never prosecuted. But while control of their sexuality was presented to the Irish people, and to Irish women in particular, as a moral issue, the virtue of chastity was in fact rooted in economic necessity. Post-Famine Ireland had learned the bitter lesson that subdivision of farms that were never large to begin with was economically unviable. The continuing tradition of rearing large families to work the land meant that, where only one son could inherit and thus marry, his siblings must remain celibate or leave the country.'

I experienced too the alarming spectre of what was described to me as the classic Irish mother. I had befriended a brilliant young barrister who had recently returned to Dublin to set up his practice after finishing his Master's in London. Owing to the penury of setting up—it takes years to be paid—he, like so many young Irish people, lived with his parents. When I appeared on the scene his mother went what can only be described as berserk. She had already seen off all the women with whom her darling son had ever become involved and I was the worst case scenario, a divorced, independent Australian. She followed him around Dublin by telephone, she constantly phoned him at my hotel, she phoned him five or six times a day at work to berate him, she listened in on another line when he telephoned me from home. She controlled the purse strings and she naturally cut off the money, ensuring immediate emasculation. She gave him hell. She was worse than any jealous wife. At the height of her manipulation and control she theatrically checked herself into hospital for heart palpitations, blaming me. Ha. She wouldn't be considerate enough to have a heart attack, I bitterly thought. As long as they can make others miserable those kind of people live until they are ninety. She later even tried to blackmail me by threatening to send letters I had written to her son (by searching his briefcase) to my editor in Sydney. It was war, pure and simple. I had never seen obsession like this, it was pathological, her whole desperate being was bound up in her son. Alexis Guilbride explained to me that since sex outside marriage was forbidden, people often made early and misguided marriages. And since divorce was forbidden they were stuck; often silent, unhappy, loveless, the husband a 'disappointment'. The woman's place was in the home and with an empty life, her intelligence wasted, her son would become her love relationship, her true love. Hence the possessive Irish mother for whom no other woman is ever good enough for her son. It was stressful and oppressive and I began to feel as Bob Geldof does in Dublin—that I could not breathe. Imprisoned by net curtains, claustrophobic in the muddy night and in the mist that wraps itself around you in the streets, stays on your shoulders as you enter the intimate fug of the pub.

'Ireland,' wrote J. P. Donleavy once, is 'a country where the dead are forever living and which is at once magical, illogical, mysterious and infuriating—a land that is mostly, and perhaps always will remain, a condition of the mind in which dreams can be your only reality.'

# ■ A Singular Man

The gravestones in the cemeteries flashed forlornly past as the train flew through the suburbs of Dublin, past the council houses, through the dreary industrial outer suburbs and into the folding green hills. The black trees moulted now for the winter reached out spindly fingers into a grey, grey sky. The mist was like cotton wool as we hurtled across the countryside, into the mystic. Across the bleak, haunting bogs.

A wet sky hung low, dark and filthy, smothering the prosperous midland town of Mullingar with its close, grey shops punctuated by elegant Georgian buildings. The phone naturally didn't work in the pub, nor the next or the next. As your man Donleavy has pointed out, it is best to keep your options open in Ireland, things might take longer than you planned.

The huge grey stone house loomed eerily out of the mist and came through the trees as the taxi twisted up the driveway. Carved stone lions, sphinx-like, guard each side of the drive, stone eagles with wings spread rising from the roof. Pound, pound, pound on the massive wooden door, like a wayfarer lost on a stormy night. J. P. Donleavy is sitting in an armchair in front of a blazing fire taking afternoon tea. By now I was getting used to the routine. The huge and magnificent house, staff discreet. More used to it than a journalist ought.

I am greeted warmly by a man—with fine snowy hair and beard and hand outstretched—who seems to be almost universally disliked. He is pompous they say, he is a chauvinist they say, he writes the same book over and over they say, he is a stage Irishman they say, a poseur, a bore. They call him a dirty old man. Basically the Irish think J. P. Donleavy a wanker.

"I have had to come to terms with discovering that I am a disliked, almost hated man in British publishing circles," he will tell me in a hurt and baffled fashion. "There has been publicity of

## ■ J . P . D O N L E A V Y

various sorts, I can't understand it, this has come to me suddenly, this hostility, feminists raving. At least in Dublin you knew you had an audience. They hated it so much they would go out and read my books. No one was going to be indifferent. I had to get used to the fact that there is a great hostility out there that one doesn't even know about, in publishers and everything. But in Dublin they took care of everything because it was always 'that no good son of a bitch'. Dublin provided an audience second to none, you know they are going to get that book and open it and read it. You lose track of where you stand and your enemies are often well worth standing because they offer a stimulus. You can have thoughts of revenge."

And J. P. Donleavy knows all about revenge.

He puts a log on the fire and sinks back into his armchair to hold forth. The long sofa stretching across the fireplace seems to envelop me as I sink further and further into the warmth. Cushions are scattered across the wooden floor. Still a handsome man at nearly 70, tall, fine-featured, dressed for company in soft expensive tweeds, a lavender silk shirt and cravat. An elegant and civilised man with impeccable manners, he offers tea from a silver pot, almost a parody of the landed country gent.

I don't know what I was expecting from this writer of bawdy, licentious books about bad behaviour, about fucking and fighting, but not this. Definitely not this. Not this lonely, lonely man. I am getting used to this too, it seems. Famous men, singular and all alone in their mansions. Rattling sadly around. And this *is* a serious mansion. Oh, yes. Languishing out here in splendid isolation.

At one point he will confess with weary resignation to having put advertisements in lonely heart columns in desperate moments. They come but they don't stay. Two wives and at least two live-in girlfriends, always beautiful and getting younger and younger. But they leave him, they always leave. One wife left for a Guinness heir, another girlfriend for a French driving instructor. Left him bereft. It is all such a terrible disappointment really. "The women in my life were always treated with the greatest consideration," he waves his glasses in his hand. "I don't have a stable situation in this place where the presence of a woman is around with children and a family life. That is stabilising, you can work within that. It is very good because all you need in life is what children bring. This place is a paradise for kids. It gets more difficult not having that. But it is a myth about women and the country house and the beautiful grounds. It is so hard to find somebody who actually likes the country because it is isolating. The true picture is that women like to have a city where they can go and visit. And if they have this carry on of a country house business they want to be in it for a day or two a week and they want to be in the city the rest of the time. My first wife actually came to like the country but the options that exist for women nowadays, well. This sort of situation is impossible unless someone has grown up with this kind of house." Well that certainly narrows it down, J. P., known to his friends as Mike. You'd be looking for your heiress then. It's obvious to *me*. Your horsy, rootin', shootin', tootin' debutante.

Well, he was a wild man once. According to the autobiographical *The History of the Ginger Man*, a vivid account of student life in Dublin where he came from the navy, a GI from Brooklyn, after the war, he was utterly mesmerised and 'bedevilled. Albeit one soon realised that to survive in the great sea of poverty prevalent in the Dublin of the time, the oft encountered sins of lying and cheating could be seen to be required.' He was wildish anyway for a man married in penury at 20. Brawling in pubs in a city 'afloat with beer and aloud with festivity . . . There were constant generous occasions of hospitality all over Dublin with very few hours ever going by without someone or something inciting some celebration. And one could drift from one to the other, frequenting the innards of drawing rooms or pubs and hotels, which were a few steps in every direction all over the city . . . And as for country houses, one needed only someone sober enough to steer an automobile straight for a few miles or around a few dangerous corners to enter some mansion beyond some wooded copse where much eccentric goings-on would be going on and, provided you were appropriately affable, you could eat and drink to your heart's content and be merry if you could and sleep where you collapsed . . . but what about literature and art. The hope to be part of which throbbed in every citizen's heart. And made the excuse for him to go on living the next day and the next with the indifferent present being made tolerable by adorning the days ahead with rosy dreams . . . There was for the citizens at large a casual carelessness about Dublin life. And with aesthetic unselfconsciousness and the previously mentioned face-breaking being rampant at the time, and wine, women and song being the priority, no one knew or much cared that a so-called literary period was then hugely in the making.' Doesn't sound to me like a whole lot has changed, tell you the truth.

But this was clearly the shining time of his life, his never-forgotten time at Trinity College. The exploits of his friends and the people he knew would form his first novel *The Ginger Man* and shape his life. His spirited, disastrous, chaotic friend Gainor Stephen Crist was the model for Sebastian Dangerfield, although Brendan Behan once claimed it was himself and threatened to sue in a night on the town in London which wound up in a fist fight in the middle of Fleet Street. According to Donleavy he walloped Behan good and proper with a hook to the jaw and, well, Behan is no longer here to argue the point is he? Afterwards, the matter settled and the police successfully lied to, they wandered off down the street arm in arm.

Donleavy writes in the same archaic way that he speaks. Except that the writing has more colour and movement. Long-winded, slowly telling meandering stories that can kind of fizzle and peter out. The same ones, you get the feeling, he has been telling ad nauseam for years and years. So often he forgets to finish them. We are talking a bad case of anecdotage here, but he is merely being obliging, seeking to be hospitable, to entertain a visitor. "I could never do journalism because I can't turn stuff out quickly," he ruefully interrupts one interminable tale. The accent veers oddly between American and Irish.

Attitudes have certainly changed since those boyos played up
in Dublin in the late '40s. Dangerfield is cruel and it shocks
even Donleavy now that his chronically unfaithful character hit his
wife and then laughed about it. Although in his book *A Singular
Country*, an idiosyncratic, satirical look at Ireland, he wrote of
the drunken Irish husband regularly bashing the nagging battle-
hardened wife when she refused sex every Friday night after he
spent his pay in the pub.

*The Ginger Man* has been published in over 85 editions and
has sold millions and millions of copies. But it has only, it seems,
caused him misery. He is a fierce litigator, Donleavy. A paper
pugilist. You wouldn't think it to look at him, but you wouldn't
want to cross him. You don't fuck with Donleavy. It doesn't matter
how long it takes, or what it takes, he will win. It took 20 years to
get the rights back to his masterwork and in the end he bought the
publishing house to do it, spectacularly trumping his nemesis. At
20 he modestly set out to 'write a splendid book that no one would
ever forget' because he was an artist but no one would buy his
paintings. At first no one would publish his book either. It had
been rejected by 35 publishers when Brendan Behan advised him
to send it to Olympia Press in Paris. There it was published as
pornography, along with Nabokov's *Lolita,* by Maurice Girodias.
An apoplectic Donleavy asked for the rights back but Girodias,
who had a watertight contract which included all overseas rights,
refused to relinquish them. Years of bitter litigation followed. In
one letter Girodias referred to Donleavy's 'violent self-pity'. Years
later the bankrupt publishing house was put up for auction.
Donleavy sent his wife and his secretary, "both stunningly beautiful women, flying to Paris with enormous drafts drawn on the
Chase Manhattan Bank." After a cliffhanger auction against
Girodias himself, who was secretly bidding to get his beloved company back for a minuscule sum, Olympia belonged to Donleavy,
who then found himself in litigation with himself. Which he soon
decided to settle.

His book free at last, Donleavy's celebrity slowly grew and his book was, naturally, banned in Ireland. "*The Ginger Man* became a tag associated with me and the fact that it had been banned was always something that attracted people. On the other hand I think any Irish man who sat down and wrote and didn't get on the banned list would be a worried man because it didn't take much."

There have been 11 novels, four books of non-fiction and five plays since. "I have done a tremendous amount of work, I am shocked and horrified when I see the manuscripts. It is because I have this routine, I write seven days a week. I have never suffered from writer's block." They are all best-selling aspects of a life plundered for literary effect and the delinquent, comic people he has known. It was they who lived fast and wild, not he, the voyeur. *A Fairy Tale of New York*, about an undertaker, is based on conversations he had with a seaman in the navy. "For some strange reason, in the navy I would confront former morticians more than anyone else. They had become medics and this particular man was a bosun's mate; he was a mortician who had never qualified as one. He had to get a high school diploma in order to go back to morticians school and then qualify. So I was commandeered to sit his high school diploma for him which I duly did. I don't think he got awfully high marks"—the briefest of smiles. "I got to know this man tremendously well. That is how I got to know about the business. He had all these dreams as to what he would do as a mortician. All those words you hear are his exactly. I got fascinated. The only job I have ever had in my life was during summer vacation at school and it was to cut grass in a cemetery. This gave me my interest in cemeteries. It is a very traumatic thing in your life, which erodes as you get older. You get less concerned about dying. One of the remaining aesthetics of American life is the fact of the cemetery. The great mausoleum in California. I automatically head there in my spare time. The great mausoleum at Forest Lawn is quite something."

But he has always been drawn back here to Ireland. 'To free oneself to its soft, moist cleanliness and not always balmy breezes,' he once wrote. And its being a tax haven for artists didn't hurt, she snidely adds. "Yes," he admits, "the tax thing was the major reason I came back. The Irish thrive once they leave Ireland. Strangely my whole thrust of life is my professional use of what is around me as a writer. But every writer looks for silence. I have made a search for this for my whole career, it is very hard to find this."

His voice echoes down the long silent room. A perfectly pro-portioned formal reception room, whose windows open onto his green and rolling acres and whose green walls are hung with his own paintings. Behind me is a grand piano that no one plays any more, now that the women and children are gone. A reception room with no one to receive. "I don't seem to have parties these days," he says wistfully, prodding the fire with his foot.

It is hard to understand this hatred around him, this hatred that consumes him. He seems perfectly harmless and pleasant to me, haunted as he is by a novel he wrote 40 years ago. "It did dawn on me that *The Ginger Man*, whatever its purpose in my life or anybody else's life, the one purpose it had in Irish life which I directly knew about was tourism. A lot of people read it and came here. There was a television thing called 'J. P. Donleavy's Ireland'. As a result of that the Discovery Channel made a programme that was seen by 22 million people."

He is an old-fashioned gentleman and perhaps that is the prob-lem. He just went out of date. His books were written and his attitudes formed before anyone had ever heard of feminism. The behaviour of his protagonists is simply unacceptable now and he, in his tweeds up here in his conspicuous country house, photo-graphed so often with wolfhound and rifle, has been folded into his books in the public mind. The priapic macho country squire. In fact, he seems rather sensitive and fragile. The other scenario is that of the dirty old man. Photographed with house and very young, very beautiful girl. The last one was 23 to his 68. Indignation now. "One loses sight of the fact of what the public might think of you. All the interview things over *The History of the Ginger Man* have been the most vile. Attacking things by women journalists. I was quite surprised when all these articles appeared. One of them had written something really terrible in the *Guardian*. I had an old girl-friend who had lived here and a new girlfriend had turned up and so there were two women in the house at the same time. So this picture didn't look all that good. I did come across as a chauvinist. None of this has changed my attitude. My mother was worshipped by my father, so there was an awareness that came later. I have never had a woman in my life who has not become a firm fast friend, and I would put my life in their hands. That goes for every single solitary one. I don't sue because I am a writer writing about people and it is give and take. They photograph me standing in front of a castle, wearing tweeds, whereas in fact if anyone comes to see me in my working clothes, they are torn to shreds and in rags because I go out and do heavy work on this place. I remember one of my secretaries had a boyfriend and she was living in the gatehouse and he would come up to the house and say, 'Where is this guy?'. One day she said, 'Oh God, you must have had a good look at him today.' He said, 'No'. She said 'He was in front of you all day.' I was mending the road. Every now and then I get a tinker who will come up and say, 'Can you get anything out of them up there in the big house?'."

And it certainly is a very big house, much bigger than it first appears, as we wander the hallways with stone floors wide as a road and through the great dark old rooms. He stands slightly stooped and so alone in so much grandeur, his white hair catching the light, the wind roaring down the freezing passages. He turns on the light to the heated indoor pool, now covered in moss. He turns the floodlights onto the full soccer pitch outside where you can smell the countryside encroaching. We cruise through the library and check out the bedrooms where the children once slept and an oval pink richly feminine bathroom, a gift to a past amorata—"she went, of course". He is right. It is a house that is crying out for people, for singing and dancing, for wild footsteps on the flag-stones, for the squealing of children, for the chink of cocktails at six, and roaring dinners for 20. The formal dining room is something else again, with a huge Francis Bacon mirror and a massive marble table, a place where wife number two, Mary Wilson Price, the one who left for the Guinness heir, would entertain after the hunt. "There are about 20 bedrooms and seven or eight bathrooms. It was built in roughly 1750. It is reputed that James Joyce spent some time in this house. It has to be looked after most of the time. I used to have a full maintenance man and a staff but now wages are very high, especially the overheads of employees, you have to pay insurance. Keeping anybody working you have to be careful. But it is a tremendously pleasant house to be in. You can work in one part of it and not be conscious of anybody else. Some writers prefer to have noises going on but if you get sensitised to the fact that someone is making noise that is interfering with your writing then you are sunk. This place does actually operate profitably as a farm. There are 180 cattle and the bulls out there are very dangerous bulls."

It is an empty house full of memories, of echoes of past happiness fragmented. We stand in a conservatory that is devoted to his 16 books: piles of original manuscripts, posters of plays, pieces of past projects, a kind of shrine to a staggeringly successful literary career that has not, in the end, brought joy. The perceived rejections and slights have conquered the sense of success. "That astonishing business in Paris was where my career began. My battle has never ended, I have never had a situation that so-called success has been upon me because after *The Ginger Man* was published my legal battles went on for 20 years. I could never sit back and say that was fine." He offers it up with that uneasy and tortuous combination of ego and humility that exists in the writer, one feeding off the other. "I am hesitant to tackle another novel or a book now because that is an immense thing, with concentration long-term, and it is a bit worrying always to do that. I remember when I finished *The History of the Ginger Man* the energy and concentration it had taken. Writers do need someone who is going to be an audience. Someone who is going to listen to you and hear you. You don't get any immediacy out of it. You are talking about another year before it even comes out. I go out and work on the farm and things come up on what you are working on and then you know you are in the swirl of a book."

We wind up in the warm modern kitchen. And there on an old wooden chair huddled next to a fire is Donleavy's handsome eldest son Phillip, who lives in New York, but is here to put together the film of *The Ginger Man*. With all of this shuffling, whispering magnificence to play with, Phillip is huddled in the kitchen.

And now it is very dark outside, an impenetrable winter dark without sky. The night descends here in seconds. And as I look back I see his shape standing in the light over the front door and see too that those fine careless days of roaming the countryside with the wild Brendan Behan so very long ago were the best days of his life. As he put it himself in *The History of the Ginger Man*: 'God's mercy, On the Wild, Ginger Man.'

The birds fly whooping across the Irish Sea as the train passes through Blackrock. The chimneys of Luggala have long disappeared into the exquisite valley behind me. Past the oil refinery on a blue winter day, the sky criss-crossed with streaks of white.

And then I was going backwards on the Gatwick express and London was flashing past, elegant houses and church spires. The dreaded fax had come from the Starship Enterprise in Sydney— 'Return'—and it was time to go home.

I sat on the plane looking at the grey coming down to the ground, at the black and orange empty trees, at the element of water, the mist that you could almost catch in your hand, and thought of Garech and Roderic arguing in the Roundwood Inn, William and Mary cruising down the Serpentine, their children transformed now into swans, the pinstriped boyos, gowns flapping behind them, hauling their legal briefs down Fleet Street, Susan and Clare laughing in Notting Hill, Berkoff fulminating in the Docklands, all the brilliant men and women who had talked into my tape, all the elegant times we had. But as the polar wind carried the plane in the jetstream across the Atlantic, over the surreal white mountains of Iceland, there was one more thing I had to do. One more adventure to be had.

It wasn't that much cheaper to get the Greyhound bus from Los Angeles to Las Vegas than to fly, but I just had to do it. There was, to my mind, no other way to get there than to be on the road. To be a midnight cowgirl one more time. To be on the road in America. They are begging at the bus station as we leave warm, shiny LA, the palm trees and cypresses blurring like a picket fence with fronds.

# Please, Please, Please

The Greyhound bus trundles through the ghostly, shimmering lunar landscape as the sinking sun flares red across bare skeletal hills then fades to Nevada night. From this slumbering ancient landscape the neon city rises, ablaze with gleaming light. The dishevelled man sitting next to me is telling me all about his covert CIA activities; crazy as a coot. Mexican eyes restlessly roam the bus in the fading desert light.

The bus cruises down the Strip, past the vast, glittering monuments to naked human greed. Past the fountains of moving lights. Las Vegas at last: temple town of the American dream. Checking into a cheap hotel I am shocked at my appearance in the mirror.

And down on to the beckoning lights and the acres and acres of gaming tables at the Sands Hotel. Mr and Mrs Iowa squealing at the slot machines, Miss Sacramento tossing hair and compulsively pulling at coin machines at the bar. At the end of a vast, cavernous, shabby room, full of smoke and noise and cheap perfume, flashing lights and low-rollers tearing at the arms of machines, a horn section can be heard blasting up the Grand Ballroom.

Tonight it is, ladies and gents, Mister Excitement himself, Mister Dynamic, Soul Brother Number One, put your hands together please for Mister *Jaaaames* Brown. The actual sex machine. Awl-right. A walking symphony of blue sequins bathed in red light and topped by an immaculately tall and curving quiff, the construction of which takes several hours a day.

"James Brown, James Brown, James Brown" chants the reverential audience as the tiny barrel-chested Godfather of Soul struts across the stage, tilts his chin and acknowledges the righteous, righteous reverence. Mister Excitement is excited. Overexcited even. "We're hot now," he informs us silkily, "we're ready to go." And six slinky sequinned babes with stratospheric voices launch into 'Living In America', the rhythm section gets down and the horn section gets up.

**J A M E S    B R O W N**

The Godfather thrusts his tiny hips, squeals and does the legendary camel-walk across the stage; even if it is, at nearly 70, on stiff and creaking legs. His electrifying, sweating, sex performances are, of course, legend; like a man possessed he would in his day be an orgiastic frenzy of pleading, shimmying on one vibrating leg, falling to his knees, pirouetting high in the air, shrieking mad and anguished; giving it up for the audience. Frenzied energy. Sex, sex, sex. Baby, baby, baby. Yes, yes, yes. The killer moves that Mick Jagger, Prince, Michael Jackson and pretty much everyone who followed would emulate. There is a clash of sequins when he dances with one of the singers.

His knees often bloodstained, he would leave the stage soaked and destroyed; unravelled. Well, he doesn't do the splits any more but those pipes are still rich and magnificent and the soul scream "owwwwwww" *almost* sacramental. The famous cape routine to 'Please, Please, Please', where in a kind of rousing ritual supplication that comes from the southern Baptist preachers, he falls to his knees, an assistant drapes a cape around him and helps him to his feet, whereupon he hurls the cape away and gives more, more, more, is somewhat gingerly handled on those tired, scarred knees, but those glittering sequinned capes are a fairly unique fashion statement still. You kinda imagine a meeting with Mr Dynamic and his friend Elvis dressed to thrill back in their heyday. All those sequins would have been blinding. The Godfather, with his coiffure and dazzling jumpsuits, has never been a man for understating his position.

He has been doing this routine ever since his gospel singing got him out of spending his adolescence in jail, sprung by the Mount Zion Baptist Church to sing in its community choir. His band, which he runs with tyrannical discipline, is as tight and funky as can be; as a stage presence his is still Mister James Brown, legend and don't you forget it, launching now into 'I Feel Good', flanked by high-kicking dancing girls in boxer shorts.

But there is something slightly sad about an old man and a Las Vegas lounge act, no matter how slick its delivery might be.

"Ah will do this till ah fall," he assures the audience before casting his eyes heavenwards and profusely thanking the Lord, with whom he appears to have an interesting and sensual relationship, in which much un-Christian behaviour is reconciled. The Lord, for example, does not appear to take a dim view of cocaine abuse or wife beating, with which he was charged more than once.

"I am a dynamic person," he tells me the next day, as he is helped down from the stage during afternoon rehearsal.

The dancers are dancing up and down the aisles of the empty room.

His extremely large and watchful minders hover on red-alert in case Mister Brown should so much as flicker his displeasure. It has been nearly a year of faxes, phone calls, I am practically on intimate terms with his manager Mr Friday, to be granted what will be a mystifying audience with the Godfather; a man without whom it is almost impossible to imagine modern popular music. Close contact with the Sex Machine, however, can raise certain questions as to the Godfather being the full quid. The man who brought funk, by kicking off from the upbeat and not the downbeat, "the old two-four situation, funk means blues and gospel together and it makes people feel good", and soul to the white middle-class by sheer guts and hard, driven work, and the man whose turbulent life takes in all the extremes, traverses the entire spectrum of American success.

From a shack with no windows and being sent home from school for being inadequately dressed, in rags, to being raised in a house of ill-repute by an aunt; from pimping, dancing and stealing, from no education and jail, to private jets, paranoia, fleets of cars and luxe to the last degree; from poor to rich to poor as the Inland Revenue Service pounced on the millions he often carried in suitcases. He has always been pursued by his leering demons and always transfigured by his music. Tough as hell. Through all his troubles, it is said, he has never cracked. The people around him have though, thanks to his tyranny.

In 1967 he played before three million people and sold 50 million records. His antics and outrageous egomaniacal persona have often seemed comical but underlying it all is, one suspects, the little motherless black boy who had no shoes for school.

There have been times, however, when he has gotten a bit far on up. As in 1988, when he was sentenced to six years behind bars for getting on up on some angel dust, carrying a shotgun into an insurance seminar (perfectly rational behaviour, if you ask me) and then leading the police on a wild car chase.

"You gotta be fearless of everything except God," he rasps in his almost incomprehensible southern drawl. "You have to watch men but you shouldn't fear a man. But God you fear because you can't see him. You just know his presence is there. You can put a man in a cage but you can't kill his spirit. When I was in prison, by the way, I became a leader because the fellas believed in me. I was straight. In prison I just had to try to keep my body loose and active. You see the demons around you and you fight and keep on fighting. The music was always in my head. It is a prison when you have ideas and bad attitude; it is a prison when you make $125 a week and you have to spend $150; it is a prison when you are only allowed a drop-out education that doesn't mean anything."

He sits at a table in his elaborate tracksuit and cowboy boots, dazzling teeth, glittering beringed fingers gesturing wildly. He has been watching the rehearsal with narrowed eyes.

Suddenly he leaps up and claps his hands. Everybody jumps nervously.

"Miss Helen," he drawls at the dancers, "Miss Holly, you act is not together. Do that passage again." Then he imposes one of his notorious fines on a singer for grievous lapses in punctuality, grooming and other crimes. "That young man has got another $25, he knows why he got it, he was drinking at rehearsal, on the job. So that is $50 now." He sits down with a flourish. "Excuse me, young lady" he says.

Brown's ascendancy in the early '60s came from an animal instinct and he had to push the sound he kept hearing in his head into the white mainstream, in a time before the civil-rights movement had gathered momentum. "It was very hard back then, but finding the music was like finding oil in your own backyard. It was like getting religion in a bar, like getting rain in the middle of the Sahara Desert. So it was an impossible task. I had a problem with the drummers, I had a problem with the guitars, I had a problem with the horn players because they were in that old two and four situation and there is nothing wrong with it, it is good music but it just comes at a different pace. When you are looking left going right, you know, when you are down we are going up, when you are going up we are going down. The music is kicked off from the upbeat not the downbeat. I had to follow my nose, I had to prove to all the other groups in the world to go on the upbeat. But I knew I was right." And it was about the feeling. Right on. Right now. "In the '60s, I had a record company that whatever I wanted to do, any time of the night I wanted to record, I could. The company pressed their own records. I recorded a record tonight, then tomorrow at the same time it would be on the market. You record now and you can't get it out until six months later—that is not the record business. You don't want the news in six months, you want the news on the day. When you feel it, that is when it should come out. When I do an album, I do a whole album in 12 hours."

The Godfather who once campaigned with Black Power, who created a black liberation theology, an image of self-respect, seems a strange combination of put-upon black man and evangelistic leader. "All rap is not bad but they did have a risqué problem and it destroyed our youth and our future because it had no respect for the mamma or the grandmother. And if you don't have no respect for the mamma or the grandmother then you don't have no respect for yourself. You see, they have no respect for the black man in this country and a lot of black men don't have no respect for themselves. There is coloured people that's afraid of their own shadow and there's Negroes that think they are better than anybody black and want to be white. They'll never be white, they gotta be who they are. And this country has got to wake up. If they have a country that don't have no religion and a President that don't have no budget, they ain't gonna last long. This is a very sad time."

James Brown has been described as being a restless soul. "Not so much a restless soul with some people," he says, his leg jiggling. "What makes me restless is to watch people have a way out and don't take it. That is what makes me restless. It makes me restless when I see some of the finest musicians of this time and a lot of them don't know why they are doing it. It makes me a restless soul when people are on welfare taking $120 a month when they could be getting $5000 a month. They have got enough talent to get it but they don't use it."

During the rehearsal the Godfather stalks up and down the stage on those skinny legs, shouting orders, cackling with laughter, jive-talking, clapping, yelling "chugga-lugga" and shrieking "ooowwww" before delighting an audience of one journalist and rows of empty aisles to a sweet homesick rendition of 'Georgia', the State where he lives on a ranch and gets into a whole lot of trouble. Mister Brown has a deep and huge laugh. He has to bend over to do it.

That night, strutting in his stacked shoes under the strobe lights, his face shining, he stops suddenly in the middle of 'It's A Man's World' and calls for a 30-second silence for "Mr Rabin and the Rabin family in the name of world peace".

Maybe world peace and domestic peace are two different things. Mr Brown is always being charged for beating up his various wives.

But on that hot Vegas night, Mister Brown, the Godfather, was dancing to the tune of self-affirmation that he has been dancing for near on 50 years. "God bless you, young lady," he says as I leave. "You got soul." Out in the garish street they are pushing and hustling and ugly. But I don't care.

I got soul. All right. Get ready. I'm coming.

■ ■ ■

And the plane powers across the Pacific towards red earth, bleached blue sky and glittering bays.

And here I go rolling home.